Projecting Race

Projecting Race

POSTWAR AMERICA, CIVIL RIGHTS AND DOCUMENTARY FILM

STEPHEN CHARBONNEAU

WALLFLOWER PRESS
LONDON & NEW YORK

A Wallflower Press Book

Wallflower Press is an imprint of
Columbia University Press
Publishers Since 1893
New York   Chichester, West Sussex
cup.columbia.edu

Copyright © 2016 Columbia University Press
All rights reserved

Wallflower Press® is a registered trademark of Columbia University Press

A complete CIP record is available from the Library of Congress

ISBN 978-0-231-17890-7 (cloth : alk. paper)
ISBN 978-0-231-17891-4 (pbk. : alk. paper)
ISBN 978-0-231-85095-7 (e-book)

Columbia University Press books are printed on permanent
and durable acid-free paper.
Printed in the United States of America

c 10 9 8 7 6 5 4 3 2 1
p 10 9 8 7 6 5 4 3 2 1

Cover images: *With No One to Help Us* (William C. Jersey Production, 1967); *The Man in the Middle* (George C. Stoney Associates, 1966); *Palmour Street: A Study in Family Life* (Southern Educational Film Production Service, 1949); *The First Thirty* (Office of Economic Opportunity, Public Affairs Dept., 1965); *A Street Academy* (Office of Economic Opportunity, 1969); *Another Way* (Drew Associates, 1967)

Contents

For Ilysia, Rosie, Dorothy and my daughters, Sofia and Dahlia

Acknowledgments

The briefest of glances at this book's table of contents will tell the tale of George Stoney's influence on me as a film scholar. He instilled in me as a New York University undergraduate a fascination with the past, present and future of documentary film. His course, 'Documentary Traditions', was one of my last as a senior and left an indelible mark. Professor Stoney's detailed notes in my modest undergraduate film journal inspired me and are indicative of a thoroughly committed educator who was always seeking to learn himself. I was humbled to be in his class and have sought to emulate him in the classroom ever since. His influence on the documentary world is legendary and I suspect I will continue to return to his life and work as a source of inspiration.

My world was rocked as well by the many energetic and brilliant film lecturers I encountered at New York University in the mid-1990s, especially David Lugowski, Peter Decherney and Joe McElhaney. Peter Decherney, in particular, deserves thanks for what has turned into a career-long advising session; his feedback on countless papers, personal statements, presentations and overall encouragement and friendship has been foundational for me and I cannot imagine being a film scholar without his help.

The faculty in film and television studies at the University of Warwick rescued me from a low-paying activist gig in Seattle. My courses there with Richard Dyer, Ginette Vincendeau, José Arroyo and Rachel Moseley were inspired and dramatically informed my own pedagogy as a film studies educator. My relationships with Chon Noriega, Marina Goldovskaya and Eric Smoodin at the University of California, Los Angeles were and continue to be sources of inspiration. I thank all three for their friendship and for their encouragement during difficult times. My peers from my time at UCLA have profoundly shaped me as a scholar and have provided much needed emotional support through the ups and downs of graduate life, so thanks to Sudeep Sharma, Emily Carman, Deron Overpeck, Agustin Zarzosa, Lindy Leong, Sharon Sharp, Jennifer Holt,

Maja Manojlovic and Ross Melnick. The work of Lynne Jackson, John Caldwell, Stephen Mamber, Steve Macek and Devorah Heitner have also been formative for me over the last ten years.

The Chicano Studies Research Center at UCLA played a vital role in providing a home for Baylis Glascock's extensive collection of Farmersville films and related primary documents. A special thanks, then, to Chon Noriega, Baylis Glascock and Michael R. Stone, the Archives Manager at the Center. Allen Fisher, an archivist at the Lyndon Baines Johnson Presidential Library, was enormously helpful in tracking down material related to Julian Biggs' and Colin Low's initial visit with the Office of Economic Opportunity in Washington. Colin and Eugénie Low graciously welcomed me into their Montreal home, where I listened to Low speak about his work with the OEO and his career in general. Spending time with them was an honour and an experience that I'll never forget. My sincere thanks to Anne Michaels, Harold 'Casey' Case and Harry Keramidas for taking time to speak with me over the phone, revisiting their work with the OEO in the late 1960s.

No single book chapter can do justice to the collective archival and preservation work, much less the historical experience, of *The Hartford Project*. From day one I was inspired and overwhelmed by the labour that went into and continues to maintain the vast collection of films, transcripts, interviews and reports held at Trinity College's Watkinson Library. A huge debt is owed to Susan Pennybacker whose work at the Hartford Studies Project made this book possible and whose generosity opened up a whole world to me that I had assumed would be closed. I am also deeply saddened by the passing of Peter J. Knapp, Trinity's College Archivist at the Watkinson Library. My brief time researching at the Watkinson was facilitated by his knowledge of the collections there as well as his good cheer. The fleeting vision of sharing this book with him was a major motivation to finish. Pablo Delano, Glenn Orkin and Christopher Moore deserve special mention as well for their support of this work.

I am also grateful to the transcriptions composed by many at the Hartford Studies Project. The benefit of being able to refer to transcripts of the dozens of films and interviews associated with *The Hartford Project* cannot be overestimated. My thanks, then, to Tara Brown, Stacey Einhorn, John Forster, Christopher J. Garr, Emily Gifford, Bart Kempf, Melissa Kotulski, Chris Legrand, Kevin Massicotte, Beth Rose, Eric Ruark, Damien Vasseur and Steven Veshoshky.

Ultimately, this book aims to acknowledge the leap of faith undertaken by many activists and artists involved with *The Hartford Project*. The recent passing of Charles 'Butch' Lewis is another bitter pill to swallow considering how his generosity made the preservation and study of these War on Poverty films possible. His recorded testimony, along with that of Anne Michaels and Colin Low, for the Hartford Studies Project helped me cobble together a narrative of the OEO's communication experiments. Ultimately, the enormity of what these and so many have accomplished will continue to yield research and creative work for many years to come.

Since my career began at Florida Atlantic University I have had the pleasure of working alongside Gerald Sim. We were hired together and immediately bonded as we helped each other navigate the perils of academic life. Fusing intellectual insight with his characteristic wit, Gerald has never failed to remind me that my labour is something that I control and that the best way to stop a calamitous action is to let it proceed. Whenever he says, 'Let's be clear...' I know I'm about to hear something good.

Chris Robé has been a stalwart supporter and friend throughout my work on this project. He consistently saw potential in this work that eluded me, especially during periods where the research had stalled. His sense of humour and trenchant insight sustained me through many challenges. Our shared love for noisy music also provided essential outlets for escape and our garage band sessions with Mark Harvey, Phil Hough and Phil Lewin over the last two years have left me smiling and my ears ringing. Susan Reilly has also been unwavering in her support for this project and my career. I am extremely thankful for her recommendations for countless fellowship and grant applications. Eric Freedman, Mike Budd and Michael Hofmann also offered valuable criticism of and support for this research at various stages.

Susan Richardson of the University of Alberta intervened with a crucial letter of support for my Fulbright application in 2011. My experience with Fulbright Canada in general spurred new insights and intellectual pursuits that would have otherwise never materialised. New friendships and intellectual partnerships came about and I am grateful to Don Holly, Brendan Kredell, Elena Del Rio, Liz Czach and especially to Jaimie Baron and Jonathan Cohn for making my brief stay at the University of Alberta so welcoming and impactful. This project would never have been completed without the support of Fulbright Canada, the Lyndon Baines Johnson Foundation and the International Council for Canadian Studies.

A handful of film scholars have also intervened at crucial points to support this project and/or my career in more recent years and they include Zoë Druick, Deane Williams, Mary Celeste Kearney, Patricia Aufderheide and Timothy Corrigan. My editor at Wallflower Press, Yoram Allon, has been such a champion for this book and his spirited emails always picked me up. Matthew Buchholz generously shared his expertise on copyright issues and assisted with the imagery in this book. I also owe a debt of gratitude to the anonymous peer reviewers who poured over early versions of this manuscript. Their efforts substantially improved the project and its faults are entirely my responsibility.

Finally, the summer of 2011 is a notorious one for my family as I found myself battling a sudden health crisis. I quite literally would not be here if it were not for the intervention of the medical staff at the intensive care unit of the John Muir Medical Center in Walnut Creek, California. The nursing staff there kept my family sane during a strenuous time. I am also in awe of the generosity of Stephanie and Mark Adams, who rescued my wife and me from an engulfing storm of medical diagnoses to provide us with a tour of Pixar Studios. We were strangers to them, but there was no hesitation on their part to give us a small reprieve. Since 2011, Dr Jair Munoz Mendoza has also been a calming force and has contributed in many ways to my life and hence this book.

My mother, Dorothy Charbonneau, has been encouraging me to write for as long as I can remember. Her never-wavering belief in my creative and expressive potential has been a gift that I hope to pass on to my own children. Chuck Holst – uncle, friend and best man – instilled in me a love of conversation, westerns and the value of 'getting out of Dodge'. Over the years, Steve and Mitzi Bauer have continued to be a source of emotional support for my family. And my in-laws, Sue and Bob Shattuck, have been pillars over the last fifteen years, through good times and bad. My sister, Rosie, and her husband, Josh, are my favourite Angelenos. Rosie, in particular, never ceases to amaze me with her creativity, sense of humour and big heart. I've been watching movies with her since we could both walk and our sensibilities are at times indistinguishable.

The biggest thanks of all goes to my wife, Ilysia Shattuck. She has been with me on this journey since 1998 and her activist spirit informs this work. Her love of dancing and social justice inspires me and is already rubbing off on our two daughters, Sofia and Dahlia.

INTRODUCTION

LEARNING TO LOOK:
THE EDUCATIONAL DOCUMENTARY
AND POST-WAR RACE RELATIONS[1]

> I am frightened by how the intellectual neatness of the philosophy is so flaw-
> less that we often seem to feel there is no need to look at our motivations.
>
> – Henry Lanford (1968)

The quote above is a reflection from Henry Lanford, a research assistant on a 1968 state-sponsored documentary film series, *The Farmersville Project*. A gradu-ate student at the University of Oregon, Lanford had been invited to join a team of Canadian and American filmmakers who were committed to testing the viability of documentary film as an instrument of conflict mediation. The setting was California's Central Valley, specifically the town of Farmersville, which was quickly developing a Mexican American majority, and the racial di-vision between the town's populace and its white power structure was a source of animosity and hostility. The farmworker jobs of retired Okies who still lived in Farmersville were now the jobs of Mexican Americans, whose working con-ditions were becoming increasingly chemical-intensive and damaging to their health. In response to such conditions, Filipino American and Mexican Ameri-can farmworkers were organising themselves and standing up for better working conditions all across the state. Within this context, *The Farmersville Project* – sponsored by the Office of Economic Opportunity (OEO) and directed by the National Film Board of Canada's (NFB) Julian Biggs and Colin Low – yielded thirty-four short documentaries about race relations, farmworkers and poverty in order to energise new lines of communication in an already polarised town. The endeavour was a new kind of participatory pedagogy but the crew consisted of outsiders. As a result, Lanford himself grew sceptical about the likelihood of the production's success: 'The essence of the danger,' he wrote at the time, 'is in [our] strange unquestioning and missionary-like devotion' (1968).

This sense of anxiety serves as both a starting point and endpoint for the project at hand. With these comments from his production journal Lanford expresses doubt about the crew's implied status as enlightened outsiders as well as the overall utility of their film series, *The Farmersville Project*. However, for me, this sentiment inspires a look back at a history of the post-war liberal documentary and its attempts to frame race relations. To this end, this volume tracks the historical development of the documentary film in the decades following World War II, with a particular focus on the maintenance of a post-war racial *look* in pedagogical settings. As we will see, the films of *The Farmersville Project* were designed to serve a unique brand of participatory pedagogy: to facilitate communication across racial lines, or to compel the town's white status quo to truly *see* as well as hear from their Mexican American neighbours. The OEO hoped that this pedagogical agenda would smooth over racial barriers to communication and ease the work of organisers on the ground as they sought to address poverty as a general social problem. Accompanying the agency's liberal reformist endeavour was a desire to stage and facilitate a particular racial look through new filmic pedagogies.

The Farmersville Project stands at the tail end of a broader history of the post-war documentary. The first half of this book analyses documentary films in the 1940s and 1950s that bear the mark of Italian neorealism, those that blend an educational mission with re-enactments designed to shadow history and capture a quotidian flavour of reality. In contrast, the second half charts the influence of new documentary approaches on sponsored educational films in the 1960s, where the intensity and urgency of that decade encouraged documentarians to record life as it unfolded in front of the camera. Nevertheless, this division should not obscure a larger continuity as the majority of the documentaries discussed here deal with race and race relations during the post-war era within particular pedagogical contexts. As a unique kind of cinema, these *educational* documentaries are sponsored by state agencies at various levels and most of them generate an address from the state to a particular audience. Or, to put it in more cinematic terms, these films produce racial looks that are expressed through specific sounds and images in order to educate and train. Studying the racial politics of post-war documentaries asks us to consider our textual analyses in terms that go beyond standard notions of representation. The conditions of reception for educational documentaries are often narrowly defined and their social impact may indeed be negligible. But while their social representational value is often limited, their unique ways of seeing – especially when held in light of their institutional and historical situation – can give us access to particular and often overlooked modes of knowledge formation. And, from a post-World War II American perspective, these ways of seeing are often coordinated with certain racial values that leave an inevitable inscription. This racial residue in educational, training and mental hygiene films speaks to an American society caught up in the contradictions of its ideals in light of the brutal realities of Jim Crow.

It is quite clear that the stakes of historicising and theorising the racial look are as high as ever. In a commentary on the events of Ferguson, Missouri and the decision not to indict Officer Darren Wilson in the shooting of Michael Brown, Matthew Pratt Guterl – author of *Seeing Race in Modern America* (2013) – makes a compelling case for approaching 'racial sight as an endemic, disturbing feature of American history and culture' (2014). Even as Guterl acknowledges that economic disparities underpin race relations in America, he insists, 'these are historically and politically linked to things as simple as sight' (ibid.). In his book, Guterl sets out to study 'racial sight in the modern United States' and the 'popular reliance on observable details and racial biometrics to classify, organize, and arrange different kinds of bodies, and the enrollment and imprinting of individual bodies with multiple markers that match a particular template, stereotype, or stock representation' (2013: 3). My hope here is to direct this cultural history of the racial look into a narrower study of documentary film history, with a particular focus on the post-war educational documentary. To a substantial degree, the pedagogical film practices assessed in this book foreground the racial 'imprinting' as well as this process's entanglement within particular frameworks of public policy.

Lanford, then, represents an example of the particular racial look under review here. For me, his testimony mobilises a broader post-war liberal anxiety. The educational documentaries featured in this book, most of which explicitly address issues of race and racism, were made by liberals working within particular institutional and historical coordinates. Sidney Meyers, George Stoney, Colin Low and Julian Biggs all, in different ways, produce a post-war racial look in flux, as it struggles to come to terms with racial inequality. In most instances, the films reviewed in this book accentuate the experiences of African Americans as well as Mexican Americans and Puerto Ricans through the lens of specific traumas. In some cases, the trauma is displaced from a social field and etched onto an oedipal core. In other cases, the trauma is tied to severe conditions of urban or rural poverty. Stoney's films often feature the latter while also exhibiting a more delicate touch. In these films, African American familial struggles highlight the interconnectedness of psychic strife and social circumstance. Low and Biggs' participatory pedagogical films for the OEO in the late 1960s – on which Lanford worked – also feature testimonies from Mexican Americans, African Americans and Puerto Ricans that compel linkages between personal, social and economic registers. A dynamic mapping of post-war racial experiences can, to some extent, be gleaned from these documentaries.

But framing these analyses in terms of the racial look reminds us of the outsider status of the filmmakers in relation to the experiences depicted, the very thing that troubles Lanford. Stitched together, the films of Meyers, Stoney, Low, Biggs and others articulate a faltering liberal racial look, one that increasingly finds itself in crisis. These filmmakers exhibit a disdain for the racism of post-war America and see their films as attempts to foreground the struggles and experiences of African American, Mexican American and Puerto Rican peoples. And yet their films are still *their* films. While the films discussed here grow more and more participatory, the cameras are still – by and large – directed at people of colour rather than by. The racial dynamic at work here is, then, complicated. The look these films mobilise is always a racial one in which a white liberal vision is constituted outright or intervenes on behalf of the state.

The historical timeline for the films considered stretches out from the late 1940s to the late 1960s, and in doing so we are able to take note of a racial look *in process* as it comes to terms with its own contradictions and implications. Here the look parallels the historical flux of post-war liberalism. Viewing liberalism as a 'complex and variable dynamic, rather than as a singular set of substantive positions' (Horton 2005: 4) enables us to be open to its post-war variations and its registration through a wide array of pedagogical, observational and participatory documentaries. And yet in spite of these variations and the contradictory nature of liberal discourses, scholars such as Carol A. Horton have correctly pointed out that the edifice of American liberalism has been and continues to be articulated through race. The spectre of racial inequality haunts American liberalism in the post-war era as both an internal contradiction in need of resolution and as a fulcrum for perpetuating economic inequality. As Horton notes, racism is both flaw and feature in the history of American liberalism, 'a complex and double-edged phenomenon' (ibid.). And a fascination that drives this book is how this fact is registered onscreen, through the use of filmmaking at a time when the medium was perceived as a key site for the inculcation of modern liberal citizenship. An assumption of this particular study is that post-war modes of liberal citizenship, at their core, seek to confront and mitigate the racial inequality on which they are based.

In the twenty-five years following World War II, the United States changed radically as a result of the Civil Rights movement. The overarching narrative of this book coincides with Martin Luther King, Jr.'s stewardship of the Civil Rights movement from – as Taylor Branch puts it – 'obscurity to … the center stage of American politics in 1963' (2006: xii). At that time, 'President John F.

Kennedy declared racial segregation a moral issue "as old as the Scriptures and … as clear as the American Constitution"' (ibid.). The passage of the 24th Amendment (abolition of the poll tax), the Civil Rights Act of 1964 and the Voting Rights Act of 1965 were testimonies to the grassroots efforts of African Americans and organisations such as the NAACP, Southern Christian Leadership Conference, Student Nonviolent Coordinating Committee and the Congress of Racial Equality. These particular reforms followed history, as grassroots actions, resistance and violent struggles reframed race relations in America. In the process, post-war liberalism's internal contradictions with regards to the principle of equality and the harsh realities of segregation were confronted and directly resisted by the Civil Rights movement. And yet, as the Kerner Report pointed out, the 'expectations aroused by the great judicial and legislative victories of the civil rights movement have led to frustration, hostility and cynicism in the face of the persistent gap between promise and fulfillment' (Kerner 1968: 204). Housing, employment and education continued to be domains of struggle as a legacy of white supremacy persisted through taken-for-granted institutional practices and social attitudes. The recognition of these limits contributed to a radicalisation of the political scene as frustration in communities of colour boiled over in the streets and in the fields.

While the nation struggled to articulate a new vision of racial equality, the motion picture was integrated into post-war modes of governance across an array of institutional and industrial sites. Nonfiction filmmaking in non-theatrical contexts became a key medium for narrating as well as managing the nation's escalating engagement with race and racism. Michele Wallace for instance notes that 'up until the release of *Guess Who's Coming to Dinner?*, there is an interesting correlation between national governmental policies regarding "race," and film portrayals of racial subjects' (1993: 258). In the decades following World War II, the *classical* documentary form – or the expository mode – both persists and is reoriented to accommodate the post-war use of film by institutions as an instrument of knowledge formation (see Nichols 1991: 34). John Grierson's famously functionalist conception of nonfiction film reverberates in the 1950s as public agencies, corporations and non-profit organisations sponsor a dizzying array of training films, classroom films and other educational documentaries. The Griersonian preference for short documentaries premised on mapping out relationships between the subject and the state – utilising formalist and realist techniques in the process – remains as a constitutive horizon for a broad cross-section of documentary culture in the post-war era. It both continues and is also transformed by a number of innovations in documentary form as French, Canadian and American documentarians develop new modalities – participatory and observational – which seek to engage everyday life more directly while restraining the classical impulse to rely on voiceover narration and reenactments.

These transformations in documentary form during the post-war years are familiar. Nevertheless, a review of post-war educational documentaries can flesh out our understanding of these stylistic transformations with an eye towards their intersection with broader social and cultural forces. Certainly, the post-war deployment of documentary as a liberal medium for knowledge production and conflict mediation – essentially, from 1945 to 1970 – continues to be a murky terrain. The same time frame also encompasses the post-war push for Civil Rights as well as its aftermath. What *Projecting Race* sets out to accomplish is a fusion of these two lines of historical development, to present case studies of the American liberal documentary and its encounter with racial otherness. The documentary filmmaking of this period occurs against the wider historical backdrop of decolonisation, which Fredric Jameson argues should include the Civil Rights movement (1984: 180). Our diachronic survey of educational documentaries during this time charts a specific post-war racial look, or, following Alessandra Raengo, a 'visual relation' (2013: 12). Raengo paraphrases Frantz Fanon by arguing that Blackness is forged through a visual encounter, an interstice resting between 'interpellator and interpellated' (ibid.). These films, then, map this post-war racial look or visual relation and remind us of the particular *work* they perform on behalf of a problematic liberal discourse whose representations of people of colour is both a source of acknowledgment as well as a strategy for containment.

This is an area of scholarship that has been neglected within critical race film history. In his study of 'black-themed cinema' in the 1960s, Christopher Sieving notes that 'much of the major scholarly writing since 1993 on black film history has focused on those periods or movements dominated by African American directors and characterised by a conscious opposition' (2011: 4). The muddled and compromised world of post-war liberal documentary constitutes one of the blank spots in African American film history and critical race film history more generally. The focus on a clearly demarcated oppositional cinema is essential, of course, and this study stands on the shoulders of the research conducted on this front. My project, then, seeks to complement existing scholarship in both documentary history as well as critical race film history. The aim is to shed light on the racial politics of educational documentaries, often sponsored by various branches of the state. These agencies or institutions are clearly part of the status quo yet also resonate with a particular post-war anxiety around race. As a contribution to our understanding of this period of documentary film history, this book will highlight the documentary form's post-war life as a managerial tool for mitigating social conflict against the backdrop of evolving race relations. In doing so, the documentaries discussed will envelope the full breadth of approaches during this time, including expository, observational and participatory modalities. From this perspective, educational documentaries represent an intensification of documentary style, purpose and history as they mine and recombine contemporary filmmaking trends to accomplish a narrowly articulated pedagogical mission. Ultimately, this volume seeks to engage in a consideration of familiar documentary styles as they reflect and inflect a bigger national drama around the struggle to end segregation as well as confront racial inequality in a pre- and post-Civil Rights America.

The Racial Look, Liberalism and Documentary Film

This book is organised with chronological and conceptual goals in mind. Conscious of the broader context of post-war race relations in America, I trace the deployment of distinct educational documentary modes to both represent as well as manage racial otherness within a shifting liberal imaginary. The classical documentary film's ties to liberalism are more fundamental than they are negligible. As Zoë Druick has noted, 'a wide range of commentators as well as institutions' facilitated the 'formation of "documentary" as an educational instrument for modern nation building' (2008: 67). The documentary idea 'was seen to crystalize an alternative to Hollywood that might be developed outside of theatrical circuits for what were deemed serious purposes' (2008: 68). Druick demonstrates how international organisations, such as the League of Nations and the United Nations Educational, Scientific and Cultural Organization (UNESCO), were constitutive sites for the emergence of documentary film as a means of liberal pedagogy, closely 'tied to a discourse of neutrality seemingly outside politics' (ibid.). The perception of documentary film as an educational tool that addresses its audience with a tone of high seriousness and a feeling of being above the fray is a legacy of the documentary tradition. This familiar affect is the by-product of documentary film's early situation within a liberal formation centered on mitigating the traumatic effects of modernity.

By and large, the methodological disposition of this work leans toward historically situated textual analyses of well-known and lesser-known educational documentaries. Without delving too deeply into the ontology of the documentary image, let me briefly note that I read documentary *imagery* as *imaginary*. The term imaginary is used here in a rather conventional manner. Christian Metz referred to cinema as a 'technique of the imaginary' and suggested this was the case 'in two senses' (1986: 3). On the one hand, there is the Lacanian association in which the imaginary refers to a pre-oedipal stage of development when the infant encounters the 'endurable mark of the mirror' (1986: 4) and is both defined and divided by the experience of misrecognition. While on the other, there is the 'ordinary sense' (1986: 3) of the term. Here 'imaginary' refers to the cinema's reliance on a signifier that is illusory 'from the start' (1986: 44). What we perceive in cinema is 'not really the object, it is its shade, its phantom, its double, its *replica* in a new kind of mirror' (1986: 45). In short, there is no there there. What cinema presents to us is the paradox of a present absence or a moving image that is loaded with 'perceptual wealth, but at the same time stamped with unreality' (ibid.). This latter and simpler construction of imaginary is what attracts me. It articulates the contradictions and complexities of moving images in a way that encapsulates the documentary dilemma as we are drawn to an experience of perceptual indexicality – of reality registered before us – even as we are cognisant of the documentary image's spectrality and unreliability. Neither strictly objective nor subjective, imagery – in this case, documentary imagery – of race relations produced by ostensibly 'neutral' or even liberal institutions played a significant role in the evolving post-war perception of racial difference in the United States. Educational films often trace a liberal discourse that is less reflective of reality and more expressive of a desired civic cohesion in the face of racial and social conflict. This book's organisation, then, is designed to explore this role of documentary filmmaking within a shifting series of educational films that mix and match expository, observational and participatory modes in the process.

However, this familiar documentary dilemma can also be tied to the spectrality of racial imagery. In fact, Raengo echoes Metz when she deploys the shadow metaphor to challenge the paradigm of the mirror and its fixation on authenticity:

> we understand racial images to be those that deliver a racial content, ultimately, a body. When the body is secured, 'racial images' perform an ontologizing function: they are understood to be as accurate as mirror reflections and yet as tethered, contiguous, and, therefore, trustworthy as shadows. Thus racial images are those that can be trusted at face value. (2013: 163–4)

The trustworthiness of the mirror eventually gives way to its counterpart of the shadow. While the mirror generates a 'structure of referral' by securing its referent and assuring the viewer, the 'alternative paradigm' of the shadow is aligned with a 'structure of deferral' and nudges the viewer away from 'photographic fixing' and towards 'cinematic becoming' (Raengo 2013: 17, 39). But the Metzian shadow and its hollow authentication is seized by Raengo and rendered in socio-historical terms, arguing that the shadow of race – and ultimately the racial look - is *the* authoriser of the photochemical index. In our ongoing historical and cultural time frame, the racial image is the guarantor of indexical 'face value' (2013: 18). Of course, it is this apparent authorisation or 'ontologising function' that needs to be undone. If the faith of the index is often assured by a racialised body, then Raengo seeks to shed light on the phantasmagoric nature of this scene or encounter:

> The complication, though, is that the mirror is the mode through which the white, Western subject encounters the Other, as a mirror image, but one that reflects back something that is skewed, frightening, opaque, and thus needs to be disavowed. As [David] Marriott's reading of Fanon [in *Haunted Life*] shows, the face-to-face encounter between the black and the white produces blackness as a specter. The native too, Fanon explains, encounters her own other as a mirror, but quickly realizes that what is reflected back is neither here nor there; the black *imago* exists only in-between, like a ghost show, a phantasmagoria. (2013: 164)

Raengo's aim in her book, *On the Sleeve of the Visual*, is to chart

> a way out of the 'black representational space' … whereby this moment of phantasmagoric visuality can be productively mobilized to turn these visual relations inside out, and blackness can be unhinged from the body and the image, but still claim its 'ontological resistance'. (Ibid.)

Seeing Blackness outside the fixity of the 'photochemical imagination' and instead from the vantage point of 'the shadow' short-circuits our unconscious slippage from visible surfaces to visual depths (2013: 3, 165). This is, in fact, one reason for couching this book's historical textual analyses in terms of a cultural history of the racial look. The idea of the racial look reminds us that what is being produced is always, as Raengo states, a visual relation between the observer and the observed rather than something fixed (a deferral rather than a referral). Raengo also empowers us to forge a critical gaze that undercuts the allure of giving ourselves over to the imagined depths of the image while also leaving the door open for imagery that foreground these visual relations in implicit and explicit ways.

Organisation

Over the course of seven chapters, this book tracks the post-war racial look in sponsored cinema as it evolves from the fixity of a therapeutic gaze to the productive uncertainty of collaboration. The narrative put forward here, then, charts the development of a liberal racial look that is increasingly unsure of itself and yet always hegemonic, never completely displaced. The last chapter comes the closest as the state-sponsored film crew for *The Hartford Project* (1969) includes a local community leader and founder of the Hartford chapter of the Black Panther Party, Charles 'Butch' Lewis. And yet the still largely unseen films were dismissed by the OEO, the agency that sponsored them, as a failed project. Nevertheless, the elements that make *The Hartford Project* so compelling almost fifty years later are the same ones that elicited disavowal at the time of its production.[2]

In essence, the first half of the book (chapters 1–3) focuses on the immediate post-war years and the influence of Italian neorealism on documentary filmmaking, while the second half (chapters 4–7) centres on the incorporation of new documentary approaches (observational, participatory) into pedagogical cinema. Chapter one – 'Documenting from Below: Post-war Documentary, Race and Everyday Life' – provides an essential historical prologue for the book and reviews key concepts that emerge throughout, including Henri Cartier-Bresson's *decisive moment* as well as David Desser's *therapeutic vision*. This section initially provides a sketch of the post-war Griersonian documentary tradition and how that interfaces with a broader history of race and film in the United States. The core thematic takeaway from this opening section not only concerns the expansion of managerial and educational cinema after World War II, but – more crucially – the emergence of a 'feeling of the new' (Casetti 1999: 75) within the documentary domain. This sensibility draws from Italian neorealism and seeks out slices of everyday life. It speaks to what I characterise as the *documentary from below* – speaking from the vantage point of life as it is lived through the textures of everyday experience – and thus impacts the post-war racial look as African American experiences are articulated through a therapeutic address to African American characters who have incurred traumas on the battlefield, in the streets and in the home. The domain of the educational documentary charts a contradictory post-war framing as the subjective experiences of African American individuals are directly acknowledged while also inoculated from the political realities of racial inequality.

Chapter two – 'The Sick Quiet that Follows Violence: Neorealism, Psychotherapy and Collaboration' – presents analyses of two key documentaries from the early post-war years that pursue distinct representational strategies. While not a typical educational documentary, *The Quiet One* (1948) is nevertheless a documentary classic whose influence is discernible in all of the subsequent films discussed in this book. It conveniently synthesises the overlapping stylistic threads reviewed in chapter one as the film draws on classical documentary techniques and Italian neorealist traits in order to highlight a particular social problem. Nevertheless, the way in which the film depicts its young African American protagonist, Donald, privileges a therapeutic approach that is more invested in tracking his familial trauma than the realities of racial inequality in the post-war years. George C. Stoney's and William T. Clifford's *Palmour Street* (1949), as a mental hygiene film produced by the Southern Educational Film Production Service (SEFPS), is similarly focused on psychological issues. Sponsored by the State of Georgia, the film's aim was to promote mental health awareness among African American families. The film also shares with *The Quiet One* a neorealist sensibility as it reenacts the daily struggles of a particular African American family. The mental hygiene credentials of *Palmour Street* continue to uphold *The Quiet One*'s focus on familial struggles and yet the collaborative nature of the production opens up the film's overall address. Rather than psychically pin down its subject through an authoritative voiceover, *Palmour Street* presents open-ended vignettes of African American family life in the south. The family's struggles are less severe than those shown in *The Quiet One* and thus more relatable. As a form of filmic pedagogy, *Palmour Street* embraces aperture over closure as the film sets out to provoke discussion and self-reflection among its audiences. In spite of the shared properties of these two films, *Palmour Street* moderates the professionalised racial look as a result of Stoney and Clifford's collaborative and deferential approach which seeks to pose questions without offering clear answers. This educational film's uniqueness and divergence from *The Quiet One* is also contextualised within a history of the SEFPS.

Chapter three – 'Charismatic Knowledge: Modernity and Southern African American Midwifery in *All My Babies* (1952)' – picks up where the previous chapter left off by focusing on another film by George Stoney, *All My Babies*. Like *The Quiet One*, *All My Babies* is a seminal American documentary film whose innovations result in part from its neorealist posture and investment in recording everyday life by restaging events as well as capturing them in real time. However, *All My Babies* shares with Stoney and Clifford's *Palmour Street* a commitment to collaboration with the African American subjects in the film as well as from the larger community of midwives and nurses. Sponsored by the Georgia Department of Health and the Medical Film Institute of the Association of American Medical Colleges, *All My Babies* was designed to encourage enhanced cooperation and dialogue between African American midwives and health care professionals, between traditional and modern practices of birthing. As such the film's educational agenda dovetails with its collaborative mode of production as a modern means of communication, and *cinema* enters the fray to better facilitate this encounter. Nevertheless, the film has not yet been fully considered in light of this controversial wave of modernisation, one that often sought to marginalise the figure of the African American midwife. Stoney's film, which has been justifiably praised for its humanistic treatment of the midwife, must mitigate its own divided racial look and constitute African American midwifery as a flexible practice with a legacy formidable enough to stand up to the modern medical establishment.

Chapters four through seven shift the focus to educational documentaries whose modes of address reflect the new observational and participatory styles that became so paradigmatic in the 1960s. Stoney reemerges here as an important figure, one who laments his inability to deal directly with what he considered to be the 'central issue of the middle 20th century,' the Civil Rights movement; in his mind, he was 'failing in [his] basic responsibility to record history as it is made' (1963). The observational and participatory modes of documentary (or, respectively, direct cinema and *cinema vérité*) reinvigorated Stoney and other documentarians in the 1960s. Chapter four – 'Full of Fire: Historical Urgency and Utility in *The Man in the Middle* (1966)' – reviews the emergence of these two modes and insists on reading them, in spite of their differences, as expressions of a desire to record everyday life. Of course, these modes dispense with the use of reenactments in earlier neorealist films and seek to minimise the rhetorical device of voiceover narration, especially the Voice of God. Instead, both modes of documentary prefer to capture events as they unfold, whether the filmmakers sees themselves as observers or active participants. These new documentary approaches presume a reality that plays out in real time and ultimately resist the pedagogical intentionality we associate with educational filmmaking. A clear example of how training films bore the mark of these new approaches comes from Stoney and his film, *The Man in the Middle*. This was one of a handful of training films that Stoney produced for various police departments in the 1960s. While most of Stoney's police training films reflect the stylistic traits of his earlier work, *The Man in the Middle* takes advantage of observational and participatory techniques to transform what might have been an unremarkable training film into a pedagogically unique project. In the end, the film marries the stasis of *procedure* with the flux of embodied history as words of protest from community organisers from South Jamaica, Queens are featured.

Chapter five – 'Training Days: Liberal Advocacy and Self-Improvement in War on Poverty Films' – continues this look at how training films absorbed new documentary modalities through a discussion of select state-sponsored War on Poverty films. Through extensive archival research I show that filmmaking was an important part of how the War on Poverty was pitched to the populace and how new volunteers were recruited and trained. While many of the documentaries were classical in style – featuring Voice of God narration, reenactments, and evidentiary editing strategies – others became increasingly inspired by new observational and participatory approaches. The narrative arc of this chapter follows the construction of the white liberal advocate whose onscreen presence eventually yields as the films grow increasingly observational in style. Films discussed here include *The First Thirty* (1965), *A Year Towards Tomorrow* (1966), *With No One to Help Us* (1967) and the Drew Associates' *Another Way* (1967).

The final two chapters expand the consideration of the War on Poverty by highlighting the OEO's experiments with participatory filmmaking in the late 1960s. Chapter six – 'The World is Quiet Here: War on Poverty, Participatory Filmmaking and *The Farmersville Project* (1968)' – centers on *The Farmersville Project*, a series of educational shorts imagined as community development films. The frustrations of which Lanford spoke at the outset of this introduction refer to one of the instances in which the OEO embraced a new participatory documentary approach – one developed in Canada – to mitigate the entrenched racial and class-based hostilities occurring on the ground. *The Farmersville Project* represents the first instance of what I call the 'OEO Communication Experiments' (OEOCE). Largely ignored by historians, the OEOCE involved the collaboration of American and Canadian administrators in the late 1960s. Specifically, in 1967, the National Film Board of Canada sponsored what became known as *The Newfoundland Project*: an experiment in participatory filmmaking conducted by Colin Low (NFB) and Donald Snowden from Memorial University. Initially expecting to make a traditional documentary about the problems facing the residents of Fogo Island and their response to a top-down policy of resettlement, Low wound up producing twenty-eight short topical films designed to promote a civil and reconciliatory discourse. The films were screened locally as well as to outside policymakers in order to open up new lines of dialogue on a contentious issue. While the crisis on Fogo Island eventually reached a resolution, the *perception* of success on the part of this filmmaking endeavour – described as the 'Fogo process' – traversed the border and drew the attention of Public Affairs staff at the OEO.

Chapter six as well as chapter seven – 'An Urban Situation: *The Hartford Project* and the North American Challenge' – review the OEO's attempts to apply the Fogo process to communities torn asunder by racial conflict and socioeconomic divisions. The two communities selected – Farmersville, California and Hartford, Connecticut – posed obvious contrasts, as the former was agrarian and rural while the latter was urban and industrial. And yet both were examples of communities where the institutionalised white status quo was threatened by increasingly organised and politically active racial minorities. The OEO's heightened anxiety in the face of its own precarious status – as the election of Richard Nixon loomed – as well as the rise of what Herbert Kramer, head of Public Affairs at the OEO, referred to as 'black militancy' (Anon. 1975: 19) compels a crisis in the agency's managerial liberal outlook. This breaking point represents a partial conclusion to our history of the post-war educational documentary and its registration of the racial look. Ultimately, chapters four through seven seek to advance our knowledge of race-themed educational documentaries in the 1960s, a decade that – according to Christopher Sieving – 'has gone largely unexplored by scholars in the field of black cinema studies' (2011: 1).

Taken together, these seven chapters give a sense of how educational documentary filmmaking evolved in the post-war era as the influence of Italian neorealism waned and new documentary approaches were developed. The documentary film activities addressed here collectively represent – in spite of their variety – a racial look transfixed by a double desire to acknowledge change while upholding a sense of stability and stasis. The dramatic fight for racial equality during these decades brought about incredible transformations while also shedding light on an entrenched white normativity across a number of everyday and institutional settings. Post-war liberal institutions were similarly caught in a series of contradictory maneuvers, taking one step forward and two steps back. And one of the best ways to access these ideological machinations is through particular modes of communication in a number of different settings at different times. This overview of educational documentary activities will help us chart a narrative of post-war liberalism's schizophrenic navigation of racial difference, entailing a dance of recognition and denial.

Documentary Studies, Film History and Participatory Culture

In remarks made at an event sponsored by the Museum of Contemporary Art in Chicago – 'Public Media 2.0: A Conversation on the Future of Urban Documentary and Social Change' – B. Ruby Rich, a noted feminist film scholar and critic, observed that the study of documentary film had evolved from an initial infatuation with 'authors' – or great documentarians – to a study of radical media and social change.[3] The former impulse was motivated by a desire to validate the documentary film as an aesthetic object of study and counter claims of realist naiveté. The subsequent response focused on the documentary's deployment by a wider range of practitioners and activists, many of whom were and are socially marginalised based on their race, gender, sexual orientation and/or class status.

Documentary form – in its cinematic, video and digital manifestations – offered and continues to offer a crucial means of intervention into the public sphere and the politics of visibility. When looked at from this vantage point, this volume combines a heuristic investment in the aesthetic study of documentary filmmakers with a materialist commitment to mobilise their filmmaking and films within a social and political field. To be blunt, many of the filmmakers highlighted here are white males working for the state. The point of this project is not, however, to simply trumpet the filmmakers' technical and aesthetic achievements. Rather, the aim is to understand the historical and political presence of their work and its engagement with race at a time when liberal institutions were evolving rapidly.

Textual analysis of key films is, then, at the heart of my methodological tool kit; but, as David E. James has written, 'a film's images and sounds never fail to tell the story of how and why they were produced – the story of the mode of their production' (1989: 5). While much of my own discourse is spent on the films' 'images and sounds', these analyses are mindful of their institutional purpose and historical situation. Whether we're talking about the SEFPS, NFB or the OEO, I read the resulting films or film series – *Palmour Street, All My Babies, The Man in the Middle, The Farmersville Project*, etc – against the historical backdrop of their production, reconstructed through archival research as well as oral history. The retroactive work of critical analysis also necessarily includes framing these film practices in relation to their historical circumstances. All of the film activities reviewed represent a post-war liberal engagement with race and race relations that fluctuates over two and a half decades from an early Cold War variation, with its 'emphasis on the strictly formal aspects of racial discrimination' (Horton 2005: 122), to the last gasps of Great Society managerial liberalism in the late 1960s.

Many of the filmmakers discussed in this book are underappreciated, if their work is known at all. George Stoney has been well known for a very long time, and yet a sustained study of his work and its significance has been fleeting, perhaps attributable to his commitment to collaboration and social activism over and above his own authorial contributions to documentary. Nevertheless, the recent critical mass of academic interest in the history and theory of educational films sets the stage for a consideration of Stoney's work at the SEFPS and later. Anthony Slide, Geoff Alexander, Heide Solbrig, Haidee Wasson, Lee Grieveson and Dan Streible have helped underscore the significance of the moving image as a pedagogical instrument throughout the twentieth century. Research centered on non-theatrical films frequently combines an exciting range of historiographic methods, attendant to the particularities of educational film form as well as the variety of its institutional situations. In this light Stoney, whose work has been sidelined or ignored altogether, assumes greater significance. For quite some time now, histories of the moving image have exceeded the boundaries of entertainment and art to incorporate other educational and communicative domains. This openness to the deployment of the moving image to manage perceptions of public health, labour and race relations in specific historical circumstances makes a fresh appreciation of Stoney as well as the SEFPS possible.

A materialist enquiry into the post-war documentary's negotiation of race and race relations, then, both renews our appreciation of familiar documentarians as well as generates new knowledge about the moving image's incorporation into an array of communicative procedures. Tracing these filmmakers' experiences also contributes an understanding of the state and its inevitable ties to social movements. Out of respect for the 'ambiguous location of Chicano cinema', Chon Noriega – in his book, *Shot in America: Television, the State, and the Rise of Chicano Cinema* – acknowledges the methodological necessity of teasing out and foregrounding the interlocking strands that bind the study of social movements to the study of the state (2000: xi). George Stoney was both an activist and a filmmaker for the SEFPS. Colin Low and Julian Biggs were employees of both the Canadian and American governments whose approach to participatory filmmaking reflected a desire to bring about social change. These are complicated individuals in very contradictory institutional settings. Their sensibilities register the flow of post-war liberalism and its dialectical embrace of change and stasis, management and malleability.

Finally, this book will risk proposing a metanarrative. As a contribution to film history, this project charts another affinity among these filmmakers in spite of the neatness of the conceptual divisions implied by its chapters. The formal distinctions acknowledged here belie a broader impulse towards a participatory cultural formation. Stoney's subject-centered production engenders a revision of documentary practices with an eye towards participation and collaboration between the filmmaker and the subjects of a documentary. In this sense, his work at the SEFPS looks ahead to his time as the head of the NFB's 'Challenge for Change' (1966–70) project, when he championed the teaching of production skills to indigenous peoples so that they may author their own films about their community. Low's work on *The Newfoundland Project* – which inaugurated 'Challenge for Change' – as well as the OEOCE, he described as 'vertical' rather than 'horizontal' (Crocker 2008: 66). By this he meant that the Fogo process and its promotion of condensed filmic portraiture diminishes the intervention of the filmmaker and places greater emphasis on the life experiences and expressions of documentary subjects. While divergent in important ways, these documentary practices also cohere around a notion of privileging voices and daily experiences that are otherwise excluded from broad historical narratives. The idea of a documentary project whose perspective on the historical world comes *from below* opens up the frame to accommodate contingency and subjective expression.

Upon his return to the United States and the fading influence of the blacklist, John Grierson recognised a similar paradigm shift in documentary production from expository norms to *cinema vérité*. He recognised that new participatory practices entailed 'decentralizing the means of production, taking the myth out of it … and making the documentary film a living tool for people at the grass roots' (Sussex 1976: 196). With the participatory turn, as Bill Nichols has put it, the filmmaking process is the result of an interaction or an 'encounter' (2001: 17) rather than something imposed. And with this an element of contingency is overtly introduced and the dream of representing reality in any totalised sense falters. The privileging of subjects' voices yields a more inductive and fractured whole, nudging the documentary project that much closer to the everyday and the actual as opposed to a presumably deeper real (see Aitken 1992: 12). This epistemic break suggests a more modest and less confident documentary endeavour that parallels cracks in modern liberalism in the 1960s and eventually engenders heightened reflexive sensitivities on the part of film diarists, essayists and ethnographers. This book's concluding sections suggest that the state's crisis mentality of 1968–69, then, found a synchronous avenue of expression in new participatory documentary practices. State agencies were seeking new ways to access the thorny issue of racism and poverty, to address as well as call out subjects caught up in untenable socio-economic circumstances. Vérité modes of production resonated with the needs of a state agency in crisis and, in turn, registered a parallel crisis in consciousness as classical expository aims were increasingly seen as untenable. The politics of visibility were changing and called for an embrace of greater expressivity, to unsettle the authority of a voice outside and above the subjective experiences conveyed. Instead the 'voice' of the documentary and the voices of the subjects depicted should meet at some point, inscribed together in new documentary practices.[4] The OEO's use of the Fogo process in 1968 and 1969 presents us with an opportunity to explore a concrete manifestation of these aesthetic and managerial crises in intersection with one another and with specific material conditions. As Henry Lanford notes, previously unquestioned motivations were coming into sharper focus.

Notes

1 Excerpts from this chapter were previously published in Stephen Charbonneau (2014) 'Exporting Fogo: Participatory Filmmaking, War on Poverty, and the

Politics of Visibility', *Framework*, 55, 2, 220–47. Reproduced with permission of Wayne State University Press.

2 The title, *The Hartford Project*, is partly a critical construction on my part. The reality is that *The Hartford Project* unlike its counterpart, *The Farmersville Project*, was left largely unfinished and partial. As we will see, this was largely because the production encountered a wide range of difficulties. Nevertheless, in spite of this sense of incompleteness, the title corresponds to a series of twenty-four films that are by any measure a coherent body of work that documents life in Hartford in 1969.

3 'Public Media 2.0: A Conversation on the Future of Urban Documentary and Social Change' was held on 6 March 2013 at the Museum of Contemporary Art in Chicago. It featured discussions with Gordon Quinn, Allan Siegel, Steve James and Michelle Citron. The event was also moderated by B. Ruby Rich, Mark Shiel and Brendan Kredell and was sponsored by the Society for Cinema and Media Studies and the University of Chicago.

4 Bill Nichols characterises the 'voice' of a documentary as a synonym for the 'social point of view' of the film (1985: 260).

CHAPTER ONE

DOCUMENTING FROM BELOW: POST-WAR DOCUMENTARY, RACE AND EVERYDAY LIFE[1]

The history of documentary film is inextricably bound up with the representation of racial otherness dating back to nineteenth-century efforts to integrate film-making into anthropological excursions. Subsequent ethnographic films, rooted in a colonialist ideology, include the Lumière-produced *actualités*, popular travelogues by Paul J. Rainey such as *African Hunt* (1912), and, of course, Robert Flaherty's romantic ethnographic classic, *Nanook of the North* (1922). John Grierson's famous coining of the term 'documentary' was in response to Flaherty's second film, *Moana* (1926), a salvage ethnography in pursuit of a pre-modern Polynesian culture (see Ellis 2000: 28). It is also difficult to disentangle race from the documentary film's broader liberal tendency to train citizens, promote cultural pedagogy and, to some extent, manage the excesses of modern life in the twentieth century. The post-war educational documentary wades into these familiar waters and exhibits an intensified documentary experience in which a procedural address is wedded to a growing infatuation with psychoanalytic and therapeutic discourses. This means that the stylistic traits of a classical or 'traditional' documentary film are all present, but the pedagogical aim is much more calibrated to a specialist audience. If a theatrical documentary film addresses its audience with the proverbial axe, then an educational documentary is allied with the scalpel.

This chapter's primary aim is to acknowledge the pre-World War II cinematic legacies that are both confronted and continued in my later case studies, particularly the films reviewed in chapters two and three. The documentaries analysed, whatever their peculiarities, participate in a broader history of film and race. They also speak to the post-war evolution of documentary filmmaking more specifically. The Griersonian documentary tradition persists in the post-war decades even as it is transformed by countless transnational articulations. Its absorption into colonial and postcolonial conflicts speaks to its pliability as the social documentary form Grierson outlined cascades from liberal managerialism to Third World Marxism. The post-war iteration of the Griersonian documentary at work here is deeply influenced by Italian neorealism. As has been noted, *The Quiet One, Palmour Street* and *All My Babies* reflect the neorealist impulse to shadow reality through non-professional actors ensconced in everyday settings. Their Griersonian credentials are clear, but varied. While *The Quiet One* and *Palmour Street* have explicit messages on behalf of the social services they depict, the former's formalism is more evidently aligned with the modernism of the Griersonian vision. Nevertheless, *Palmour Street*'s educational mission fulfills the Griersonian call for documentary films to teach and ultimately seal the breach between citizens and the state. *All My Babies* similarly participates in a wave of medical modernisation and pedagogy sweeping the south even as its celebration of the African American midwife hedges on this aspect of its sponsored mission. A proper framing of these films, then, calls for a clear orientation in terms of documentary history, the Griersonian tradition, as well as the history of American film and race. The educational films highlighted by this book should be viewed at the intersection of these three strands where a post-war cinematic *feeling of the new* is experienced in light of a core 'American Dilemma', in which the white majority is simultaneously representative of 'enduring political values and deeply ingrained anti-African prejudices' (Horton 2005: 122).[2]

Post-war Grierson and 'A Feeling of the New'

If we step back and take a broader view of post-war documentary filmmaking in the United States, it is possible to read the innovations of this period as part of a re-calibration of the classic Griersonian model for documentary. Grierson's formulation of the documentary film as a medium uniquely suited for promoting citizenship as well as functional communication between the state and the public continues to resonate as a foundational touchstone for Western nonfiction filmmaking.[3] And yet this model clearly evolves in light of a constellation of transnational cultural influences during the post-war era. From the vantage point of the United States, formal and practical innovations developed by filmmakers in Canada, France and Italy influenced American documentarians and redirected the Griersonian notion of documentary towards the recording of everyday life, energised by *cinema vérité* and direct cinema or, respectively, the participatory and observational modes of documentary. The epistemologically distinct paths of the participatory and observational modes revised the Griersonian project even as many of the latter's core principles remained intact. Despite their modal differences, these adjustments to documentary form are expressions of an inertial movement towards a representation of everyday life that challenges the strictures of classical documentary exposition.

This claim is not unusual. Many scholars of documentary film history have offered similar insights into how *cinema vérité* and direct cinema revised the orientation of documentary film in the post-war era.[4] My point is that this paradigmatic swing in favour of everyday life produces particular echoes in the racial politics of many American documentaries during this time. From within the post-war bubble of American racial politics, this broader cultural swing towards the registration of everyday life in documentary film is inscribed in particular ways around the issue of race. If the post-war liberal admission of racial inequality is constrained by its focus on the 'formal aspects' of racial discrimination – i.e. blind to the affective, cultural, social and economic ramifications of white supremacy – then post-war nonfictional representations of race challenge this constraint by venturing beyond the juridical sphere and into a socio-psychic one. The emphasis on the 'everyday' in post-war documentary accrues a significant political edge when the experiences depicted and the emotions on display are those of oppressed racial minorities. In such instances, we can discern a tension inherent to the post-war liberal tendency to understand racial inequality in strictly legalistic terms, often occluding social, cultural and psychological reverberations.

Of course, any reading of the racial politics of post-war documentary must account for the historical ebb and flow of Grierson's influential ideas about what the documentary film can and should do. The way in which the Griersonian model of documentary film changes in the post-war period is a crucial context for understanding the linkage between the liberal documentary and race. The primer on Grierson that follows will emphasise his relationship to the United States as well as his contribution to the definition of documentary film as a mechanism for stabilising national identity and citizenship in an increasingly turbulent twentieth century. We shall see how the Griersonian model was revised in light of new filmic and photographic practices in Canada, France and the United States. My focus on Canada reflects a desire on my part to correct the tendency of film historians to overlook the contributions of Canadian filmmakers to world cinema, but also speaks to the cultural entanglement of Canada to the United States which is at the heart of the last two chapters of this book.

John Grierson may have been born in Scotland, but his canonical perspective on filmmaking was forged by his post-graduate years in Chicago, Hollywood and New York. As Jack C. Ellis has recognised, Grierson returned home from the US with three fundamental premises having been solidified: 'citizenship education was the broad necessity, film the chosen medium, documentary its special form' (2000: 21). Grierson's arrival at these premises was both a product of his encounter with new trends in global cinema (Hollywood, Eisenstein and Flaherty) as well as indicative of a climate of liberal elite angst in light of the encroachments of modernity, specifically dramatic social transformations wrought by industry, technology and mass culture.

Most famously, it was Grierson's absorption of Walter Lippmann's ideas on modern society and citizenship as articulated in his book *Public Opinion* (1922) that made the biggest mark on his thinking. In short, Lippmann argued that the American democratic process was no longer practical in the wake of significant changes incurred on the country's path to modernity. In his view, the romantic notion of cultivated and informed voters rationally conducting themselves in the voting booth was untenable given the pace and labyrinthine nature of modern societies, where the issues of the day (foreign policy, finance and the workplace) rendered the classic democratic, educational model obsolete. What was now needed – from this point of view – was a new and more modern pedagogical framework: specifically, a medium capable of mobilising the frenetic details of quotidian life into new narrative structures out of which an elusive deeper truth could emerge. For Grierson, Hearst newspapers were a model in this regard. In them he claimed to have discerned 'a deeper principle' in which a 'complex world … could be patterned for all to appreciate if we only got away from the servile accumulation of fact and struck for the story which held the facts in living organic relationship together' (qtd. in Ellis 2000: 22). The medium of cinema, Lippmann suggested to Grierson, provided the kind of spectacular 'dramatic patterns' that could be replicated in educational discourses with the support of the state or other non-commercial institutions (ibid.). Through his initiation and management of the film units for the British government's Empire Marketing Board (1928–34) and the General Post Office (1934–38), Grierson fine-tuned a pedagogical and propagandistic cinema premised on promoting and consolidating a sense of national identity among viewers through the use of short films in non-traditional exhibition settings. While deploying an array of formalist techniques – montage, poetic narration, visual composition – films like *Night Mail* (Harry Watt and Basil Wright, 1936) articulated a new vision of modern citizenship to smooth over the rough edges of daily life in an increasingly complex industrial and colonial era.

In the late 1930s Grierson advised the Canadian government in the design and establishment of its National Film Board (NFB), serving as the board's first commissioner from October 1939 until 1945. Through his work with state institutions – from 1928 to 1945 – a Griersonian documentary frame proved enormously influential and increasingly pliable to an array of transnational articulations. Following his departure from the NFB, Gary Evans notes that while 'some felt anchored to the Grierson tradition of making public-service films in the national interest', there was a new generation of filmmakers who believed in 'breaking out of past patterns and in anticipating future trends' (1991: 67). Specifically, Evans continues: 'Many of the Quebec filmmakers were falling under the spell of *Nouvelle vague* (New Wave) in French cinema and felt that change was at last imminent in their tradition-bound province' (ibid.). The NFB's 'Unit B' would be home to new innovations in documentary form during the 1950s. Colin Low got his start at the NFB as an animator and his first live-action film, *Corral* (1954), is indicative of a shift away from classic Griersonian documentary. Centered on the topic of horse training, *Corral* was initially envisioned as an expository documentary in the Griersonian tradition, specifically through its use of voiceover narration to 'explain the training process' (Delisle 2007). However, Low and Tom Daly – the executive producer of Unit B – came to the conclusion that the imagery, in conjunction with the film's musical score, were best served without the burden of voiceover narration (ibid.). The signification conveyed by the visual composition, editing and the music was sufficient for the film's purposes. *Corral*, then, is indicative of the emergence of a new paradigm in documentary filmmaking whose piecemeal definition came together through a transnational circuit of cultural developments in Canada, France and the United States.

The allure of *Nouvelle vague* cinema for Canadian filmmakers is central. But a related and equally important French influence was that of the photographer Henri Cartier-Bresson. Specifically, Cartier-Bresson's book *Images à la sauvette* (*The Decisive Moment*) was cited by several filmmakers of the NFB's Unit B as an influence on their approach to documentary filmmaking (see Evans 1991: 70). This publication 'paid homage to surrealism and the principles of photojournalism in the recording of daily ephemera', deploying techniques such as the 'rapid-fire 35-mm camera to document the drama of the ordinary moment' (ibid.). Cartier-Bresson wrote many years later in 1976 that the 'camera is a sketch book, an instrument of intuition and spontaneity, the master of the instant which, in visual terms, questions and decides simultaneously' (2005: 15). With an insistence on capturing the 'absolute ambience of real life', Cartier-Bresson's work prompted the Canadian filmmakers of Unit B, Roman Kroitor and Wolf Koenig, to consider whether 'documentary film could not also embody the concept of "the decisive moment", that instant in which reality can be spontaneously and wholly rendered' (Evans 1991: 70). For Koenig, it was possible to trace 'a line from Cartier-Bresson to John Grierson's dictum that in documentary you

must serve the public and make subjects of peace as exciting as those of war'
(ibid.). Developing an indexical cinema that was open to the singularity of moments reflecting fleeting human experience and daily life felt – to Koenig at least
– like an extension of Grierson's humanitarian documentary aesthetic. And yet,
centring the camera's gaze upon 'ephemera' and 'decisive moments' carves out
a space for a *structured incoherence*, for allowing small everyday details to hang
within the architecture of the film without any clear explanation.

Incorporating resistant moments of everyday life, reflecting the present-ness
of experience, into a new documentary form held out the possibility for a more
open and inductive mode of address, less invested in communicating a reductive message. Evans continues to note that Koenig and Kroitor were not alone
in their desire to rethink their assumptions about what a documentary film can
be (see Evans 1991: 71). Others, such as Georges Dufaux, Gilles Gascon and
Michel Brault, drew similar lessons about being more receptive to the vicissitudes of everyday life from 'the neorealism of Rossellini's *Open City* and de Sica's
Bicycle Thieves, and were intrigued with Carol Reed's and Garson Kanin's *The
True Glory*, a documentary newsreel that had shown the possibilities of merging
dialogue with documentary' (ibid.).

These post-war aspirations on the part of some documentarians in North America do not, it must be emphasised, contribute to a fading of Grierson's influence. Rather, Griersonian principles are re-calibrated to accommodate these new desires, technologies and interests. Even as post-war documentary practices began to embrace the representation of everyday life – aided by the deployment of lightweight 16-mm cameras and wireless synchronous sound systems – the Griersonian tradition persisted as a normative paradigm available for re-interpretation rather than dismissal. In the United States, for instance, the post-war years carried forward the Griersonian tradition in documentary while also redefining it. In 1946 Philip Dunne, for instance, proclaimed in the pages of *Hollywood Quarterly* that 'three Britishers' – Grierson, Raymond Spottiswoode and Paul Rotha – had said 'almost everything that needs to be said about the documentary per se, analytically or historically' (1946: 166). During this time institutional support on the part of companies and state agencies produced a wide array of health, human services, human relations, mental hygiene and vocational films. Often exhibited in non-theatrical settings – such as classrooms, libraries and factories – these films registered a continuation of a modern liberal discourse invested in managing modernity while also re-configuring this familiar discourse around new social theories of human management. The Griersonian triad of film, documentary and citizenship education was embraced by the state during World War II and went on to be incorporated into a new post-war corporate culture, imported under the guise of an apolitical address to viewers. This discourse was steeped in scientific modes of expression and helped turn, for instance, 'sociological *theories* of worker-management interaction [into] material *practices* through the narratives and exercises of industrial media products' (Solbrig 2007: 28).

Both *The Quiet One* and *Palmour Street* – discussed in the next chapter – animate the twin lanes of post-war Griersonian documentary. On the one hand, the impulse to educate and train audiences in service to a state agency is a defining feature of these films. *The Quiet One* was produced to support the Wiltwyck School for Boys in New York and its exposition is designed to convince audiences of the school's mission in light of a particular social problem. Stoney and Clifford's *Palmour Street* is equally conversant with the Griersonian tradition and the film embraces a classical documentary approach through its use of exposition and re-enactment. On the other hand, these films' respective production teams embraced approaches that – while divergent – sought to access the experience of everyday life for their featured subjects in a way that nudges the Griersonian project in a new direction. For their part, Janice Loeb, Helen Levitt and Sidney Meyers wanted to ground the exposition of *The Quiet One* in the singular experience of an African American boy whose struggles would be central to the film. *Palmour Street* evokes this turn towards the everyday with its incorporation of elements associated with Italian neorealism. As Jonathan Kahana notes, in many of his films Stoney had emulated the neorealist impulse to focus on ordinary people (or non-professional actors) and forge a performative space in which real people re-stage events from their lives, or *shadow reality* through cinematic reenactment (2009: 46). Robert Sklar (2012) has similarly written about *The Quiet One*'s neorealist credentials.

One implication of the hybridic nature of these films is a reversal of the Griersonian insight that the chaos of modern life necessitates subjugating the everyday to the hermeneutic power of modernist interventions. *The Quiet One* and *Palmour Street* both represent reality through a discourse that is profoundly personal, subjective and embodied. Their films' narrative worlds are dialectically interwoven with the everyday experiences of their African American protagonists and, thus, compel the documentary project towards the *decisive moment*. But, interestingly, they are still very much a part of the classical Griersonian tradition in light of their films' pedagogical aims, which are advanced by these films' investment in personal portraiture.

Documentary, Blackness, and the Therapeutic Vision[5]

As mentioned earlier, this representation of everyday life acquires a certain political resonance in light of the racialised experiences depicted. And the politics of these representations actually parallel the post-war liberal moment in the US. In these films the reality of racial inequality in America is both acknowledged and unacknowledged. It is recognised in the form of the struggles and everyday experiences of the African American personalities depicted onscreen, as the ultimate frame for the difficulties registered on film. But the historical reality of racial inequality is also obscured by the emphasis on specific African American individuals. The psychological experiences of these films' main characters holds the broader backdrop of racism at a canted angle, slightly out of view and yet ever present. In the end, the films are designed to have a particular social utility for particular institutions, thus to some extent blunting the critical ripple effects of their films' subject matter. This dynamic traces the racial politics of post-war liberalism in which anxiety over racism and segregation is narrowly expressed in legalistic terms, acknowledging racial inequality and yet not grasping its full historical, cultural and economic consequences. Furthermore, this highly limited discourse of regret and embarrassment is prompted by a critical mass of historical circumstances, including the heightened scrutiny given to the US in light of its elevated status after the war as well as the new political clout of African Americans in the north (see Horton 2005: 124). These historical conditions compelled a broader acknowledgement of the country's 'racial situation' in order to attract Black votes as well as pass international scrutiny as a preeminent world power. The prevailing post-war culture of embarrassment among liberal elites was a far cry from the revolution in consciousness needed in order to address the legacy of white supremacy in the US.

The documentary representations of Black subjectivity under review in chapters two and three tap into a history of racial representation and Black stereotyping in American film. It would be a mistake to abstract these representations from this history as they are elementally interconnected. D. W. Griffith's *Birth of a Nation* (1915) is the seminal film text in this regard and, as Donald Bogle has shown, the film not only draws on previously established Black stereotypes, but also contributes the 'final mythic type, the brutal black buck' (1989: 10). The constellation of racist stereotypes in this film – the 'faithful souls', the 'brutal black bucks' and the 'mulattoes' – have continued to resonate through American film history, prompting Bogle to note that 'one can detect in this single film the trends and sentiments that were to run through almost every black film made for a long time afterward. Later film makers were to pick up Griffith's ideas – his very images – but were to keep them "nicely" toned down in order not to offend audiences' (1989: 13). The persistence of this racist kernel in American cinema is a common theme in critical race film history. Manthia Diawara insists that the release of *The Birth of a Nation* 'defined for the first time the side that Hollywood was to take in the war to represent Black people in America' (1993: 3). Griffith's toxic film, he continues, 'became Hollywood's only way of talking about Black people' (ibid.).

Black independent cinema mobilised an array of counter-representations in response to Hollywood's entrenched white supremacist formal and narrative conventions. As the leading producer of race movies during the 1920s and 1930s, Oscar Micheaux created imagery and narratives of and about African Americans that challenged the prevailing assumptions about race in mainstream Hollywood films. Micheaux, however, was not alone and was joined during the silent era by 'resourceful African American entrepreneurs such as William Foster (also known as Juli Jones) ... Emmet J. Scott, and George and Noble Johnson' (Everett 2001: 8–9). Anna Everett writes that 'this early entrepreneurial activity' (2001: 9) of African American filmmakers was eventually diminished by the creation of an oligopolistic studio system. Once the vertically integrated Hollywood studio system effectively marginalised the independent African American film movement, the racial politics of narrative cinema perpetuated racist mythologies and affirmed the aesthetic tracks laid by Griffith. As Judith Weisenfeld notes, '[by] the 1930s, when the Hollywood studio system had solidified what scholars refer to as the classical Hollywood style, race had become a central and unremarked component of silver screen images of Americanness' (2007: 4).

Documentary cinema is not immune to these traditions of racial stereotyping. As mentioned at the outset, documentary film – like the cinema more generally – was bound up with the desire to manage representations of racial difference. The ethnographic impulses of early cinema and, later on, the work of Robert Flaherty were forged upon white attraction to images of difference as well as a circumscription of such difference, holding it at bay for safe contemplation, consumption and fetishisation. The Griersonian impulse later gravitated towards the constitution of a national imaginary and downplayed any address to the experiences of marginalised subjects, thus upholding white normativity in the process. A formation of radical thought and cultural production in the 1930s spawned oppositional interventions that often dealt with race and racism. Radical documentary film collectives, like the Workers Film and Photo League, had their work touted in the 1930s by left-wing black newspapers such as the *Harlem Liberator*, who 'invariably stressed the need for black spectators to resist the ideology of capitalism codified and reified in mainstream Hollywood films' (Everett 2001: 10). The work of African American photographer and filmmaker Edward Lewis was unique during the 1930s as a counterpoint for white-generated images of African Americans. In 1939, Lewis – 'working as a one-man production company' (Bowser 1999: 20) – produced a documentary series entitled *Life in Harlem* tracking the everyday experiences of African Americans in Harlem. He also went on to produce two more documentary series, *The Colored Champions of Sports* and *Colored America on Parade*. The former series, according to Pearl Bowser, 'brought to the screens of neighborhood theaters the players most viewers had only read about in the entertainment sections of black newspapers' (ibid.).

World War II ultimately prompted a 'short-lived but self-serving' (Everett 2001: 10) revision to the cinematic racial conventions of the 1930s. According to Everett, Hollywood felt pressure from the military brass to help 'enlist maximum African American support for the war effort' (ibid.). Weisenfeld writes that 'Theodore M. Berry, African American liaison officer in the OWI [Office of War Information], produced 'Blue Print of Program for Strengthening Negro Morale in the War Effort' (2007: 164):

> Berry called attention to the disjuncture for African Americans between the discourse about the war as being 'genuinely prosecuted for practical

democratic principles' and the reality of second-class citizenship at home and of European colonialism in Africa and Asia. In laying out his blue-print for raising morale, Berry identified a number of 'sore spots' for African Americans, including segregation in the army, the relegation of black men in the navy to menial labor, black men's lack of access to service in the marines, discrimination in the workforce at home, and the segregation of blood dona-tions by the Red Cross. [...] Why, then, those black leaders who considered the question of morale asked themselves, should African American men and women participate in a war effort aimed at achieving the liberty of some while they themselves continued to live under the strictures of segregation and racism? (ibid.)

The military's filmic response to this contradiction famously included *The Negro Soldier* (1944), produced by Frank Capra and written by Carlton Moss for the OWI. Moss originally entitled the film *Colored Men to Arms!*, but was overruled by the War Department 'lest it be interpreted as a call to arms against white people' (Bowser 1999: 24). Thomas Cripps and Peter Culbert write that 'the movie served the Army as propaganda for both black and white troops and as a teacher of comradely regard across racial lines without explicitly violating Army policy toward racial segregation' (1983: 118). While Bowser characterised the film as a 'historically accurate account of black soldiers' participation in every conflict that involved American soldiers, including the Civil War' (1999: 24), Weisenfeld emphasises the film's use of religion to compel 'viewers to imagine military service as a sacred act of black manhood that should rightly result in African Americans' full inclusion as Americans' (2007: 166).

Of course, the US military and many other war documentaries upheld a broad civic address to the imagined community of the nation and sidelined ques-tions about the experiences of African Americans and other racial minorities during the war. John Huston's *Let There Be Light* (1946) partly disavows soldiers' racial identities and enmeshes these individual experiences within a therapeutic frame. One facet of this disavowal has to do with the elevation of psychoanalytic modes of address within the post-war public sphere. Michele Wallace insists that additional scholarship should explore 'how the increasing prominence of a psychiatric and/or psychoanalytic discourse impacted on definitions and criteria of "race" as a national "problem" within dominant film practices' (1993: 268). In some cases, the popularisation of psychoanalysis in post-war America held representations of subjectivities within a narrow lens of individual pathologies abstracted from a broader field of social and political forces. A certain conve-nience resulted whereby the realities of racial inequality were buried under a torrent of individualised portraits and visual diagnoses. This recourse to psycho-analysis and the manner in which thick readings of individual psyches displaced social considerations parallels the post-war tendency to acknowledge such in-equality only within particular legal parameters. In this sense, psychoanalytical and legal discourses overlapped in their blindness to the social, cultural and economic legacies of racism.

Writing more generally about cinema of the 1940s and John Huston's output during the decade, David Desser identifies a predominant 'therapeutic vision' whose presence provides a sense of uplift in the face of a countervailing 'noir vision' (1993: 20). For us, this therapeutic vision impacts representations of race in contradictory ways by both fleshing out and adding depth to racialised subjects even as the realities of racial inequality are repressed. In *Let There Be Light*, for instance, a therapeutic vision is upheld as a means of obscuring racial difference and bolstering racial equality within the military. Originally titled *The Returning Psychoneurotics*, Huston produced the film for the US Army and the intent was to ease some of the stigma attached to combat veterans suffering from mental health afflictions as a result of their service (see Desser 1993: 27). As Lesley Brill notes, 'the Army wished to reassure anxious civilians, especially po-tential employers, that soldiers who received treatment for acute, battle-induced "nervousness" were not dangerous lunatics or permanently damaged personali-ties' (1997: 111). While the army was still segregated, the picture produced of the hospital showcases an integrated patient population. Scott Simmon notes that one of the 'most surprising aspect[s] of *Let There Be Light* is its confident and casual mix of races' (2007: 3). Simmon continues to note that the 'prominence of African American soldiers in the film is more than just socially progressive' as this 'racial mix [ultimately] helps structure the film' (ibid.). He astutely points out the subtle ways in which race and the realities of segregation filter into the film.

> A unifying theme is introduced through the first interview with a black soldier, a man named 'Griffith'. [...] Griffith movingly describes how his 'sweetheart ... has been the one person that gave me a sense of importance'. It's understandable enough that an African American private in the segregat-ed wartime Army might well find himself lacking any 'sense of importance' – but the need to recover this sense turns out to be a bond across all the troubled men. (ibid.)

Simmon ultimately reads the film's inscription of a bond across racial barriers as a progressive 'subcurrent', one that is ultimately suppressed by the Army's remake of the film, *Shades of Gray* (1948); in that film, Simmon is struck by the removal of 'any significant African American presence' (2012: 6).

Nevertheless, the undeniably progressive elements of the film are both enabled and limited by their therapeutic framing. Even as the denotative significance of the film's discourse is directed towards the interior psychic strife of the soldiers – or their binding 'battle neuroses' – racial connotations rear their head. Specifically, in one of the film's group therapy sessions, Griffith reflects on his childhood:

> I have in mind my own childhood ... coming from a moderate family, moderate in the sense that the family had some sense of security. [...] We were told that ... we couldn't just play with any of the kids we wanted to play with, unless their parents in turn had the equivalent of what our parents had. And, as a result, we were kept in a narrow circle, very very narrow. However, I have found that there's been a strong yearning on my part to break out of this environment, to be able to play with Tom, Dick and Harry.

The therapist responds:

> Your mother did not feel really so superior. She felt inferior when she tried to make you take the attitude [that] you were better than the other children. So that now certain experiences in the Army have brought that out more clearly because you have been thrown in with Tom and Dick and Harry. [...] It's not necessary to be in the Army. It's not necessary to be in the war. These kind of troubles have always gone on, in all time, through all the centuries.

Griffith's statement directly references class barriers whose psychological toll reminds one of the indignities of racial segregation. The white therapist's response resonates along these lines as he heaps these frustrations upon the shoulders of Griffith's mother, ultimately naturalising her 'sense of inferiority' as a historical constant for 'all the centuries'. The therapist's application of psychoanalytic assessment abstracts Griffith's relationship to his mother from a historical and cultural perspective in which African Americans are subjugated and held within a 'narrow circle'. This narrowness is instead rewritten by the therapist as an expression of an ahistorical psychic kernel that eternally persists, or has 'always gone on'. The film, in this regard, flirts with an acknowledgement of the indignities and hardships faced by African Americans, but ultimately repackages this as a universal experience disentangled from race as well as class. This observation dovetails with Brill's assertion that the patient testimonies in *Let There Be Light* continually assert the 'centrality of family and home to psychic health' (1997: 116). Oedipal and heteronormative familial references cut both ways, teasing out bonds across racial barriers while also turning a blind eye towards the social and cultural divisions that overwhelm the realities of life outside the hospital. Gary Edgerton's general assessment of the film also straddles a similar tension in the film as he acknowledges its 'major flaw' (1993: 49). *Let There Be Light* exudes a 'strong disposition to believe in the unfailing powers of the various military psychiatrists', while also failing to flinch 'at the struggle of each of these GIs with his own personal neurosis' (ibid.).

The documentary films discussed in the following chapters reflect and contribute to the broad currents outlined here. Despite the fact that they are sponsored educational films designed with a particular utility in mind, they are nevertheless not hermetically sealed off from more familiar trends in post-war world cinema. This is, in part, a reason for their selection as they bridge the gap between nontheatrical and theatrical films. Employing a diverse set of aesthetic strategies and pursuing divergent pedagogical aims, the films highlighted in this book pursue the *decisive moment* and can be characterised as belonging to a broader post-war trend towards what I would characterise as the *documentary from below*. Emulating the New Historicist notion of a *history from below*, all of these films privilege subjective and affective experiences on the ground. In her book, *The Archive Effect: Found Footage and the Audiovisual Experience of History*, Jaimie Baron has shown how the priorities of New Historicism and the ideals of telling history 'from below' are evident in documentary filmmaking. 'New Historicism,' Baron writes, 'begins from the premise that there is no single, universal history but rather there are many histories' (2014: 110). Moreover, she argues that the New Historicist pursuit of 'eccentric anecdotes and enigmatic fragments that interrupt and exceed the homogenizing force of grand narratives' (ibid.) is reproduced in particular appropriation films where similarly destabilising archival footage is privileged. The same interruptive and excessive drives are also at work more broadly in post-war documentary cinema and is evident across a broad array of documentary modes and styles as the Griersonian project evolves. And it is not a coincidence that we see this in educational documentaries, where sponsoring agencies use cinema to blend policy with the everyday life of the audience. Given the post-war American Dilemma and its founding gulf between the promise of equality and the reality of segregation, new modes of civic training and health education juggled a desire for social cohesion with an acknowledge of quotidian stresses. As we will see, here is a chasm that defines the liberal racial look of many educational documentaries as they aim to manage workplace relations, train specialists and engender communication.

Notes

1 Excerpts of this chapter were previously published in Stephen Charbonneau (2014) 'John Grierson and the United States', in Zoë Druick and Deane Williams (eds) *The Grierson Effect: Tracing Documentary's International Movement*. London: British Film Institute. Reproduced with permission from Palgrave Macmillan.

2 Gunnar Myrdal's 1944 study, *An American Dilemma: The Negro Problem and Modern Democracy*, famously made this observation and its prevalence is felt throughout this study. Also, for more on post-war new wave cinemas, see Francesco Casetti on a 'feeling of the new' (1999: 74–88).

3 Indeed, this persistence has been oft bemoaned and criticised. Brian Winston notes the Griersonian documentary's 'burdensome' legacy and its stubborn entrenchment in the public's perception of the documentary experience (1995: 255). Writing about documentary filmmaking in the 1960s, Winston observes how Griersonian ideals were so enshrined in the 'public mind as boring that there was no easy way within the counter-culture to move people away from that perception' (ibid.).

4 Ian Aitken, for instance, argues that Grierson's understanding of documentary film stands in stark contrast to 'cine-*vérité* ideologies' (1992: 7).

5 Although this book discusses representations of African Americans and Latinos in pedagogical documentary filmmaking, the first three chapters centre on the former. Hence, this condensed historical survey of race and film here privileges the treatment of Blackness in American documentary.

CHAPTER TWO

THE SICK QUIET THAT FOLLOWS VIOLENCE: NEOREALISM, PSYCHOTHERAPY AND COLLABORATION

Michele Wallace's call to examine the ways in which the language of psychotherapy shaped representations of race is most easily approached in mental health films of the 1940s (see 1993: 268). *The Quiet One* (1948) and *Palmour Street* (1949) both address social problems from the vantage point of mental health and conjoin their therapeutic vision with neorealist aspirations. In the case of *The Quiet One*, we can glean the post-war dilemma of a nation ensnared by a collision between its stated values and prejudices. Its therapeutic mode of address acknowledges a social context for its African American protagonist's struggles, but ultimately enmeshes these within a psychoanalytic framework managed by a professionalised narrator. *Palmour Street* was produced by the Southern Educational Film Production Service (SEFPS) to educate and generate discussions among African Americans on the issue of mental health. This film coordinates a racial look that both reflects and addresses an emotional range of African American experiences in spite of its utilitarian purpose. As we will see this speaks to the African American expertise and talent brought to bear on the film by William T. Clifford and George C. Stoney as well as its direct address to African American audiences. Furthermore, in contrast to *The Quiet One*, the film's mental hygiene credentials lend the film a pragmatism that inhibits it from falling into the trap of therapeutic condescension. In this sense, the inclusion here of a more traditional documentary in the form of *The Quiet One* helps us appreciate the politics of a film like *Palmour Street*. It also moderates any tendencies to automatically condescend or mock such mental hygiene films. Counterintuitively, the procedural emphasis in *Palmour Street* steers the film towards aperture rather than closure. Whereas *The Quiet One* seeks to explain, *Palmour Street* seeks to initiate. Its final image of a question mark leaves no doubt that there is doubt.

The Quiet One: Neorealism, Race and African American Urban Life

The Quiet One is an important film for this book. As we will see, it embodies many of the trends and traits that are evident in this volume's later case studies. For starters, the film meshes Griersonian documentary purpose with the aesthetics of Italian neorealism. Its narrative is designed to both educate and privilege a view of African American urban experience that is too often kept out of view. *The Quiet One*, through its association with photographer Helen Levitt, wears Cartier-Bresson's influence openly. An unseen reality is represented not simply from above – from the perspective of an overarching Voice of Authority – but also from below. Irreducible moments of play as well as trauma are featured prominently in the film's narrative. *The Quiet One* can also be seen as the inverse of *Let There Be Light* by virtue of its referral to and depiction of a world beyond an institutional setting. While both films are staged in and around institutions, *The Quiet One* depicts scenes that exceed the confines of the Wiltwyck School and acknowledge the social conditions that contribute to so-called delinquency. The outside world is spoken of and represented in Loeb, Levitt and Meyers' film; whereas, in *Let There Be Light*, the soldiers' experiences outside of the mental institution remain largely out of frame. Of course, *The Quiet One*'s treatment of race is similarly enmeshed with a therapeutic vision. While the outside world is registered by the film, its understanding of the conditions that foster delinquency are limited by the fixed determinations of a racial look that seeks to cure. Before delving further into the film's racial politics, it is important to briefly review the film's production history and the roots of its neorealism.

Robert Sklar has argued that the influence of Italian neorealism was registered in post-war America through the 'practices of film criticism and independent nonfiction filmmaking' (2012: 73). For Sklar, James Agee – 'the preeminent U.S. film critic' – is the 'figure who inaugurates the critical discourse [on neorealism] and serves as a link between aesthetic theory and production' (ibid.). As a screenwriter on *The Quiet One*, Agee participated in an American adaptation of Italian neorealist principles. This transnational conversation was noted by American critics at the time. For instance, as Sklar notes:

> Calling *The Quiet One* 'a genuine masterpiece in the way of a documentary drama,' Bosley Crowther of the *New York Times* went on to link the film with 'those stark film dramas which we have from Italy since the war.' He pointed to its nonprofessional actors and location shooting. But as a critic who often regarded moral issues as paramount, he gave greater emphasis to the connection in ethical terms, relating [*The Quiet One* and *Sciuscià* (*Shoeshine*, 1946)]

on the grounds of 'a clear and candid eye,' 'compassion but utter clarity,' and 'an honest conclusion.' *The Quiet One*, he wrote, 'might be reckoned the *Shoeshine* of American urban life, with the fade-out less fatal and tragic because of our more fortunate state.' (2012: 76)

Agee's work on *The Quiet One* as well as *In the Street* (1948) resulted from 'his friendship with the photographer Helen Levitt … and Janice Loeb, a painter of private means who, according to some accounts, financed the making of both works' (2012: 73–4). Agee, Loeb and Levitt had previously collaborated on *In the Street*, a documentary featuring scenes that echo 'images from Levitt's book, *A Way of Seeing*: a woman with a baby carriage, a couple standing in a doorway, an open fire hydrant, an old woman hanging out on the stoop, a grandfather with his grandchild, and the ubiquitous children' (Horak 1997: 145). In both instances – *In the Street* and *The Quiet One* – Agee had been engaged to compose the written commentary, narration as well as intertitles (see Sklar 2012: 74). For *The Quiet One*, Richard Bagley was brought on board as the film's cinematographer while Levitt filled in where needed with a second camera; Sidney Meyers directed with financing provided by Loeb (see Horak 1997: 149).

According to Jan-Christopher Horak, Levitt and Loeb 'develop[ed] a script about a fictional young boy by reading numerous case studies … in the offices of the Wiltwyck School for Boys in Esopus, New York' (ibid.). No doubt, the agenda of the production team reflected Loeb's 'desire to support and publicize the Wiltwyck School, a private residential treatment center for boys in Upstate New York' (Sklar 2012: 77). This predisposition is reflected in the film's see-saw between, following Sklar, an 'uplifting' resonance rooted in a realistic attitude about the elusiveness of 'easy cures' (ibid.). Such a complex ambivalence in the film is mirrored in its treatment of race, which is both textual and sub-textual, both overt and covert. Donald Thompson plays the young African American protagonist, Donald Peters: 'a troubled, virtually mute, young black boy, abandoned by his parents and living with an overworked and unsympathetic grandmother' (Horak 1997: 149). But for Crowther the use of race in the film is only a 'circumstance'. Another critic – Vincent de Moraes, writing in the *Hollywood Quarterly* – wrote that while the filmmakers' intent to universalise Donald's struggles sidestepped the issue of race, his own critical view of the film tugged in the opposite direction. For de Moraes, *The Quiet One* undoubtedly 'attacks the racial problem with the most powerful and precise of weapons – poetry' (qtd. in Sklar 2012: 77). These views represent the range of racial interpretations of the film at the time and Sklar concludes with his own retroactive take:

A question for the present-day spectator is how much it is possible to endorse de Moraes's view that beyond the filmmakers' aims and perhaps even their awareness, the film can be read as an impassioned cry for social justice. He describes Donald's Harlem world as an 'urban cancer' and asserts that 'it is not merely love that the unhappy child needs, but justice, equality of treatment, respect, and dignity, in order to live in the community of men without distinction of color or creed.' One can come away from the film with this conviction, but does the film itself support this view? Or is it more likely that the 'unfriendly society' that the *Phylon* writer [William Couch, Jr.] describes is a fact of life for the filmmakers, a circumstance of broken families, angry grandmothers, and a bleak environment that the film does not seek to interrogate or ameliorate except to extract Donald from it for psychiatric adjustment on an individual basis, far from home. (2012: 78–9)

Sklar can only insist on the persistence of an 'unexplained gap … between Donald's final acts of delinquency on the street and his arrival at the school' (ibid.). For his part, Horak admires the 'film's completely understated handling of race,' which contrasts with 'Hollywood's one-dimensional stereotypical view of minorities' (1997: 150). Its depiction of an African American family is 'very realistic and accurate', argues Horak, 'without ever making race an overt issue' (ibid.). Although Horak notes Levitt's own 'antipathy to the film', he reads this as a likely response to its 'pop child psychology' (ibid.).

My own critical intervention insists on reading this ambivalence as indicative of a post-war liberal racial look that sees racial inequality while receding from full comprehension. The visual relation implied by the staging of Donald's social and psychic traumas ricochets outwardly and inwardly, enabling as well as inhibiting an acknowledgement of racial pain in a racist society. Therefore, my sense is that the covert reading of the film's racial politics – its 'understated hand-ling of race' – is correct. However, we must also acknowledge in the same breath that the covert status of the film's racial commentary is indicative of a particular post-war moment. In fact, this film comes at a time when the aforementioned American Dilemma circumscribes discussions of racial inequality within certain limits. This productive contradiction is further inflected by the documentary form's own encounter with a 'feeling of the new' as the Griersonian project absorbs influences from Italian neorealism as well as Cartier-Bresson's photographic pursuit of the *decisive moment* (see Casetti 1999: 74). Photographer Helen Levitt's involvement in the production of *The Quiet One* consolidates this aesthetic lineage as her own development was directly inspired by Cartier-Bresson (see Horak 1997: 141). In sum, rather than insist on the film's accuracy or bemoan an interpretative gap or blockage, it strikes me as more useful to read the film as indicative of a particular racial look with its own unique powers and perils. This way the gap of which Sklar writes is more productively read as a symptom rather than a problem.

The Quiet One introduces its protagonist with a full shot of an African American boy settling down to fish at the side of a riverbed. The narrator announces that the film will tell 'the story of one of ... eighty boys, Donald Peters, ten years old'. The narrator insists that the film wants to convey

> how he lost his way and how, at last, he began to find it. We learned this story very slowly, by bits and pieces. But we'll try to tell it as it happened to Donald, secretly in his loneliness, in a lost child's bewilderment. In all these months, Donald has made no friends. We have never seen him smile. He has hardly spoken. He is one of the quiet ones. In all these months he has never had a letter. But he is learning to endure disappointment. He used to hide himself to suffer. Now he wants me to know he is unhappy. This boy wants all my attention. At this stage, they are painfully jealous. If Donald is ever lucky enough to open up, he'll have to go through that too.

The spotlight then falls on a young African American boy, although no mention is made of his race. As 'one of the quiet ones', Donald is characterised as emotionally distant on the one hand ('He has hardly spoken') and overly attached to the narrator on the other ('This boy wants all my attention'). In this manner, the film establishes Donald as a kind of mystery but one that is eminently knowable. The medium for this knowledge about Donald is the white therapist, whose self-proclaimed intimacy with the child reinforces his authoritative position as the narrator. (At this point in the film, the narrator is clearly defined as a *voice of authority* for the film, as an embodied yet transcendent commentator.) The 'story' of Donald's condition of morose quietude is one that has been supposedly 'pieced' together by the therapist in the manner of a detective. The fragmentary characterisation of Donald's story 'as we learned it' calls to mind the fractional abstraction of a boy's eyes peering at us through the leaves in a previous shot. As an act of filmic narration the components of Donald's story will be *made whole* by the documentary. And, in a similar vein, the goal of therapeutic intervention is to *make Donald whole*, or to help him 'find' his way. The expository form of the documentary, then, is synergistically bound up with the body and voice of the narrator, whose white investigatory paternalism is both a characterisation and an expression of classical documentary discourse. While Donald is metonymically positioned as the poster child for the boys served by Wiltwyck and urban poverty in general – and in this sense he has some power – his subjectivity is conferred from the outside and at the outset by the white narrator.

Nevertheless, the narrator largely evaporates from the *mise-en-scène* of the film and functions primarily as a Voice of God commentator with occasional first-person references to his own role as a school therapist. Once conferred, the subjectivity of Donald remains as a foundational focus for the rest of the film and its overdetermination by social forces oscillates from concrete to amorphous. Our initial introduction to the psyche of Donald is aural as the narrator speaks about Donald over imagery of him on the riverbed. The narrator's verbal description of Donald seeks to *fix* him in both senses of that word. First, the narration opens by defining (or fixing) Donald as 'the quiet one', as a mentally ill subject in need of intervention. Second, the narrator proclaims that the school's efforts, as well as his own, are geared towards healing Donald or helping him come to terms with the unstable familial and communal circumstances that contributed to his mental state. This objective fixation and fixing of Donald by a white paternal expert speaks to the post-war liberal context of the film. *The Quiet One*, from this point of view, expresses a liberal discourse in which an empathic identification with the psycho-social plight of Black subjects simultaneously restages their subjugation. Donald's struggles are spotlighted with a nod towards their generative conditions. And yet the displacement of Donald's voice in favour of a white man's – coupled with the refusal to speak of race directly – produces a different kind of silence and disavowal. Ambivalence abounds and registers a recognition as well as an obfuscation of America's post-war racial situation.

The opening constitution of Donald through the verbal commentary of a white authority figure establishes a pattern for the rest of the film. From the outset, the imagery's relationship to the commentary fluctuates between evidentiary and contrapuntal. As the film moves indoors – introducing the audience to the Wiltwyck classroom – this shift from the outside to the inside metaphorically presages the commentator's shift in discourse about Donald from his outward physical (in)activity ('he has hardly spoken') to his inner retention of painful memories. This shift is matched by the image track as subjective shots are generated to reflect Donald's mental state. Such a turn of events is notable for the way in which the scene dramatically manoeuvres from the objective discourse of a classroom film into the subjective world of Donald's trauma. Our initial view of the classroom renders it an overtly racialised space: all the students here are African American as is the teacher, Mrs Johnson. However, the narrator continues to speak of the 'boys' in a general sense without acknowledging the racial dimension of their social experiences. This distancing mingles with the film's slippage into a psychological zone as the scene intercuts close-ups of Donald

Figure 2.
The bracketing hands
of the teacher in
The Quiet One
(d. Sidney Meyers,
1948).

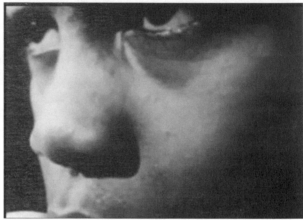

Figure 3.
"And behind the
feelings rise memories
which still hold
him in terrible hunger
and hatred." Donald
in *The Quiet One*.

with shots of the teacher's hand, writing on the blackboard. The depiction of the writing slides into a subjective space by virtue of the focus on the hand. Once we see the hand sketch the word 'baby' on the board, we hear the narrator state that 'such a word as "baby" arouses a deep turmoil of feelings. And behind the feelings rise memories which still hold him in terrible hunger and hatred.' This statement binds the shots of the words on the blackboard and those of Donald. The close-ups of Donald are notable for their canted framing of his face, which have the effect of both bonding the spectator to Donald as well as upholding a sense of distanciation. All of the shots in this small series refuse a complete view of his face and generally crop the image at his eyes. The shifting angles of the camera register the inner 'turmoil' spoken of on the soundtrack. Furthermore, the actions of the teacher's hands underscore the power of a single signifier by performing a bracketing action. In one of the close-ups, we see the teacher's hands frame one of the words ('bring') in a sentence written on the blackboard.

The fact that we don't know what the entire sentence says on the board speaks to the film's insistence here on the psychic impact of a specific signifier or word abstracted from its syntagmatic context. With the teacher's hands operating as a kind of iris-in, our look is aligned with the look of Donald as a particular word compels him inward, towards a memory of a particular familial trauma.

These shots give way to an image of a cropped photograph. In it we see a family on the beach. Donald can be seen playing in the sand at the feet of a man whose head is held out of frame. Two women, one younger and the other older, are standing and smiling at the camera with only the tops of their heads cut off by the edge of the screen. The cropping of the image is rationalised by the narrator who comments: 'The vanished father whose face he can't even recall.' With this line the indexical value of the image is laced with a subjective dimension registering Donald's distance from his father. Following another close-up of Donald in the classroom, the film returns to the photograph and abstracts two separate static medium shots of the young woman and the older woman respectively. Over the image of the former, the narrator notes that this is a 'mother who has no room for him [Donald] in her life'. In the case of the latter, the verbal description is equally dire. 'Grandma and his home with her,' the narration claims, 'a home he hates so much that even at night he seldom comes back.' Quite clearly, in spite of the photograph's denotative status as a record of a smiling, happy family, the narration in conjunction with the blunt cropping and dissection of the image encourages us to distrust our eyes and, instead, see past a misleading surface to get to a deeper psychic truth of resentment and alienation.

Throughout the film Donald's subjectivity emerges somewhere betwixt and between the fixity of the narration and the imagery presented. And in spite of the narrator's best efforts, the verbal commentary does not fully envelop the visual

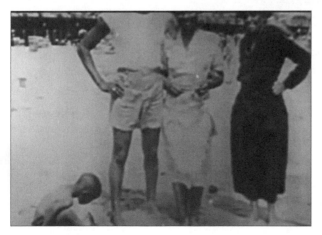

Figure 4.
The "vanished father"
in *The Quiet One*.

imagery and other aural elements on the sound track. Here a gap persists, but by design. The narration, for instance, frequently shows restraint and is silenced for significant periods of screen time as scenes from Donald's life are reenacted. Circuits of repetition also register the film's therapeutic discourse and blunt any perpetual expository churning. For instance, the photograph described above continues to rear its head throughout *The Quiet One*. It not only appears, as we have seen, in the early classroom scene with Mrs Johnson, but also re-emerges in two other instances as a crucial reference point for the film's ongoing characterisation of Donald.

The inaugural usage of the photograph functions as a sort of narrative rabbit hole, taking us deeper into Donald's character. And its insertion into the film violates the spatial logic of the classroom scene, implying that it works primarily as a mental insert signifying Donald's loss and familial alienation. A subsequent reference to the photograph similarly coincides with an action, more creative than destructive. Here the sequence features Donald 'in crafts class' sculpting a mound of clay. 'He wanted to make it look like a sea shell,' the narrator states, 'he couldn't say why.' A gradually darkening close-up of Donald's contemplative face cuts to his hands working on the clay. The focus on the hands fosters a graphic match to Donald's hands in the sand. 'Donald seemed to be doing fine,' the narrator states. 'Suddenly the hands that were working in the damp clay of the unborn shell drew him into a deep quicksand.' The diegetic sound emanating from the film denotes Donald's location on a beach and the subsequent shot renders the familiar recurring photographic image in cinematic terms. What was a family snapshot is now a kind of home movie, albeit with stagnant figures in the frame. The wind registered on the soundtrack is equally visible in the image as the dresses worn by Donald's mother and grandmother ripple in the breeze. The film returns to an over-the-shoulder shot of Donald's hands digging ever more deeply into the sand. A third hand enters the frame to assist Donald, but its owner is ambiguous. Suddenly, a voice is heard calling, 'Donald!' Following a return to Donald in class at Wiltwyck, we hear a second call that finally snaps Donald out of it, stating: 'The bottom of memory has opened and engulfed him.' The voice that retrieves Donald from the 'bottom of memory' is Clarence, a new counsellor at Wiltwyck with whom Donald has bonded. As the lone positive representation of Black masculinity, Clarence is positioned to fill several crucial gaps. First and foremost comes the patriarchal and parental gap. Clarence is depicted as a loving father figure for Donald, who in one scene is shown caring for Donald with 'warmth', as the narrator describes it. Donald's biological father is only partially represented in the film thanks to the cropped photograph as well as a restaging of a traumatic encounter between Donald and his father in the first half of the film. There, Donald observes his father and mother from within their apartment, but they barely notice him and treat him with indifference. The juxtaposition of presence with distance is rendered obsolete in the case of Clarence, who openly exhibits concern for Donald and whose voice intervenes into Donald's memory slide.

Clarence also intervenes into another gap without necessarily filling it. Here we confront a racial gap that persists in the film and yet remains unacknowledged. The voice of the white psychiatrist yields a diagnostic authority that sits at an uncomfortable distance from Donald's Black familial life and yet presumes to have full access and understanding. As a positive Black father figure, Clarence activates a double displacement as a stand-in for Donald's abusive biological father as well as for the white paternal narrator. Nevertheless, the therapeutic address of the film continues to disallow a full acknowledgement of the racial gap. The complete weight of the socio-historical legacy of discrimination is cast out from the film's interpretative gaze and this disavowal is partly facilitated by the introduction of Clarence. While Clarence functions superficially as a mediation, massaging the racial divide at the heart of the film by displacing the narrator, his character ultimately re-routes the film's analysis away from a socio-historical framing of Donald's experience and toward an oedipal narrative in which hatred for one father yields love for another.

Clarence's status is underscored by the nature of his interruption into Donald's memory-scene, triggered by the photograph. As discussed above, Donald snaps out of the scene thanks to Clarence's aural interruption of 'Donald!' The casting of Clarence's voice into the scene reproduces the transcendent position of the narrator while retaining a sense of his immanence in Donald's world. Pulling Donald out of his daydream also introduces him to a new symbolic order of familial normality as represented by Clarence. This strange recollection is rife with gaps. Here the gap between Donald's parents and himself is most pronounced as his dynamic movement – plowing into the sand – contrasts with the static poses of his parents and grandmother. The looks of the latter are affixed by an absent camera whose presence is reciprocally constituted. The moving image camera initially reproduces the static image yielding an uncanny combination of dynamism and fixity. But quickly the staginess of the photograph is abandoned in favour of the subjectivity of cinematic movement. In the end, Clarence's intervention into the scene retrieves Donald from this world of discord, fear and fragmentation – from the photograph – and seeks to reclaim him for a new world of restoration. The scene transitions courtesy of the good father, whose retrieval of Donald speaks to his proximate location to the boy and the narrator.

Both *Let There Be Light* (see chapter one) and *The Quiet One* can be read as classic Griersonian documentaries, whose mode of address is expository in nature and wedded to the ideals of good citizenship as articulated by their featured institutions (United States Army and the Wiltwyck School). And yet these films, each in its own way, exceeds the functionalist aesthetic of the Griersonian tradition. Certainly, the subsequent censorship of *Let There Be Light* speaks to the film's dangerous surplus of meaning for authorities at the time who were, at a minimum, simply not prepared for the full disclosure of mental illness and psychological trauma afflicting many returning veterans.[1] *The Quiet One*, in spite of its empathic tone and willingness to acknowledge a social backdrop for its protagonist's psychological struggles, reproduces a problematic post-war racial dynamic precisely by ignoring race. The paternal white narrator speaks for Donald, 'the quiet one'. In this sense, 'the quiet one' is not necessarily silent. The diagnostic narration envelops Donald and, not only speaks for him, but dissects and penetrates him. While Donald's subjectivity is staged for the screen, it is also by definition created and constituted through an outside voice whose authority is never questioned internally and is, instead, reified or re-channeled through the figure of Clarence. While there are references to the socio-historical framework for the breakdown of the Black family, these are largely occluded by a therapeutic vision. Here, then, the wealth of psychic depth – rare for African American characters in American film – comes at a cost as the film's gaze penetrates too deep too fast.

The SEFPS and *Palmour Street* (1949)

> We have many films on child care, family life and aspects of what we now call 'mental health'. Too often these films are not only unsuited to the needs of our audiences, they are also useless as stimulators of thought because they try to give all the answers. People are in the habit of resigning themselves to the screen, forgetting themselves in the entertainment it brings. This habit clings even when we show educational films in our P.T.A. meetings and our club and church gatherings.
>
> – Dr W. A. Mason (qtd. in Anon. 1950a)

The quote above from Dr W. A. Mason, an African American doctor working for the Georgia Department of Health, registers the post-war documentary's affinity for everyday life and aperture over closure. For Mason, mental health films need not simply prescribe behavioural attributes for an audience. Rather, they should be seen as 'stimulators of thought', inaugurating discourse on a topic that is otherwise ignored or disavowed. Mason was able to put these ideas into practice through his work on William T. Clifford's and George C. Stoney's film, *Palmour Street*. This was produced by the Southern Educational Film Production Service (SEFPS), a regional public agency designed to meet the demand for educational films on the part of local state programmes. Its depiction of African American families – when compared with *The Quiet One* – is more positive and less bleak. While co-directors Clifford and Stoney are white Southerners, the film is intended for southern African American audiences and the production featured several key African American collaborators such as Dr Mason and the Reverend William Holmes Borders as the narrator. In this context, the racial look engendered by the film contrasts with the enclosed penetrating address of *The Quiet One*. In the case of *Palmour Street*, the film's 'look' has been substantially co-authored by a bi-racial crew with the intent of harnessing the 'look' of southern African American audiences. Rather than affirm the documentary authority of the film's racial look, the filmmakers' sought to fulfill Mason's vision of a modest mental health film that provokes thought and compels discussion.

In the summer of 1950 *Film News* featured a profile of SEFPS. Under the heading, 'Looking South', the editor, Rohama Lee, opens the issue with a general comment about the state of filmmaking in the south:

> When we first trained our sights southward it was with the idea of surveying that entire area. It didn't take much looking to convince us that this just

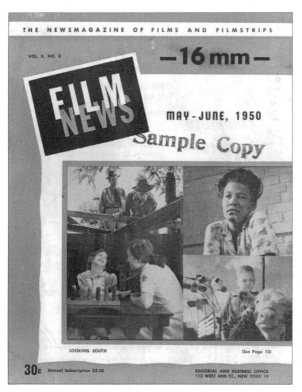

Figure 5.
Films News: The News Magazine of Films and Filmstrips. George C. Stoney Papers, 1940–2009. The Louis Round Wilson Special Collections Library, University of North Carolina at Chapel Hill.

could not be done in one issue of this magazine without at least quadrupling its size. The amount and extent of film activity below the Mason-Dixon line is not simply amazing. It is a revelation – particularly as it is not something superimposed but is practically indigenous. [...] This, we think, is the paramount difference between the film pattern of the South, and elsewhere. (1950: 3)

While many affinities with the North are noted, the most remarkable difference between the two regions is the south's unique 'spirit', one 'that carries over from other fields of activity and keynotes the *production* of films, as well as their use' (ibid.). Given the breadth of film activity in the south at the time, the editorial board decided to focus this particular issue on the SEFPS. For the board, the SEFPS's work with a number of different Southern states as well as their co-operative association with so many state agencies is reflective of the myriad of ways in which 'the South is learning to solve many of its problems cooperatively' (ibid.). This broader context of cooperation and change is redirected back at the documentary film project as Lee concludes her opening commentary with the remark: 'What a region for the use of documentary, and its growth!' (1950: 30).

In the magazine's profile of the SEFPS, 'Yoke Fellows of Athens', Ted Scythes positions the film production service within the broader context of a post-war south in transition. Scythes notes that the 'more agricultural' south is, in fact, 'not as thickly populated [as the north] and is losing more people' (1950: 7). Furthermore,

it has a larger proportion of Negro population taken as a whole; has a more homogenous white population, predominantly Anglo-Saxon; is largely Protestant in religion; has a much larger proportion of children; a lower per capita income; and a different way of looking at things which, though changing, still places family above monetary success. Most outstanding thing about the region is that it is rapidly, basically changing. For acceptance of new patterns films are regarded as a necessity and are widely used as an instrument for making the transition less difficult, for help in building a healthy, happy and successful future for the area and its people. (Ibid.)

The launching of the SEFPS is attributed to a broad array of 'Southern leaders in education, industry, science and agriculture' (1950: 6). Scythes writes that the initial spark for a southern film service came from the Georgia Agricultural Extension Service (GAES). The GAES recommended to the Tennessee Valley Authority (TVA) that they 'establish a regional film production organization

– with the idea, at first, of it specifically serving the needs of the agricultural extension services of the seven Valley states' (ibid.). The resulting institutional conversation yielded the insight that 'Southern audiences needed films to show the land they know, the problems they are facing, and to make suggestions for practical solutions of these problems' (ibid.). The *New York Times* characterised the SEFPS's output along similar lines, noting that the organisation delivered 'to the people of Dixie a shadow-report on their regional resources and problems, both human and material' (Popham 1950).

In light of the broad support for the idea among southern educational agencies, TVA encouraged the formation of a film production unit that would serve multiple public agencies. This 'broadening of the original idea' allowing the SEFPS to grant membership 'without financial obligation to *all* tax-supported public agencies, thus bringing in – additional to agriculture – public health, labor, welfare, colleges, libraries, highway departments, etc' (Scythes 1950: 6). SEFPS was eventually 'charter[ed on] February 20, 1946 in Tennessee … as a non-profit corporation' (ibid.). Seed money was secured in the form of a $40,000 grant thanks to the Rockefeller Foundation's General Education Board (see Popham 1950). A home base for the SEFPS was established at the University of Georgia at Athens because of its 'central location' (Scythes 1950: 6). In addition to Tennessee, participating states at the time consisted of Alabama, Florida, Georgia, Kentucky, Mississippi, North Carolina, South Carolina and Virginia (ibid.). The initial vision for the SEFPS 'stressed the fact that its product would constitute an enduring medium that would remain useful for many years and would be seen by many people, thus making its cost per person reached exceedingly small' (Popham 1950).

By 1950 – within five years of its establishment – the SEFPS had produced twenty films (see Scythes 1950: 6). *Film News* described these as being 'among the most functional and usable of information films extant – and produced on surprisingly small budgets' (ibid.). Many of these deal with agricultural issues in light of 'the needs of the agricultural extension services of the Southern State' (1950: 7) and their rapid evolution in the post-war era. Such films include:

> *Twelve Months Green* [1948], a very neat and even entertaining lesson for the farmers of Mississippi on building pastures and raising cattle; *Lonnie's New Crop* [1948], demonstrating a new plan of farm management that calls for planting unused land in pine woods; *Farming to Stay* [1948]; *Timber Growing Today* [1947], further expanding the agricultural horizon, etc. (Ibid.)

Other films dealt with education (*Books and People: The Wealth Within*, 1947), nutrition (*The School That Learned to Eat*, 1948), a study of industrial development in the state of Florida (*Florida: Wealth or Waste?*, 1947), and state health programs (*First as a Child*, 1948; *We See Them Through*, 1948).

The *New York Times* also made a special note about the SEFPS's work with African Americans. Under the heading 'Negroes' Roles', the article observed that 'Negroes take prominent parts in most of the films, not as special treatment but as the inevitable consequence of making factual documentaries about the South, where they comprise a third of the population' (Popham 1950). Here the newspaper insists that the documentary enterprise, if it were to maintain any credibility with audiences in the south, was compelled to feature African Americans 'prominent[ly]' and not merely as an afterthought or as recipients of 'special treatment' (ibid.). The article continues to state that a goal of the SEFPS was to elicit an 'identical response from white and Negro groups that have the same occupational or sectional background' (ibid.). In order to do so, the SEFPS explicitly avoids 'views that Negro audiences feel are caricatures of themselves and [eliminates] in early sequences any cuts that emphasize race above everything else' (ibid.). The desire for broad appeal – for white and black audiences – compelled the SEFPS to avoid stereotypes of African Americans as well as discuss race explicitly. On its surface, it would seem that the former is designed to appeal to African American audiences while the latter soothes the sensitivities of southern whites who are less likely to question their own privilege in the Jim Crow era.

But the issue of racial representation and address grows more complicated when the focus turns to SEFPS productions geared specifically towards African American audiences in the south. The first SEFPS film of this kind was *Feeling All Right* (1949), sponsored by the Mississippi Board of Health. Featuring a 'cast of Delta Negroes', it sought to educate audiences on the dangers of venereal disease. The September 1949 issue of *Film News* summarises the plot:

> Roy, a young farmer, is friendly with a worldly Jim of wrong values; goes out with him for a good time; gets himself into trouble; unwisely tries to cure himself with a patent medicine Jim recommends. Roy's mother, worried, pursuades [sic] him to accompany her to a health lecture. There he signs up for a blood test at the health department, finds he has syphilis, agrees to stay at the Treatment Center for cure. Finale is on the happy note of a healthy child. [...] This, baldly, is the story of *Feeling All Right*, and in words it sounds almost cliché. (Anon. 1949b)

'In pictures', however, the magazine insists the film is 'truly absorbing' (ibid.):

Here are Negroes presented for the first time on screen with verity and naturalness as farmers, shopkeepers, young people, old people, professional people, just people … and their story is so fundamentally right and human that, in this Mississippi Delta version or in other translation, it can help people anywhere in the world, whatever color their skin. (Ibid.)

The review continues to quote US Surgeon General, Dr Leonard Scheele, who proclaims *Feeling All Right* is 'one of the best educational films in the field of public health produced in recent years' (ibid.). While the film's denotative 'function' is notably admirable – 'to encourage voluntary blood tests on the part of the million Negroes of the Mississippi, some 300,000 of whom have seen the film since its first showing in late January' – the poetic impact of the film and its 'natural' representation of African Americans compel *Film News* to suggest 'it is a milestone in the annals of the U.S. screen' (ibid.) The film also received an 'honorable mention for creative achievement in production of documentary films' by the City College Institute of Film Techniques, New York' (Southern Educational Film Production Service 1948).

This hyperbole was tempered somewhat by the reaction of the National Association for the Advancement of Colored People (NAACP), who generally found the picture to be 'an educational document filmed in a dignified manner' (Wilkins 1949). Nevertheless, the NAACP objected to the film's exhibition 'in commercial film houses … to the lay public' (ibid.). The organisation was concerned about the film's reception outside of 'selected audiences of social workers, doctors, nurses, public health officers and other professionals; or to subscription groups; or to churches, clinics; and theatres patronized exclusively by Negroes, such as exist in the Southern states' (ibid.). From this vantage point, the white media's insistence on the film's progressive racial politics may have been a bit overstated and blind to the ways in which a mainstream audience may interpret the sounds and imagery of an educational documentary. Certainly, the NAACP's cautionary note reminds us of unruly audiences and the vicissitudes of reception. The National Urban League was similarly calculated in its response, noting that 'members of the staff of the National Urban League who have seen the film *Feeling All Right* are of the opinion that, *properly used*, it can contribute much toward bringing factual, urgently needed information on a specific health problem to the rural Negro community' (Granger n.d.; emphasis added). Like the NAACP, the National Urban League stresses the need for care when it comes to the film's particular outlets. Nevertheless,

The film has used characters and scenes familiar to the Southern rural audience, while at the same time it has not detracted from the simple dignity of the people [nor has it] neglected to acknowledge the contribution of the Negro doctor and clergyman to those whom they have pledged to serve. (Ibid.)

Even more notable, both critically and historically, was the SEFPS film *Palmour Street*, co-directed by William T. Clifford and George C. Stoney. The *New York Times* identified Clifford as the SEFPS's 'production director, and guiding light' (Popham 1950). During World War II Clifford, the newspaper notes, had worked for Bell Aircraft Corporation as head of its motion picture division (ibid.). Stoney, one of Clifford's colleagues at SEFPS, was described as being from 'Winston-Salem, N.C., [and] a former newspaper reporter' (ibid.).

> The principal script writer, and ... director ... Mr Stoney knows his rural South from long service with the old Farm Security Administration. During the war he served overseas with the intelligence section of the Air Force, and a year ago he took a leave of absence from SEFPS to study documentary film production techniques in England on a Rosenwald fellowship. He is a graduate of the University of North Carolina. (Ibid.)

Stoney's commitment to documentary filmmaking was rooted in his experience during the Depression when he worked for the Farm Security Administration (FSA). His core responsibility 'was to convince middle-class people to support programs that benefited sharecroppers and tenant farmers, people who didn't or couldn't vote because of poll taxes or race' (Boyle 1997: 29). Stoney came to this position with impressive credentials, having worked for Ralph Bunche researching 'how pols kept Blacks from voting' (ibid.). In Stoney's travels to 'Alabama, Georgia, and South Carolina, his meetings with ... Rotary Clubs, churches, and unions ... began ... by screening Pare Lorentz's classic documentary, *The River*' (ibid.):

> He showed it hundreds of times, and it never failed to work. Stoney concluded it was because the film had the form of an evangelical sermon: given Eden, man despoils it, but when he understands the evils of his ways, he can then correct them and start life anew. Because the issues of soil conservation and economic exploitation in *The River* were shared by all Southern communities, the film universally spoke to people; because the film was so emotionally resonant, it opened people up who otherwise would have rejected such an appeal because of differences in class or race. Stoney was able

to get middle-class audiences to see that these sharecroppers were the people who buy groceries or furniture in their stores. And they can't buy anything if they aren't making enough growing cotton.

At that time Stoney had no interest in making documentaries himself, but his job was providing him with a unique opportunity to study a film classic, gauge the power of film as an educational tool, and learn how to use it to advocate for social change. (Ibid.)

Stoney continued to work with film after the war when he met up with an 'old school friend Nick Read' (Boyle 1997: 30), who had 'spent the war in the Signal Corps and then went to Canada for four years to work for the National Film Board' (ibid.). Eventually Read 'came to Georgia to help state agricultural agencies use films for education' and 'realizing he needed someone who could write for farmers, he hired Stoney, and thus the [SEFPS] became Stoney's baptism as a filmmaker' (ibid.). Stoney's most important takeaway from his time working with Read was the importance of screening 'films in the community where they were made, which taught [Stoney] to be sensitive to local feelings' (ibid.).

In 1948, with the support of a Rosenwald fellowship, Stoney was able to make the aforementioned trip to the UK where he had the opportunity to learn from the likes of Basil Wright, the co-director (with Harry Watt) of the classic *Night Mail*. Stoney later remarked that he was drawn to the British documentary's Griersonian blend of creativity and utility:

Almost every time they touched something, there was an extra element of creativity in it. They seemed to know that if their films didn't have some stature beyond being useful films, they wouldn't get anywhere. (Ibid.)

Stoney subsequently travelled to Canada to learn about the National Film Board of Canada (NFB) and posted reports to the SEFPS's newsletter, *Southern Film News*. While in Canada, Stoney paid particular attention to the NFB's model of 'education film production and distribution abroad' (n.d.). Stoney was most impressed by the latter, making special note of the NFB's 'effective distribution of [educational films] to fourteen million Canadians, and through foreign exchanges, to people all over the world' (ibid.). This remarkable reach, Stoney notes, is accomplished for a relatively small amount of funds: 'For all this Canada appropriates a little less than three million dollars a year … less than the states of Florida, New York and California combined spend on official tourist advertising' (ibid.). The closest approximation of the NFB in the US was, for Stoney, the Office of War Information 'at the height of the war' (ibid.). These experiences as well as his formative years at the SEFPS informed his work in the 1950s and beyond.

Both Clifford and Stoney continued to collaborate with Dr Mason of Yale University, an African American 'who heads the Georgia Department of Health's Special program of health education for Negroes' (Southern Educational Film Production Service, 'Palmour Street'). Mason served as the SEFPS's 'chief contact man, medical advisor, counselor and friend during the shooting of [*Feeling All Right*]' (ibid.). In an anonymously authored organisational history of the film, the racial dynamics at work heading into *Palmour Street* are clearly laid out:

> In most of our films Negroes are included pretty much as a matter of course but – perhaps for 'documentary' reasons, perhaps not – they have appeared in minor roles. With Mason helping, we worked out in 'Feeling…' an approach entirely different from the usual one taken either by Hollywood or the New York documentary boys to Negro life in the south. For remember, we were making this film primarily to motivate southern Negroes, to persuade them they ought to come in for a blood test. So they had to like the main characters, they had to feel it a good thing to identify with the young fellow who caught the bad blood and got cured. (Ibid.)

The document continues to note that this approach – in which the African American characters are 'likeable, admirable … people, and fellow human beings' – contributed to the film's positive critical reception (ibid.). Nevertheless, the authors insist the film 'isn't all that good', despite the fact that 'for once educated Negro groups seem satisfied to see members of their own race on the screen treated with some degree of naturalness' (ibid.). At this point plans were hatched with Dr Mason to make 'more films especially for southern Negro audiences' (ibid.):

> The difference would come chiefly in working … in more humble settings and in the use of people who were obviously both Negro and southern. Identification, he believed, could become more than the escape-to-dreaming it usually is for people when they see movies. By creating the reality of situation films, when shown to southern Negro audiences who gather for 'discussions' in their copies of white PTA's, white lodges, white community organizations of all kinds, might jolt them out of the prayer-meeting testimonial sessions they usually become into a genuine time of thinking aloud about things they dare now think of only in silence. *Palmour Street* is our first effort to make such a film. (ibid.)

This 'mental health' production' does not seek to merely inform African American audiences about mental and physical ailments and their public health implications (ibid.). Rather, the goal is for the film to compel discourse on topics that are shrouded in secrecy and 'silence' (ibid.). And while 'discrimination … is the primary reason for the difficulty in self-revelation', the intent here is to delve further into the collective African American psyche, to access 'such uncertainties as [Richard] Wright's *Black Boy* describes as dominating his own childhood' (ibid.).

The goal, then, was to ensure that African Americans in the south felt 'that the film … is really theirs, not just a thing made *for* them' (ibid; emphasis in original). To further this end, the producers hired Reverend William Holmes Borders, 'a leading Negro minister in Atlanta, as the commentator' (ibid.). Borders was selected, in part, because of his status in the African American community as an organiser of the 'first mass meetings for Negro voters in Atlanta, [ensuring] that some 3,500 of his congregation got on the polling list' (ibid.). His presence 'will carry the word through the Baptist community of the south' (ibid.). Beyond the role of narrator, the producers wanted the cast and crew to be primarily African American. 'All credit names,' the SEFPS noted after the production was finished, 'appearing on the film … point to the large part played by Negroes in the making of the film and we are toning down talk of our own part in it' (ibid.). The producers also insist that the film 'should have been made by a Negro unit' and they have, as a result, 'been trying to get a foundation interested in starting one at Atlanta University' (ibid.).

In addition to the SEFPS's work with Dr Mason,

the script was prepared in collaboration with physicians and specialists of the Georgia and U.S. Public Health Services and several psychiatrists on the staff of the Emory University Medical School. Negro school teachers and social workers doing graduate work at Atlanta University contributed their experiences and observations. Finally the script was checked carefully with 14 Negro specialists on rural life meeting at Tuskegee Institute.

Special mention is being given on the final print to two Negro physicians who were in great measure responsible for the successful completion of the production: Dr A. A. Butler, outstanding leader in Gainesville who introduced the idea of the film to what might have been an understandably suspicious community, helped to choose the actors and served as chief local adviser; Dr W. A. Mason, Director of Georgia's special program of health education for Negroes, has been the chief person responsible for the production. (SEFPS, 'Palmour Street (A Study of Family Life)')

Dr Mason was adamant that the film should be 'designed especially to stimulate discussion,' rather than simply inculcate or dictate to an audience (ibid.). The hope was to 'spread more widely among the Negro parents of Georgia certain basic concepts of 'mental health' as they relate to family life' (ibid.). Foremost in the producers' minds was the sense of a generational shift or a new post-war world with attendant new powers and perils for young African Americans. From this vantage point, the producers felt that the 'kind of life young Negro children know is vastly different from the childhood of their parents' (ibid.). A post-war 'social riptide' is upon them and with it comes 'more and more opportunities' coupled with 'more and more situations where they must face discrimination and denial of rights' (ibid.). With this observation close at hand, the film set out to avoid offering clear-cut solutions. Instead, the producers aimed to show 'by means of a few simple dramatic incidents the fact that parents *do* have an overwhelming influence in shaping their children's personalities' (ibid.; emphasis in original). The coherence of these dramatic incidents into 'a narrative of simple family life' is specifically coordinated to 'meet the most pressing needs of southern Negro audiences' and to inspire discussion on a host of parenting issues facing African American parents. Nevertheless, the producers also insist on the film's pertinence for 'most parents and children in America, especially those with moderate incomes' (ibid.).

The sparing use of Borders' narration in *Palmour Street* parallels the narrational rhythms of *The Quiet One*. While the Voice of God narration in *Palmour Street* often intervenes to establish exposition, its usage in this film frequently undermines the narrator's own authority in order to challenge the viewer to think for herself. To begin with, the relative infrequency of the narration was important to the producers, who wanted scenes to unfold unencumbered by the verbal scaffolding of the commentary. The producers were quite clear that the narrator should 'only occasionally [speak] to ask a question or underline the significance of a situation' (Anon., 'Palmour Street (A Study of Family Life)': 3). But here we stumble upon another unique trait of this film's narration: its constant posing of unanswered questions. Throughout the film, the narrator refrains from simply telling the audience what to think. Instead, the discourse of the film aims to be generative rather than conclusive. For instance, an early scene takes place in a local clinic and contrasts the behaviour of various mothers. The first shot of the clinic features a doorway, through which the first mother/son pairing walks. Here the mother gently guides her son to one of the empty seats in the waiting room. She's quickly followed by another mother who is berating and shaking her young son on their way through the waiting room and continues this behaviour even after they are seated. The only commentary the audience hears is open-ended: 'What makes this difference in children? Could it be this difference in their parents?' Later, the benevolent mother and her husband (played by the Merritt family who are the focus for the film) are squabbling in the kitchen while their children look on. The scene eventually shifts towards the children, framing them in close-up shots to prompt the viewer to consider their perspective: 'Wonder what he's thinking about? What does this mean to Dorothy? Even Vernon isn't too young to know that something has gone wrong.'

These questions and the vague assertion that 'something has gone wrong' traverse a series of close-ups of the children. Rather than produce a definitive discourse of the characters' interior lives, *Palmour Street* withholds complete enclosure and allows the audience some ambiguity and room to maneuver for post-screening discussions.

Of course, the dialogue swells in significance in light of the curtailing of the voiceover. It was imperative for the producers that the dialogue exhibit 'naturalness' (ibid.). From this point of view, the goal was to minimise the gap between the script's artifice and the fullness of the actor's real lives:

> First the script was reviewed with the main characters: their intention of each sequence was discussed in detail. Often minor changes were made to better fit the personalities of the children or to take advantage of actual situations as they arose. Before each scene requiring dialogue was shot the actors were asked: 'What would you say in a situation like that?' Their answers often had to be shortened or sharpened, but the phrasing remained essentially their own. This helped them to avoid a common tendency of amateurs to 'read' their lines. It enables them to sound convincing even when – as often happened – as many as a dozen takes were necessary before cameraman,

Figure 6.
"A narrative of simple family life." *Palmour Street: A Study in Family Life* (d. Bill Clifford and George Stoney, 1949).

sound recordist and director were all satisfied with the performance. (Ibid.)

This approach was designed, then, to maximise the film's registration of everyday life as a way to advance its pedagogical project. The film's suspension of its own narration allows quotidian scenes in the kitchen, on the porch, and in the street to play out with a sense of real duration. *Palmour Street* risks incoherence as a *documentary from below* – pursuing reality from the vantage point of an intimate domesticity – while also harvesting educational significance from the scenes filmed. Nevertheless, the film bridges the divide between these two approaches by embracing aperture over closure through the narration's questioning tone as well as the minimisation of its own harvesting impulses. Finding dramatic scenes through collaboration, for instance, upholds the film's neorealist tendencies, but also builds credibility with the audience. It also seeks to establish a surplus of meaning, one that goes beyond the traditional mental health incitement to inform and, instead (following SEFPS's stated goal for the film), plumb the uncertainties about which Richard Wright wrote regarding his own childhood.

The racial look activated by *Palmour Street* is harnessed to promote mental health awareness among African American families in the south and such an address reroutes the look away from interrogating the psychic life of one subject and towards a critical awareness of everyday familial struggles. Here it could be said that *Palmour Street* succeeds where *The Quiet One* fails. The family dynamics depicted are less extreme and more ambiguous, in line with the subtle pressures and strains of life. Similarly, the embrace of aperture over closure cracks the confidence and the fixity of *The Quiet One*'s staging of racial experiences. Here *Palmour Street* is more overtly invested in initiating a dialogue rather than launching a monologue. This is clear not simply in light of Dr Mason's intentions, but also because of the uncertainty of the film's discursive address. That pursuit of irreducible tension registers a neorealist aesthetic that is less dogged in its psychic mining of the subjects depicted and thwarts easy conclusions as an incitement to discuss. The film's final image – a looming question mark – pulls the rug out from under the audience and emphasises the relationality and contingency of the racial look. The visual relation that subtends the racial look is foregrounded by the aperture of the film's discourse, its self-conscious address to African American audiences, as well as the bi-racial collaborative nature of the production.

In the April 1950 issue of *The Survey*, a magazine dedicated to 'family training for parent and child', *Palmour Street* is featured as a filmic document of 'a real street … and real people' (Anon. 1950b: 188). A few paragraphs accompany a photo spread of stills taken from the film and the writer insists that the 'simple incidents of the picture are not much different from the day-to-day experiences of leading actors' (ibid.). The key roles of *Palmour Street* were played by 'Mr and Mrs James Wesley Merritt and their four children' (Anon., 'Palmour Street (A Study of Family Life)': 3). The Merritt family lived in Gainesville and the film was primarily 'shot in and around their own house' (ibid.).[2] The production itself had to be arranged with Mr Merritt's work schedule in mind. At the time, he was running a 'shoeshine concession in a white barbershop' and needed to 'be at his stand during rush hours' (ibid.). The article continued to note that the film premiered at the Fair Street School, 'a few hundred yards from the Merritts' home, the film's main location' (Anon. 1950: 189). The film's utility is underscored as the 'Department of Health will use it in many Georgia communities as the basis for discussion groups dealing with parent-child relations' (ibid.).

As the producers noted, the utility of the film was of utmost importance and was far from being taken for granted. Through a review of the film's post-screening materials, we recognise a complicating factor for the production, one that disavows the racial identity of the individuals represented and reaches for a universal frame. On 30 August 1950, [Bill Clifford] wrote to Stoney and emphasised 'an urgent need for some sort of guide to point the way' for post-screening discussions of *Palmour Street* (Clifford 1950: 1). Before completing the guide Clifford hoped to 'introduce the film to one or two groups of Health Educators' (ibid.). In the resulting 'Discussion Outline for "Palmour Street"', a few principles are easily sketched. First comes the insistence on the *documentary* value of the film. *Palmour Street* 'attempts to show family life experiences as they actually occur' (Anon., 'Discussion Outline…': 1). Out of this commitment to recording real life comes the recognition that the experiences depicted do not lend themselves to easy solutions. Rather, a realist ethos compels viewers to confront particular knots or entanglements of familial life that compel discussion. Once the film begins, the prompt states, 'you will immediately realize … that no one answer solves the problems which come up in this family or your family or mine' (Anon., 'Discussion Outline…': 2).

Another value implied by the above and then explicitly stated is an insistence on the universality of experiences depicted. If the events on screen are readily applied to 'this family or your family or mine', then it is clear that the producers wanted to facilitate a dual address for the film (ibid.). On the one hand, the film needed to fulfill its promise as a film about African American families in the post-war south. To this end, the producers hired African American performers as well as the aforementioned team of African American advisors and researchers. And yet on the other, there remained a desire for the film to frame the experiences on the screen in such a way that viewers who weren't African American would be able to relate to the supposed rock of parent/child relations. The familial challenges screened in the film 'present basic experiences and in the discussion which follows the film we hope to look for principles relating to human behavior, rather than answers to specific situations' (ibid.). Race is avoided altogether by the discussion questionaire, supplanted by the prompt's referral to a constitutive 'human behavior'.

For the 'Discussion Period (Following Film)' the questions direct consideration towards this theme of universality and the 'emotional needs of children' (ibid.). The prompts in the guide are thematically arranged and are supplemented by multiple choice options for the participants. For instance, one passage asks the audience to consider which 'needs were met, and how?' (ibid.):

    a. Security
        1. 'Mama told me about that a long time ago.'
        2. The whole family eats happily together.
        3. Mother-daughter relationship.
        4. Father-son relationship.
    b. Love
        1. Mother-daughter and father-son relationship.
        2. Care of the infant.
    c. Recognition (Permitting children to do the things they are able to do)
        1. All share in planning for party.
        2. Pea shelling scene.
        3. Removal of dad's shoes. (Ibid.)

Here it becomes clear that the film avoids a polarising approach in which the life experiences depicted are presented as either ideal (worthy of emulation) or cautionary (demonstrative of dangerous or risky behaviour). Rather, the representation of the family as well-intentioned and yet beset by everyday struggles carves out a significant degree of interpretative freedom for the audience and ultimately grist for discussion.

Thankfully, the archival record includes some audience responses. On 2 August 1950, a student in the School of Public Health at the University of North Carolina wrote a letter of gratitude to the SEFPS 'on behalf of the class' (Montgomery 1950: 1). The student, Meadie Montgomery, specifically thanks Ledford C. Carter – 'Asst. to Director of Production' – 'for [his] help to us in obtaining the film *Palmour Street* for preview' (ibid.). The letter continued to convey the class's general reaction to the film:

The class as a whole was very favorably impressed with the film. However, there was some sceptism [sic] about the use of *Palmour Street*. It may be that we are too inexperienced to realize its many potential uses. Perhaps this sceptism [sic] will be erased when we assume our jobs in September and discover for ourselves where such a film will fit into the picture. (ibid.)

No doubt the film's ambiguity frustrated the class and thwarted their expectations. One of the students wrote the following on an index card:

Beginning was good. Film has educational value with parent study groups in colored race. *IF* the last idea of the tragedy is *cut out completely*. It contributed absolutely nothing to the film. (Anon. 1950a; emphasis in original)

The end of the film and its refusal to bring about a conclusion frustrates the student and leaves her hanging. But the student is correct to emphasise the value of the film as a prompt to study groups, while also underscoring the racialised experiences depicted on screen. The racial look of the state pulls in two directions in that there is a recognised need to specifically represent and speak to the multi-dimensional experiences of African American families in the south without condescension and through collaboration. And yet the state flinches at the doorstep of transparency and direct address to the specific conditions of Jim Crow and how this overdetermines the stresses and struggles of everyday life

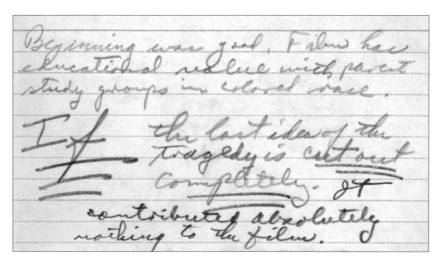

Figure 7. Student feedback on *Palmour Street: A Study in Family Life* (d. Bill Clifford & George Stoney, 1949). George C. Stoney Papers, 1940–2009. The Louis Round Wilson Special Collections Library. University of North Carolina at Chapel Hill.

for African Americans. The neorealist impulse – the *feeling of the new,* the *documentary from below* – is even more concentrated here in Clifford and Stoney's educational film. Its treatment of the African American family and the African American subject is less penetrating and arrogant than *The Quiet One.* This moderation of the film's racial look can be read as an extension of the producers' awareness of their own privilege and the realities of racism in the south.

Notes

1 *Let There Be Light* was famously withheld from the public by the Army in 1946 and was not officially screened until 1980. A screening at the Museum of Modern Art in New York was thwarted when, according to Huston, 'two military policemen arrived and demanded the print' (qtd. in Simmon 2007: 5).
2 Lynne Jackson has written that the selection of Gainesville, Georgia was largely motivated by Stoney's friendship with Silva Meyer, 'managing editor of the paper there'; the hope was 'that this friendship would at least guarantee the endorsement of the project by the local paper; he felt he could count on some protection from that end' (1987: 370).

CHAPTER THREE

CHARISMATIC KNOWLEDGE: MODERNITY AND SOUTHERN AFRICAN AMERICAN MIDWIFERY IN *ALL MY BABIES* (1952)

George C. Stoney's lifetime of educational film production was only in its infancy with *Palmour Street*. He would soon produce and direct what is considered to be a classic American documentary film in *All My Babies* (1952). The film has continued to receive praise and accolades in recent years as it was added to the National Film Registry in 2002 and in the summer of 2013 the Brooklyn Academy of Music included the film on its programme, 'A Time for Burning: Cinema of the Civil Rights Movement'. As mentioned earlier, the film follows the lead of *The Quiet One* as an educational documentary that exhibits a number of neorealist traits, including a commitment to shadow reality as a *documentary from below* and its deployment of nonprofessional actors to reenact realistic scenarios drawn from everyday life. And yet *All My Babies* continues Stoney and Clifford's use of collaboration in *Palmour Street* by drawing on the expertise and experience of African American midwives and nurses. As a film sponsored by the Georgia Department of Health and the Medical Film Institute of the Association of American Medical Colleges, *All My Babies* set out to promote greater coordination between traditional midwifery and the modern health care system. And the production of *All My Babies* echoes this institutional goal as the cinema, a modern communicative technology, and its practitioners collaborate with 'traditional' African American midwives to spread this message about professional medical care. Such a collaboration models the desired collaboration between traditional and modern birthing practices. Stoney's film, which has been justifiably praised for its humanistic treatment of its midwife protagonist, must mitigate the racial look of the medical establishment and constitute African American midwifery as a flexible practice with a legacy formidable enough to stand alongside the modern medical establishment. And the collaboration at the heart of the film privileges the voice of the midwife, critically thwarting the initial purpose of the project as a whole.[1]

On the one hand, the film's continued appeal might be viewed as out-of-step with the trends in documentary filmmaking that soon followed. Its reliance on reenactment as well as its specific pedagogical purpose would seem to align it with documentary classicism and preclude the pursuit of fleeting everyday experiences. And yet Stoney's approach, as discussed in the previous chapter, inverts the Griersonian formula by privileging an investment in the *decisive moment* over and above the envelopment of the viewer with information. The information is there, but it's enmeshed in the expressivity and experiences of the film's subjects which compel a sense of *aperture over closure*, leaving room for the audience to come to their own conclusions. In this manner, Stoney's films powerfully stage a conversation between documentary paradigms and, therefore, resonate beyond their immediate designation as educational or training films. Following an overview of the film's production, this chapter will analyse the film's aesthetics in light of its historical situation within the broader push to modernise and professionalise birthing practices in the post-war south.

All My Babies was commissioned to educate both southern midwives and health care professionals with an eye towards encouraging greater cooperation between the two groups. As Stoney later noted, at the time of the film's launching 'a majority of the Negro children in the south were still being delivered by "granny women"' (1959: 79):

> Fully two generations after doctors and hospitals had almost completely replaced the folk midwife among the white population, these little trained, largely illiterate, traditionally elderly women were attending a quarter of a million births a year. (Ibid.)

Stoney felt that 'these women, the dedicated and the damned alike, had something undeniably grand about them' (1959: 81). Such encounters with southern midwives deeply affected Stoney and when the opportunity finally came to produce 'a simple training aid' (ibid.), he embraced it. The contract for *All My Babies* was 'executed' on 21 June 1951, 'by and between the Georgia Department of Health, Atlanta, Georgia ... and the [Medical Film Institute]' (State of Georgia 1951). The document stipulates that the intent is for the Medical Film Institute to 'produce a film on the subject of lay midwife teaching and nurse instruction, designed to promote the use and understanding of recommended techniques for home delivery, to improve methods of maternal and infant care, to incourage [sic] a wider cooperation between midwives, doctors and public health nurses and to stress a better understanding by midwives of danger signals and methods of referral' (ibid.). The 'motion picture [is] to be photographed on 35mm black and white film [and the] total length of this film is to be ... no less than 27 minutes screen time and no more than 33 minutes screen time' (ibid.). Ultimately, the 'subject to be portrayed is the work and techniques recommended for use by lay midwives in the Southeastern United States with particular attention given to the Negro midwife' (ibid.). The document explicitly identifies 'George C. Stoney as [the Contractor's] representative who shall consult with the Advisory Committee on any matters' (ibid.).

Five months later – on 7 November 1951 – Stoney completed a summary report entitled, 'A Film for Midwives'. Here Stoney defines the 'central problem' as the persistence of a 'gap between precept and practice, between the way things are demonstrated in the training classes and the way things are actually done in the homes during deliveries' (ibid.). Given the impracticality of 'direct supervision by a group of experienced nurse-midwives', Stoney suggests that the 'motion picture is the best way to show this audience [of midwives] how the instructions they are given by the nurses can be carried out in the kinds of real – and far from ideal – situations in which they must work most of the time' (ibid.).

In order to accomplish this task, Stoney makes the case for cinematic realism. 'It is proposed, therefore, to make the film as realistic as possible, without sacrificing emphasis, repetition and generalization that are needed in any teaching medium' (1951: 5–6). Nevertheless, the realism of the proposed film will need to contend with a necessary process of *idealisation* whereby the protagonist will be a 'midwife who ... will know her job more thoroughly than most and her techniques will be those given general approval by medical authorities' (1951: 6). However, Stoney adopts 'a simply story framework' in order to temper the pedagogical elements of the film and ensure that the 'demonstration will become for the moment reality for the midwife viewers' (ibid.). This narrative frame will keep the midwife at the centre of the action and ultimately 'encourage the members of the audience to identify with the midwife heroine, to respect her, to experience both her misgivings and her triumphs at the same time that they are watching the details of her work' (ibid.). Here we have a clear articulation of Stoney's unique educational film aesthetic. His approach, as we've just seen, pulls the audience in two polar opposite directions, blending realism with heightened idealisation.

The narrative structure Stoney had in mind was less invested in the 'building of conventional dramatic effects through surprise, tension and excitement' (1951: 6–7). Rather, Stoney felt that the film should be able to maintain an audience's 'interest' through multiple viewings, or 'through many repetitions'

(1951: 6). This would preclude a conventional narrative structure premised on the viewer's ignorance of the story. In its place, Stoney felt the focus should be on 'character and the capturing of reality in exact detail' (ibid.). Such a level of precision would be achieved primarily through casting:

> All characters will be played by 'real' people, whose acting will consist for the most part of reliving incidents that might well be a part of their everyday life. Since both the midwife group in the southeast and the vast majority of their [patients] are Negro, our principled character and the families she helps will be Negro. Medical and nursing personnel shown in the clinic sequences and in the home will be drawn from the staffs of health departments near the film's main location. Most of these, of course, will be white. It is hoped that, without departing from the guiding principle of reality, at least one Negro nurse and perhaps a Negro doctor can be included. (1951: 7)

According to an article in the *Independent* – a retrospective look at Stoney's career – the way in which *All My Babies* 'uses re-enactments and a dramatic script, owes much to the style and subject matter pioneered by [Pare] Lorentz in *The Fight for Life*, but it is notable for Stoney's signature understanding of sensitive issues around race, class, and gender' (Boyle 1997: 30). The article continues:

> For example, realizing that white women would be projecting a film about Black women giving birth, he was careful not to include anything that might prove embarrassing for Black women watching it in 'mixed' company. The film is a beautiful study of a remarkable midwife, made at a time when strong female role models, especially African Americans, were rare to find. The film is also notable for being, in an age of scripted documentaries, far more natural: Stoney went straight from his story outline to his subjects to find out what they would and wouldn't do, and then revised his shooting plan. (ibid.)

On 15 February 1952, Stoney reported on the challenges as well as successes of the production for *All My Babies* up to that point. On the one hand, Stoney notes that the film is slowly taking shape as he had originally intended: 'More and more as the production goes on the rushes approach more closely the ideas I had in my mind' (1952). Nevertheless, he wrote of struggles with his cinematographer, Peaslee Bond. As Lynne Jackson has pointed out, Stoney 'took a chance on Bond [who] had been doing some documentary work, but most of the jobs he had filmed were industrials for commercial use' (1987: 375). Stoney wrote that it was clear 'Bond is really a superb craftsmen' (1952). However, his skill as a cinematographer did not necessarily prepare him for Stoney's unique approach to documentary, one that eschewed the constraints of traditional exposition in favour of a subjective, embodied realism. 'The difficulty,' Stoney wrote, 'has been that he isn't used to being treated as an artist … given responsibility, given a chance to contribute ideas, and not blamed excessively when he makes mistakes' (ibid.). Stoney's film practice, this implies, is as invested in its aesthetic and stylistic connotations as it is its pedagogical denotations. This entailed a unique blend of open experimentation, collaboration and rigour that was initially overwhelming for Bond. 'He is so used to "playing safe" with commercial guys,' Stoney continued, 'that for the first month he hardly knew how to take my method of working' (ibid.). While Stoney initially 'had to take over complete responsibility for framing and basic lighting as well as action', Bond eventually caught on and – at the time of Stoney's writing –

> interestingly enough, most of the frames are his originally, rather than mine, and the ideas for lighting and camera movement are generally *his*, and yet we are getting almost exactly what I want. Evidently he has finally absorbed the story, the mood and the chance to be a really independent artist. I'm tremendously pleased. (ibid.; emphasis in original)

The collaborative nature of the production extended to the midwives serving as consultants. Stoney noted that 'Miss Mitchell and/or Miss Cadwallader, nurse-midwives from the state office, have been with us on the shooting of almost every scene' (ibid.). While there were times when their presence was 'a bit hard to take', their contributions were 'wonderfully helpful' and they were sensitive to the 'slightest of technical errors' (ibid.). Furthermore,

> both of them, and especially Mitchell who is with us most of the time, have thrown themselves into the production in a remarkable way, doing make-up, costuming, helping cart people around, etc. as though they were a part of the team. (Ibid.)

The collaboration was both a reality of the production and a central theme of the finished film. As we have seen, the founding impulse for making the film in the first place was to engender 'wider cooperation between midwives, doctors and public health nurses' in the process tethering the modern medical establishment to everyday life in southern black communities. As a virtual training ground, the film racialices this encounter and initially contrasts white modernity with African American social traditions.

Figure 8. Mary Coley, the featured midwife in *All My Babies* (d. George Stoney, 1952). George C. Stoney Papers, 1940–2009. The Louis Round Wilson Special Collections Library, The University of North Carolina at Chapel Hill.

This encounter is a charged one and occurs against the broader background of the 'destruction of the African American midwifery tradition and its replacement by medicalized, hospital-based births' (Fraser 1995: 42). Gertrude J. Fraser has written extensively about 'how white medical and public-health professionals in the first half of the twentieth century defined the "midwifery problem," linked it to other social ills, and provided racial and scientific rationales for medicalizing pregnancy and childbirth' (ibid.). This broader historical context compels us to read Stoney's film critically and be alert to its resonance with this trend towards modern rationalisation. Stoney's reference to these women as 'traditionally elderly', for instance, has been disputed by subsequent historical and ethnographic research into the history of African American midwifery. Most notably, Fraser argues that it 'was not the case in most southern states' that midwives were 'always elderly' (1998: 11). For Fraser, the 'use of the phrase "granny" implies that these women were harnessed to a static reproductive tradition' (ibid.). Rather, Fraser demonstrates that African American midwives 'practiced a rather flexible birthing philosophy, incorporating techniques and protocols from their training in health and hygiene by public health departments and through their association with local physicians' (ibid.).

Fraser argues that 'a reading of medical journals, county records, and legislation from the period' says less about the real practices and conditions of African American midwives in the south than it does about the tendency of public health officials to 'disparage the personality of the "Negro" midwife or the details of birthing "superstitions"' (1998: 6). The condescension of such materials for Fraser ultimately reveals the 'mind-sets of southern professionals involved in midwifery control and public health' as well as the contested nature of 'southern society and everyone's proper place within it' (ibid.). The 'figure' of the midwife was often the critical fulcrum in this larger discourse about the south (ibid.). During the first half of the twentieth century, anxiety over the 'preservation of racial boundaries and fears about the insufficiency of white fertility went hand in hand with the vital statistics [population data, birth and death certificates] and maternal health movement' (1998: 20). The attention heaped on the African American midwife in the south testifies to her ubiquity and importance in African American families as well as the encroachment of modernity and the 'administration of American lives' (1998: 21). The midwife's possession of a kind of 'charismatic knowledge identified as "mother's wit"' was viewed 'as an essential feature of a successful practice' (1998: 26). And yet this charismatic knowledge was anathema to an increasingly aggressive and professionalised white medical establishment.

If we let this historical frame impact how we look at Stoney's *All My Babies*, then the film's political implications swell with clarity. Suddenly the film's entanglement of procedure with the charismatic knowledge and labour of the African American midwife *grounded in the historical world* seems to echo the broader tensions at work throughout the south. No doubt, Stoney's task with the film is to help seal the breach between midwife and nurse, midwife and doctor, with all the racialised implications just reviewed as a white medical establishment sets out to regulate African American midwifery in the south. To some extent, *All My Babies* could – on a first pass – be seen as a participant in this broader history of white medicalisation and its gradual but definitive intent to cast African American midwifery to the dustbin of history. By encouraging greater 'collaboration' and, implicitly, a certain amount of oversight on the part of the professionalised white medical class, *All My Babies* would appear to gently nudge this southern black tradition towards absorption by a new scientific and technological regime. The film is part of a wave of 'federal and northern philanthropic infusions of funds and programs into southern health' that, in many instances, pursued the 'long-term goal of phasing out midwives and replacing them with clinics, hospitals and medical doctors' (1998: 27). Nevertheless, the associative 'short-term goal' of educational campaigns was often more positive as they sought to 'improve African American child and maternal morbidity and mortality rates' (ibid.). In this sense, the use of music by such campaigns mirrors the use of film. Fraser notes that some '"Negro spirituals" or nursery rhymes [were adapted] to drive home the message of hygiene, limitation of practice, and prenatal care to midwives' (ibid.). *All My Babies* similarly slides into the same historical framework as its 'short-term goal' seeks to engender the sort of collaboration that prevailed on the film set between the African American midwives and health professionals *and* the film producers. In this sense the happy co-administration of patients that prevails within the film between the African American midwife and the white medical professionals does seem to reflect the collaboration that occurred without, between Stoney and the film's midwife protagonist, Mary Coley. The film reproduces a regulatory racial look that also loses momentum in light of this collaborative nature of the production, but also thanks to specific formal decisions that subordinate the figures of the medical establishment to the work of Coley. Elements of Stoney's film underscore the subjection of African American bodies to the 'shared structural conditions of ill health, racism, political neglect, and economic distress' (ibid.). The film prioritises and upholds Coley's subjectivity and, in the process, bucks a trend that haunted the use of music in midwifery campaigns where the 'simplicity and repetition [of such songs] indicated a view of the midwife as not only illiterate but stupid' (1998: 28).

The film explicitly combats this tendency. But it is also caught between the push and pull of endorsing regulatory oversight on the one hand while engendering affective identification with the African American midwife on the other. In this sense, the film animates a more dynamic portrait of African American midwifery as – following Fraser – a *flexible* tradition mindful of the possibility for change as well as its own historical legacy. This open and productive tension is staged in the film through the use of Mary Coley's commentary in conjunction with scenes featuring white medical professionals. No doubt the visible presence of a white masculine doctor in certain scenes promotes a fleeting, but authoritative paternal presence that reverberates with *The Quiet One*. However, the commingling of the presence of white professionals with the spectral authority of Coley's voiceover narration privileges the midwife's perspective even as she is seen cooperating with a white medical establishment. Early on the audience is treated to a classroom scene in which a white health officer lectures a dozen or so African American midwives. He opens by announcing a tragedy:

Two days ago, a baby delivered by a midwife died when it ought to have lived. As your health officer, it was my duty to find out why that baby died. My examination showed that its cord got infected and you all know what that means: something wasn't clean. Maybe the midwife didn't boil her scissors long enough. Or it could've been that the dressing she used wasn't sterile. Or it might have been that she got in a hurry and didn't wash her hands well. Now you midwives in this county have built up a wonderful reputation. You work hard, and I know how difficult it is to keep things clean in some of the homes where you have to go. But your record shows that you can keep clean. And when something like this happens, it's a warning to all of us, to us doctors and nurses as well as to you midwives. It shows us how very easily we can slip back when we get careless.

While the monologue hedges its critique (note the use of the first-person plural as well as the recognition of the midwives' work ethic and hard earned reputation), the focus of the address is on a deadly oversight. The paternalism of the scene is undeniable as a white health officer lectures this assemblage of African American midwives about the importance of hygiene in their work. The condescension of the white therapist/narrator in *The Quiet One* temporarily rears its head for a moment. And yet the authority and awkward formality of the health officer's speech pales in comparison to the affective power of Mary Coley's voiceover narration, which saturates the film from beginning to end. Even the health officer's speech is immediately absorbed by Coley's spectral commentary on the soundtrack.

I've been doing the same thing about eighteen years, but I still know I can slip if I don't keep checking on myself. These young girls who are just starting out, they have an advantage because they're learning the right way at the beginning. But you know old folks can change too, if they just put their mind to it.

Coley's words are spoken over imagery of the midwives – including herself – as they practice tying umbilical cords on mannequin newborns. The paternalism of the scene persists as a white nurse oversees the work of the midwives, young and old. Nevertheless, Coley's perspective, and the way in which it is conveyed on the soundtrack, is paramount. It is her interiority that subsumes everything else in the film and exudes an openness to learning and evolving that upholds African American midwifery as a tradition that looks ahead as much as it looks back.

This productive tension plays throughout the film, but its expression during the opening scenes is instructive. The film opens with a fleeting use of the Voice of God in which a disembodied authoritative commentator establishes the key characters and their relationship to one another. Here the beginning is notable for the way it establishes Coley as the protagonist, as the individual at the centre of the film's narrative universe. It's Coley's actions that matter here and how they help young mothers. The health officials are tertiary and presented as background professionals whose aim is to facilitate and support Coley in her work.

> I want you to meet Mrs Mary Coley, a midwife who lives in Albany, Georgia. This is a story of how she helps people: people like Ida Fleming, who engaged Miss Mary to deliver her third child; people like Adam and Marybelle Dudley, newcomers to Dougherty County who bring their troubles to this midwife. In the country health department are doctors and nurses who help Miss Mary do the job which she and thousands of other midwives all over the south have dedicated their lives: the birthing of healthy babies.

Coley's work as a midwife is also metonymically positioned as indicative of a broader community of southern midwives whose work is neither marginal nor disposable, but essential to the 'birthing of healthy babies'. In this manner, the opening helps trump the white paternalism of the classroom scene just discussed.

However, the transcendent voice of the outsider gives way immediately to Coley's own voice. At the conclusion of the above introductory comments and the accompanying visual survey of the main characters, the screen is overwhelmed by a multitude of photographs featuring African American children and babies. The photographs fill and exceed the frame, leaving the spectator briefly overwhelmed by the number of children. Further enhancing the shot's power is its spatial abstraction: we aren't clear of the spatial orientation of the image as it commences the first full scene of the film. The feeling passes as the film cuts to a shot staged in depth of a pregnant Ida looking at the same photo collage, framed and displayed on a wall in Coley's living room. Ida turns to Coley, held in the foreground of the shot, and asks if the babies are all hers. 'Yes,' Coley replies, 'these are all my babies, delivered about 1400, counting the ones [that] come this year.' The initial sense of visual overwhelm that accompanied the shot of the photographs is intensified by Coley's numeric summation. If our view of two or three dozen babies can impress, then the thought of 1400 babies heightens the abstraction of the image. We, like the film, simply can't keep up and the boundaries of the frame parallel the boundaries of our cognitive abilities to fully imagine the totality of Coley's work as a midwife. Our view of the photographs, of all of Coley's babies, returns at the end of the film as well. When Coley adds a photo of a recent newborn – Adam, Jr. and his father – to her collection on the wall, the film ups the emotional ante by pressuring the viewer to amplify and multiply the individual experiences just depicted by both the number of photographs as well as Coley's own recollection of the number of babies delivered. The indexical value of this new photo is charged by its connection to a parallel filmic shot of father and son, reminding us of the individuals and experiences represented by the photographic image. As in *The Quiet One*, the photograph is presented here as an indexical trace that cuts to the heart of the matter. However, whereas the photograph in *The Quiet One* is therapeutically constituted and cuts deep within Donald, the photograph here ricochets both within and without as it reflects the unique personal experiences of Marybelle's family while also adding depth to the social abstraction of the whole photographic collage adorning Coley's wall.

Coley's voice on the soundtrack transitions us to the next scene. From this point on, it is Coley's voice that explains the imagery and sounds from the film. The implication is that Mary deserves to speak about herself, her clients and their shared experiences, trumping the authority of any outsiders. As the film introduces us to the health officer – Dr Andrew – it's Coley's commentary that directs and explains the imagery. The pattern continues throughout the sequence

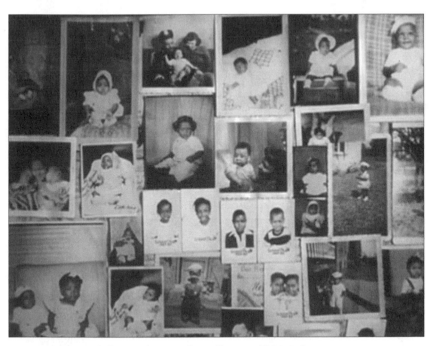

Figure 9. An overwhelming photographic collage in *All My Babies*.

and the rest of the film as scenes of African American mothers in modern medical facilities are catered to by white nurses and doctors. It is Coley's perspective that undercuts the procedural nature and the authority of these scenes. No matter that many of her lines are pedagogically pointed and specific ('Every time a mother comes to the clinic they measure her blood pressure'). Even when that is the case, her inflection is her own and the presence of her voice and authority is maintained during these brief reprieves from her work with her mothers. While the arrangement of sights and sounds here could be construed as a strategy for the phasing out of midwives – ushering in a modern era of health administration – my sense is that Coley's charismatic knowledge envelops and traverses the procedural knowledge of the medical establishment. Again, this careful entanglement of midwifery and modern medicine is not unlike the collaboration associated with the film itself. Here, a means of modern communication – cinema – is mobilised to represent the experience of southern midwives. The film's narration is after all crucial not simply for pedagogical reasons, but also for the way in which it transitions the audience from an exterior view of Mary to an internal identification *with* her.

While the commentary ensures the primacy of Coley's perspective and insights, other elements of the soundtrack elevate the film's affective resonance above and beyond the procedural. While it is often the case that scenes withhold diegetic sound, gospel music frequently swells to fill in the aural gap. In this sense, the music and Mary's voice seem interdependent and coextensive with one another. Both comment on the visual events of the film and even overlap as we hear Mary sing softly to Ida, one of two featured mothers. This alignment of gospel music with African American experience is a representational choice on the filmmaker's part and a number of problems immediately rear their head. To begin with, this should remind us – as Judith Weisenfeld's work shows – that 'religion was central to American film's representations of African Americans' (2007: 3). While Weisenfeld is specifically addressing the period of the late 1920s to the late 1940s, *All My Babies'* release year of 1952 still resonates with her insights. This near constitutive association of African American life and gospel music in film occurred for good reason. Weisenfeld writes that the 'presence of [black religious practices] in American popular culture reflected the longstanding importance of religion for many members of African American communities both as an expression of an individually held spiritual commitment and, institutionally, as a route to forming communal identity, exercising corporate political and social influence, and fostering economic development' (ibid.). Thus, Stoney's decision to overlay Mary's experiences as well as those of the African American mothers featured with gospel music is indicative of a broader representational trope that reflects the historical and political realities of African American life. And given that this film's intended audience was that of the African American midwife in the south, the gospel music speaks directly to the cultural life of the film's viewers. Nevertheless, the historical and social referentiality of African American religious traditions should not necessarily inoculate the film from an ideological assessment. As Weisenfeld points out, the way in which Hollywood affixes 'black religion' and African American experiences 'served broader ideological functions' (ibid.). Without a doubt, the use of religion to signify to the viewer the intrinsic blackness of a character or social situation often leads to a stabilisation of racial identity, ensuring smooth and uncritical consumption on the part of white audiences. 'The coupling of religion and race at certain moments in film,' Weisenfeld notes, 'authorizes and naturalizes American racial categories and works to describe and prescribe the boundaries of the category of religion' (2007: 4–5).

Nevertheless, the way in which gospel music appears in the film acknowledges the significance of religion in the social lives of the characters without reducing the latter to the former. Of course, one could imagine an educational documentary about midwifery without the music. There is nothing about the work of midwifery that specifically mandates the incorporation of gospel music and its associative feelings of religiosity. In fact, if anything, the music might be seen as distracting from the procedural demands of the film's pedagogical mission. However, this feeling of excess casts the music in a specific light. The music erupts on the soundtrack and plays out in an overt fashion, in contrast to the typically covert and complementary role we are accustomed to film music fulfilling. Gospel music in *All My Babies* signifies African American experience, but the way in which the film marginalises the role of religion in the characters' lives allows it to chart a different path from that of Hollywood. Whereas Hollywood films, following Weisenfeld, insisted on a reductive bond between religion and African American life (functioning as a kind of shorthand), here the presence of the gospel music acknowledges the rich legacy of the form and its expression of African American religious community without any explicit mention of religion in the film itself. In this manner, *All My Babies* slips and slides past what might otherwise be reductive tropes. What continues to anchor this film is its framing of procedure by Coley's charismatic knowledge and presence.

This blend of Coley's knowledge and presence is on full display in the scenes depicting her work with her mothers. The birthing scene at the heart of the film registers the affective rhythms of the birth and labour as well as Coley's masterful guidance. As Ida's labour intensifies, the representation of the midwife's role is not unlike that of a film director working with an actor: guiding, encouraging and supporting with technical skills and emotional connection. The film's tracking of Ida's labour foregrounds time and renders it elastic. On the one hand, as an educational documentary, the film deploys time procedurally to acknowledge its importance in charting the labour and the pace of the mother's contractions. However, as the rhythm of the birthing scene plays out through the coordination of imagery and sounds, a different sense of time takes hold. Here, through shots of the clock and scenes of mother and midwife waiting and singing, an affectively charged sense of time develops and sharpens as the contractions accelerate. Our experience of time intensifies and its function as an ever-shortening unit of measurement overlaps with its emotional buildup towards the moment of birth. As the scene progresses towards this moment, the film carefully balances shots of Ida's womb with her face and thus insists on reminding the viewer that the woman giving birth is more than a body, but rather a person. Stoney's own remarks on this scene makes this point:

> I doubt that a delivery has ever before been so beautifully and so fully covered. Your [Mr Tall Bob] Mitchell stuff is magnificent. There is one pan from Martha's face (smiling) to the vaginal area, where we see the baby lying, still attached to the cord that goes inside the mother. Even more impressive to me is a longer take that begins with Martha smiling; her face tightens as a contraction begins; she begins pulling on her legs manfully and the camera moves down to show the results; we see the head bulging from the vagina; it doesn't quite come out; the legs relax; camera pans back up to Martha's face to show her relaxing from the contraction and breaking into a smile again. My wife thinks that should be shown, without a cut, to classes of expectant mothers. She believes nothing could be of more reassurance to them.
>
> Lordy but it was lucky we had the two camera coverage, for the Aeroflex coverage of the actual birth gives out exactly when the baby's head is exposed and the shoulders are beginning to appear. You covered it all completely from your angle. Despite your worries not a single one of your shots were out of focus. (1952b)

It's worth noting here that Stoney, at the suggestion of his wife, is made aware of the film's value not simply for midwives in training, but also for expectant mothers. As a result, the film's procedural address is augmented by an affective resonance designed to humanise the mothers as well as the birthing process itself. The film is made for both a specialist and a *special* audience, one that responds to the film on an affective as well as a cognitive level. Coley's physical and spectral presence throughout the film harnesses these two planes of address. We hear, see and feel her thoughts, fatigue, knowledge, empathy and authority. Of course, it is not simply *really* Mary Coley that we see and hear in the film. It is also an ideal Mary Coley, who actively performs and re-enacts scenes from her life. Perhaps paradoxically, Stoney records history through his reenactments as Mary Coley both recites and performs her life experiences as a midwife. And, as is often the case, this act of recording – of reenacting, of staging everyday life – entails an intervention into rigid racial schemas. The racial look is both acknowledged and deliberately turned on its head as the film shifts gears from being *about* Mary to being *of* her: an extension of her life, voice and work. Reenactment is, then, a gain and not a loss.

A 'sneak prevue' of *All My Babies* was held by the Georgia Department of Health for the State and Territorial Health Officers Association on 8 December 1952 (State of Georgia 1952). In a pamphlet for the screening, the film's 'objectives' are clearly listed and they include a desire to facilitate a mutually beneficial relationship between the community of midwives and the modern medical establishment (ibid.). The film hopes to 'help the midwife appreciate that her job is not just "catching the baby," but that she is part of a team, made up of the patient, the patient's husband, family, the public health nurse and the doctor' (ibid.). Conversely, the film also wants to educate doctors about 'what is expected of a midwife, technically and emotionally' (ibid.). And at its core, it remains 'a teaching film':

> *All My Babies* is a teaching tool which shows clearly and simply the methods a midwife should follow from the time she takes the case until the baby is taken to its first Well Baby Clinic.
>
> The team approach in meeting the emotional needs of the family and patient are so well integrated into the film that it might also be listed as a mental hygiene film. The film successfully combines human interests and the best in normal obstetrics.
>
> Since the obstetrical techniques are so clearly detailed it is felt that the film will be useful in fields other than that of midwife teaching by the public health nurse. (ibid.)

The teaching this film sets out to perform does not simply chart specific 'methods', but it also couches such techniques within a broader consideration of 'emotional needs'. Clearly, the film's blend of pedagogy, mental hygiene and portraiture is a chief reason for its influence and resonance as an educational documentary. In this instance, cinema's affective power resists easy labelling and upholds the work of the African American midwife in the south at a time when the modern medical establishment was seeking to marginalise her. Lynne Jackson concludes her production history of the film by observing that this is its most significant accomplishment. Specifically, *All My Babies* made the case that 'if they worked with midwives, [doctors] could get a variety of clinical experience that they couldn't have otherwise' (1987: 388).

While this chapter concludes our discussion of films that generate a specific medical or therapeutic vision, we will soon see how this legacy persists in War on Poverty films, where producing well-rounded citizen-subjects is a core feature of their liberal advocacy. Nevertheless, *All My Babies* must be regarded here as an educational film that openly engages with the contradictions of its liberal racial look. The specific visual relations manifest in this film traverse and work against the material campaign of modern medicine to marginalise southern African American midwifery. The neorealist impulse in *All My Babies* foregrounds Mary Coley's charismatic knowledge in a manner that tempers the polarising and colonising momentum of the medical establishment, highlighting midwifery's flexible and humanist birthing philosophy. If the racial look falls short of turning its visual relations 'inside out', then at least it actively resists its charge. Coley's presence and work are privileged by the *documentary from below* and Stoney's continued reliance on collaboration and his acknowledgement of the limits of his own experience models a racial look in retreat as well as showcases Coley's look back.

Note

1   Lynne Jackson's work on the production history of this film is seminal. In her article, 'The Production of George Stoney's Film *All My Babies: A Midwife's Own Story* (1952)', she explains how Stoney's prior work on the film, *A Concept of Maternal and Neonatal Care* (1951), 'indicated that Stoney was able to handle the scientific details of the subject' (1987: 369).

CHAPTER FOUR

FULL OF FIRE:
HISTORICAL URGENCY AND UTILITY IN
THE MAN IN THE MIDDLE (1966)

On 9 March 1960, Michael A. Roemer sent a letter to George Stoney praising two of his films, *All My Babies* and *Still Going Places* (1955). 'Along with *The Quiet One*,' Roemer wrote, 'they seem to me just about the finest and most moving documentary films I have seen – and among the very best work done in America since the War' (1960). Roemer found it 'encouraging … to see a subject approached so forthrightly, with so much feeling, and with so strong a sense of what is important in life and what is not' (ibid.). Roemer, a seminal educational filmmaker in his own right, goes out of his way to praise Stoney's work. From the vantage point of 1960, with fifteen years of post-war documentary film to consider, Roemer views Stoney's films the most inspiring.

This letter was written during a period of transition for documentary film-making as it was caught between its classical legacy and new modes centered on the recording of everyday life, specifically direct cinema and *cinema vérité*. As Stoney continues to produce educational and training films throughout the 1960s, his aesthetic swells to incorporate some of these techniques. This chapter, then, introduces a critical transition. The educational films highlighted here and in subsequent chapters represent a shift away from the neorealist leanings of *The Quiet One, Palmour Street* and *All My Babies*. Recall that Italian neorealism was a major influence on each of these films as was reflected in their shared invest-ment in re-enacting reality through the use of non-professional actors. While the politics of the films vary from *The Quiet One*'s stifling therapeutic treatment to Stoney's collaborative approach in *Palmour Street* and *All My Babies*, their neorealist aesthetics are similar and feature a blend of evidentiary and continuity editing strategies. In the remaining chapters of the book I consider educational documentaries that are more distinctly observational and participatory as they move away from the neorealism of the works discussed earlier.

And yet, even as we've reached a crossroads, Stoney persists as a major figure for this chapter and the book as a whole. While his sponsored work drifts into new arenas and takes on new stylistic traits, the participatory bent of his film practice continues alongside a commitment to address racial inequality. In fact, the intensity of the 1960s and the fight for civil rights lead Stoney to express frustration at what he perceives to be his own failings. On 10 May 1963, for instance, he authored a letter to Elizabeth 'Betty' Marchant, who worked at the Methodist Church's Office of Visual Education. In a response to a query from Marchant he writes: 'Meanwhile, what am I doing? Exactly what all of you are: – making a living … supporting the status quo … and failing in my basic responsibility to record history as it is made' (1963). Taken at face value, the quote strikes one as unsurprising. It is hardly news that a politically committed documentarian such as Stoney would bemoan his own feelings of complicity, inadequacy and powerlessness in 1963. Decades later, in his supplemental commentary for Jack C. Ellis's book, *The Documentary Idea*, Stoney reminds readers that many post-war documentarians produced films for industry that belied their supposed left politics (1989: 302). He notes that he, along with Joe March and Alex North, made substantial contributions to *The American Road* (1953), a film that commemorated the Ford Motor Company's fiftieth anniversary and 'enshrines Henry Ford as a folk hero' (ibid.). In light of such capitulations, Stoney transparently comments that he and his peers in documentary production likely 'lost the respect we once had as documentary filmmakers on the part of the intellectual and artistic community' (ibid.). For Stoney, the turning point was prompted by a 'new approach ("direct cinema") and a new concept ("the independent filmmaker") to inspire us and refresh our resolves' (ibid.).

Stoney's retrospective comments, then, dovetail with his 1963 letter to Marchant. Both are confessional in tone as Stoney foregrounds his own structural position as a producer of sponsored documentaries. Nevertheless, the older Stoney is in a better position to identify the light at the end of the tunnel. As we see above, he highlights the reinvigorating effects of a 'new approach and a new concept'. The new approach of direct cinema tackles the representation of reality from a different perspective and its innovations speak to Stoney's dilemma as articulated in his letter to Marchant. His perceived 'responsibility to record history as it is made' is a laconic summation of a documentary practice in flux. Direct cinema, or the observational mode, eschews reenactment and pursues the decisive moment more aggressively. The staging of neorealist scenarios within a pedagogical framework resists the active, mobile and searching camerawork of observational documentary. This new approach, in turn, dovetails with the historical conditions of the late 1950s and early 1960s in the United States. Stoney's reference to the *making of history* in 1963 clearly resonates with the heights of the Civil Rights movement and registers an overwhelming sense of social and political urgency. While Stoney's letter does not specifically reference the assist of new documentary approaches, his retrospective account does and it is easy to see how the observational and participatory modes of documentary would appeal to filmmakers who were living during a period of such extraordinary change. In short, the historical world Stoney wishes to represent is in crisis and has reached a breaking point. If it is correct to critique the observational and participatory documentary modes for a tendency to evacuate historical context in favour of the intensity of concrete everyday experience, then that critique falters when the material conditions for the emergence of these modes are considered. Both modes register the historical pressures of everyday life at a critical juncture in the ongoing fight for racial equality and decolonisation. The *decisive moment* touches history as the singularity of individuals' experiences in the streets is charged with the weight of revolution and social change.

Stoney's recognition of direct cinema and *cinema vérité* as sources of rejuvenation for American documentarians on the left compels us to take a slight detour to review their ideological underpinnings as distinct observational and participatory modes of documentary filmmaking. While both modes represent a break away from the neorealist influences reviewed in the first part of this book, they nevertheless continue to advance a post-war narrative of a pursuit of the decisive moment. The desire to record and document everyday life from the vantage point of marginalised subjects through the *documentary from below* persists. And rather than view this continuity and intensification as a development engineered by individuals, it is most fruitful to perceive such formal and practical innovations from within specific institutional parameters. I am also interested in isolating a more elusive post-war structure of feeling that arises at the intersection of documentary film and race, one that is reflected in the activities of individuals and yet transcends them at the same time. And it strikes me that one advantage of studying educational documentaries is that they intrinsically tip the scale in favour of their institutional bedrock through a heightened sense of utility.

As we have seen, these educational films express varied takes on the liberal racial look after the war. The psychoanalytic racial look of *The Quiet One* is articulated through the figure of the white therapist who defines the African American protagonist from the outside. Here the racial look fixes the protagonist from a therapeutic and paternal standpoint. The liberal trajectory of the racial look is modified in *Palmour Street* and *All My Babies*. While medical discourses continue to define the core address of these films, Stoney's collaborative approach produced a racial look that was compromised and uncertain. That uncertainty is positively registered in *Palmour Street*'s ambiguous punctuating image of the question mark as well as a fuller and more complex representation of an African American family in the south. Stoney's collaboration continues and reaches its most potent expression in *All My Babies*. Here the racial look continues to fracture under Stoney's 'team approach' even as it seems to reflexively restage the medical establishment's confrontation with the tradition of African American midwifery. As we will see, the racial look's ambiguity and uncertainty in the latter films is simultaneously intensified and submerged in the observational and participatory modes of documentary. Here the racial look is further troubled by the liberal documentarian's retreat to the role of observer and/or mere participant when confronted with an immediate reality. And yet, ambiguity in the face of a social and political crisis is not necessarily subversive and may in fact lean in the opposite direction, towards a liberal retrenchment of white authority. From this vantage point, the observational mode – through its fly-on-the-wall posture – reconstitutes the white therapist's authoritative voiceover from *The Quiet One* as a new structuring absence.

While the politics of these modes and specific films will vary, the crucial point is that the stakes are higher in the wake of direct cinema and *cinema vérité*. And this speaks to their aesthetic tensions as well as their historical situation as the fight against segregation and racial inequality reaches a fever pitch. The rest of this chapter will attempt to map these tensions through an overview of the historical emergence of the observational and participatory modes of documentary (respectively, direct cinema and *cinema vérité*) and a critical discussion of George Stoney's work in the 1960s with a particular focus on his film, *The Man in the Middle* (1966), a sponsored film with observational and participatory traits designed to train police officers.

Neutral Observers and Filmmaker-Divers

The rise of the 'new approach' in documentary filmmaking, as Stoney describes it, reflects a post-war pursuit of the decisive moment, to record reality as it unfolds before the camera without recourse to heavy-handed narration or reenactment. To repeat, for my purposes, both the observational and participatory modes represent an aesthetic and practical departure from as well as a continuation of broad Griersonian principles. We can initially trace this dynamic through the work of Robert Drew, a journalist in the employ of *Life* magazine during the 1950s who sought out documentary filmmaking as a new and exciting medium for representing the events of the day. As Robert Allen and Douglas Gomery write:

In 1954, Drew took a leave of absence from *Life* to prepare a sample magazine-style documentary program for NBC. The idea was to bring to television the excitement and spontaneity of the still photo-essays that had made *Life* one of the most popular magazines ever published. However, spontaneity was not possible with the cumbersome equipment then available. 'The only real surprises that took place in front of the camera,' Drew recalled later, 'were the shock of the clap sticks and outburst of the sound man shouting "Cut!"' NBC was unable to sell the pilot Drew prepared, and he returned to *Life*. Shortly thereafter Drew took another leave to become a Neiman Fellow at Harvard for one year. This sabbatical gave Drew the opportunity to discuss television, drama, philosophy, politics, and film with the other journalists studying under Neiman Fellowships. The problem with the documentary in particular, Drew concluded, was that in traditional documentary films the logic and rhetorical power was carried by the narration rather than by the images themselves, reducing documentaries to little more than illustrated lectures. (1993: 224)

Drew's interests paralleled those of Wolf Koenig and Roman Kroitor, Canadian filmmakers who were directly influenced by the photography of Henri Cartier-Bresson and his characterisation of the decisive moment. Allen and Gomery highlight Drew's interest in a 'spontaneous' photography and the possibility it held for resuscitating the status of the image in documentary cinema. The novelty of this gesture should not be overstated as it harkens back to the role of the image in modernist poetic documentaries of the 1920s. And yet at the same time the desire to rewrite the rules of expository documentary filmmaking so as to loosen the rhetorical grip of narration spoke to a post-war fatigue in Western culture with authority, with a discourse of expertise. François Truffaut derisively labeled the 'Tradition of Quality' in commercial French cinema 'le cinéma du papa'. In the UK, the 'Free Cinema' movement trumpeted a film practice that diverged from industrial norms and openly bore the scars of everyday life, of the real social conditions of the working class in the here and now. Francesco Casetti has suggested that a 'feeling of the new' was palpable in post-war world cinema and traversed a wide array of disparate film movements, including Italian neorealism, the French New Wave, British Free cinema and New American Cinema (1999: 75). This was, then, a constellation of cultural practices that expressed a similar yearning to resist staid industrial norms ('the shock of the clap sticks') through a new cinema of the everyday.

In the documentary tradition, this transnational critical mass produced a slew of techniques designed to embrace the representation of everyday life and downplay narrational imposition. Such techniques were aided by the deployment of lightweight 16-mm cameras and wireless synchronous sound systems. A barrage of labels inconsistently applied over the decades followed and referred to a developing set of distinct and unique documentary styles: direct cinema, cinéma direct, cinéma vérité. Bill Nichols' critical intervention helps us delineate – through the fog of nomenclature – two distinct documentary modes at work here: observational and participatory (2008: 109–23). While indicative of two varied and, to some extent, opposed documentary traditions – technically and epistemologically – both the observational and participatory modes reflect a cultural turn towards the everyday and a desire to render documentary filmmaking more spontaneous and in the moment. But, in doing so, these two modes endorse significantly different paths. The observational mode, for instance, upholds the ideal of the neutral observer, whereby the documentarian assumes a 'fly on the wall' posture and eschews any form of interaction with the subjects of the film. Nichols notes that one of the benefits of this approach – from the vantage point of documentary filmmaking – is that the viewer is given 'a sense of the duration of actual events' (2008: 112). The enhanced mobility of documentary crews – thanks to the conceptual and technical innovations of figures like Ricky Leacock – set the stage for observational documentarians to be more spontaneous and to film events as they unfold in real time. The concern with recording everyday activities prompts observational documentaries to 'break with the dramatic pace of mainstream fiction films and the sometimes hurried assembly of images that support expository or poetic documentaries' (ibid.). While narration was sometimes used in seminal observational documentaries such as *Crisis: Behind a Presidential Commitment* (1963), the aim was to minimise the rhetorical power of narration by devoting the bulk of the film to events recorded in real time by a documentary crew uninvolved in the action. This mode disturbs the Griersonian approach by virtue of its skepticism towards the formal intervention of the filmmaker and its insistence on allowing viewers to come to their own conclusions about what they have seen.

The participatory mode takes a different approach and upholds a vision of the filmmaker as an agent, as a force that compels the revelation of new insights and new experiences. A film such as *Chronique d'un été* (*Chronicle of a Summer*, 1961) by Jean Rouch and Edgar Morin deliberately promotes filmmaking as an interactive endeavour. In the case of this film, the audience watches as one participant is invited to join the production and she finds herself in the streets of Paris, microphone in hand, asking strangers if they are happy ('Excuse me, are you happy?'). Here what matters is not the truth of an event uninhibited by the camera, but rather what Nichols has termed, 'the truth of an encounter' (2008:

118). The camera becomes a stimulant, inviting subjects to express themselves in ways specific to that moment of engagement. Morin has described Rouch in similar instances as a kind of diver who actively participates in the image and discards the notion of the filmmaker as a passive recorder.

> The great merit of Jean Rouch is that he has defined a new type of film-maker, the 'filmmaker-diver,' who 'plunges' into real-life situations. Ridding himself of the customary technical encumbrances and equipped only with a 16-mm camera and a tape recorder slung across his shoulders, Rouch can then infiltrate a community as a person and not as the director of a film crew. He accepts the clumsiness, the absence of dimensional sound, the im-perfection of the visual image. In accepting the loss of formal aesthetic, he discovers virgin territory, a life that possesses aesthetic secrets within itself. (2003: 230–1).

The neutral observer of the observational mode is displaced by the filmmak-er-diver, an active presence that engages the subjects of documentary. A more reflexive stance is adopted as the film crew is depicted as not a witness to everyday events but, rather, an interventionist force eliciting responses. Rouch's voiceover narration in *Chronicle of a Summer* maintains that this is a film 'without actors', and was, in fact, 'lived by men and women who devoted some of their time to an experiment in filming the truth'. This encapsulates both a shared affinity for ev-eryday life – on the part of both the participatory and observational modes – as well as a critical difference between the two as the film itself is something 'lived' that involves, rather than follows, these 'men and women'. The filmmaking pro-cess and the 'truth' it purports to record are bound together, inspired by Dziga Vertov and his insistence on kino-pravda, the notion that cinema accesses and calls forth truths otherwise inaccessible to our anecdotal and everyday existence. Nevertheless, in spite of this unique participatory ethos, this stance shares with the observational mode a feeling of the new and a desire to open up documen-tary practices to the fluctuations of pro-filmic bodies, spaces and expressions.

It was this opening up of the documentary frame that wound up appeal-ing to American news organisations on the lookout for fresh ways to represent an historical world in crisis. The varied reasons for such institutional support (chiefly Time, Inc. and ABC) has been reviewed from multiple angles – tech-nological, aesthetic, institutional and ideological – by Allen and Gomery. Once Drew had 'persuaded [Time, Inc.] to finance the experiments that would carry the candid photography tradition of *Life* magazine forward into film' (Barnouw 1993: 235), these experiments in observational documentary were first broadcast on television as shorts on 'The Tonight Show' and 'The Ed Sullivan Show' (see Allen and Gomery 1993: 223). By 1960, a partnership was forged between Time, Inc. and ABC in light of a number of factors. These included the latter's position 'as a distant third in the [network] ratings race' as well as its lack of a legacy in news and public affairs programming (as compared to CBS and NBC). Furthermore, ABC found a sponsor, Bell and Howell, whose product line (amateur 8-mm home movie cameras) dovetailed effortlessly with the style of the observational mode, which embraced a more amateurish cinematography (see Allen and Gomery 1993: 226–9). The authors also note that the motivation for ABC to produce such a public affairs series, entitled *Close-Up*, must be seen in light of broader regulatory tensions in the wake of the quiz show scandals of the 1950s and calls from the Federal Communications Commission for the networks to bolster their public affairs offerings (1993: 227).

Allen and Gomery round out their overview of the emergence of 'American *Cinema Verité*' with an ideological assessment of its unique 'aesthetic problems' (1993: 233). On one level, they note that the observational mode appealed to ABC as a way for the network to 'have its cake and eat it too' (1993: 231). *Close-Up* fulfilled ABC's responsibility to cover the most pressing issues of the day while also sidestepping the divisiveness of editorial comment thanks to its purported 'objectivity' (ibid.).

> Controversial issues were discussed, but no ostensible position taken on them could be determined from the films. The 'objectivity' of *verité* also assured that a sponsor would not be called upon to identify itself willingly or unwillingly with a particular social or political position. As one advertising executive commented in 1960, '[broadcasting] has a deep underlying fear that a potential advertiser might be driven away by something the station or network says.' (ibid.)

Of course, such objectivity comes with an asterisk. This mode of documentary practice is premised on the 'implicit assumption that if right-thinking people become aware of the way things really are, they will take steps to correct injustices and inequities' (1993: 234–5). Robert Drew, the authors note, saw his innovations in light of the liberal philosopher Walter Lippmann's proclamation that new and more modern forms of journalistic practice should 'inform the populace about social issues in such a way that rational decisions could be made and acted upon by a unified nation' (ibid.). This appeal to rationality and 'right-thinking' audiences – and the appeal of Lippmann – links Drew's practice to classical documentary form and forges a bond between Drew and John Grierson.

And yet Grierson's embrace of modernist cinematic techniques still helps us differentiate his documentary aesthetic from the observational mode. Such techniques afford a sharper avenue for advocacy as documentary films intervene into a wide array of social and political issues. 'American *Cinema Verité*', by contrast, simultaneously says too little and implies too much. It says too little as its passive style inhibits the direct expressivity of the filmmakers and leaves the final assessment up to 'right-thinking' viewers. But this approach also implies too much because, as Allen and Gomery state, the 'style of *cinema verité* accommodates a liberal philosophical view in that it assumes that whatever inequities are revealed through the cinematic observation of reality can be solved by adjustments in the social system' (1993: 237). What fascinates me, then, is the confluence of observational modes of documentary with Griersonian pedagogical schemes as educational and training documentaries of the 1960s integrate the reinvigorating 'new approach' into familiar institutional agendas.

Documenting Procedure: George Stoney's Police Films

The ripple effects of new observational and participatory documentary techniques are discernible in George Stoney's training films of the 1960s. In spite of his frustrations, noted earlier, that he was 'failing in [his] responsibility to record history as it is made', Stoney used these new techniques in his sponsored work to great effect and found creative ways to record the history he was witnessing. The realisation and idealisation of Mary Coley in *All My Babies* establishes a particular aesthetic strategy that Stoney continues to deploy in subsequent work. This is especially notable in his police training films of the 1960s. While the limitations of this sponsored work is obvious – procedurally oriented films for an audience of police is not typically a site for innovation and social commentary – the way these films work through their limitations and operate subtextually to address issues of race and social change imply an engagement with history that surprises. The films discussed below – *The Cry for Help* (1962), *Under Pressure* (1965) and *The Man in the Middle* (1966) – are worth studying for their imbrication of real and ideal, history and procedure. They masquerade as mere inscriptions of proper police behaviour, but ultimately strike out at the historical world in which Stoney is ensconced. As we will see, Stoney was frustrated during these years. He was witnessing the intensification of history and participating in the movement towards greater racial equality as segregation was overcome and new hurdles unveiled. While likely unsatisfied with his police training films as true historical records, his work on these films reflects his stylistic preference for re-enactments that suggest the texture of everyday life. His films here also evolve along with the documentary project, shifting away from re-enactments towards the immediacy and contingency of observational and participatory approaches.

The fierce urgency of the historical moment drove Stoney and, although his efforts to make more films that dealt overtly with race were often frustrated, his police films of the 1960s resonate with the dramatic wave of social change sweeping the country. Most of these films were sponsored by the Louisiana Association for Mental Health and the International Association of Chiefs of Police with additional support from the National Institute for Mental Health (NIMH). The second of these, *The Cry for Help*, was produced with the Chicago Police Department and it orients police officers to the realities of mental illness. The film openly states that an encounter with various forms of mental illness is an inescapable aspect of police officers' 'regular duties'. While its most prominent features are classical and pedagogically directed – Voice of God narration, informational content, re-enactments – the film's intensive portraits of mental illness jolt its educational structure, both reinforcing its stated aims as well as exceeding them. This element of intrinsic excess that is so common to Stoney's films reflects his mode of production since his years with SEFPS. In an interview with Alan Rosenthal published in 1971, Stoney describes his status as an independent producer seeking backing from sponsors:

> The problem is that every film begins to be shaped the moment you start talking with the person who has the money. The only reason I produce my own films is that I have found that's the only way to have any control over the end product. The reason I don't have a big office or a large staff and all that sort of foolishness is that I know I have to be in a position where I can stall on the film and argue for things I believe are necessary to it. I don't want to be under the pressure of having to get that next payment just to meet office expenses, and therefore pleasing the sponsor just to get that sustaining check. Every dollar that goes into the film is like a link in a chain around your neck. It's that kind of dirty business finally. (1971: 228).

Stoney, therefore, developed a way of working that sustained his artistic vision for the films, or upheld a modicum of autonomy, even as he pursued successful collaborations with his sponsors. As he points out, the first step for him was realising the nature of the business and the intrinsic restraints that come with funding, or the inevitability of 'shaping' once the conversations begin.

> In working with sponsors, I think the first thing to keep in mind is this: Is the film worth making? Once you start, there is so much blood, sweat, and

tears that you can spend the next six months getting all the chores done, kid yourself into thinking this is a great film, and then look at the answer print and think, 'Oh my God, there goes six months of my life for something that wasn't worth the time.' (1971: 229).

Stoney's insistence on making films that are worth the 'blood, sweat, and tears' that go into their production speaks to their value beyond their immediate expository utility. His savvy business practice maximised his flexibility and leverage over his sponsor, putting him in a position to produce educational films that achieved a level of artistry and nuance that was rare. Furthermore, the fact that many of his films were designed to compel discourse among audience members – and were frequently paired with discussion questionnaires and materials – provided a context in which the films did not need to be the final say. Rather, they could embrace ambiguity and stage re-enactments that problematised principles as much as they reinforced them. The rationale being that, in this manner, the film leaves the audience in a bind and draws them into an intense discussion about professional practices in light of real world situations.

For his police films, Stoney sought a realistic texture that went beyond the standard 'procedural' emphasis. The typical police training film, Stoney notes, zeroed in on the 'accuracy of the detail in terms of *procedure*' (qtd. in Rosenthal 1971: 231; emphasis in original). In such a film, any scene featuring a policeman exiting his vehicle will feature him 'turn and close the door of the car very quietly, because this is supposed to be the way you get out of a car' (ibid.). Such an exacting approach to procedure had the effect of rendering the films mere adaptations of manuals, but 'would have no reality' (ibid.). The challenge for Stoney was to 'illustrate the theory [of proper police procedure] in practice' while also depicting a 'cross section of types and a cross section of situations', which is what precisely draws him into the dialectical crosshairs of the resulting films (ibid.). One way in which Stoney succeeded in staging this particular tension was through his use of non-professional actors and improvisation. Working with non-professional actors, and – in the case of this film – actual police officers, prompted Stoney to set aside the script and simply ask, 'What would *you* say in a situation like this?' (1971: 234). One of the film's examples of mental illness centres on a 'motorcycle cop who is contemplating suicide' (ibid.). Stoney immediately recognised some friction between himself and the real life cop whom he had to direct.

> The cop didn't like me, and I knew he didn't like me. I weigh around 130lbs., and I'm not particularly masculine as he sees it. I played into that. I admitted

that I couldn't do all kinds of things he could do. I told him *I* wouldn't know what a man would do. '*You* would know. You tell me what the dialogue should be.' You play into their ego structure. (Ibid.)

By opening up the process to these kinds of contributions from his performers, Stoney's 'realism' can be framed as a pursuit of the decisive moment. *The Cry for Help* resists the denotative closure of a typical instructional film and highlights affective moments of pain and suffering that are excessive and irreducible and yet affirm the film's pedagogical agenda. The character of the motorcycle cop ultimately breaks down and recklessly speeds away on his bike. The film concludes with a dramatic chase through the streets of Chicago as his fellow policemen seek to corral him. By the end of the sequence, and the film as a whole, he's trapped on a racetrack and pointlessly laps around until he gives himself up. *The Cry for Help* concludes on an ambivalent note, on a psychological breakdown as opposed to a procedural transcription.

Of course, Stoney's police films increasingly recognise the frequency of protests and social disobedience over both the fight for civil rights as well as the war in Vietnam. Here the recording of history intervenes more directly through the backdrop of the real. This is most clearly evident through the way that Stoney's films evolve stylistically from his particular use of re-enactment towards a more observational and participatory documentary lens. The flux of history infiltrates Stoney's films here, moving from background to foreground. Consider *Under Pressure*, a training film produced by Stoney for the Louisiana Association for Mental Health and shot in Cleveland. The pedagogical agenda for the film is articulated at the outset by the narrator's overview of a policeman's double life. Here the film sets out to prepare the audience for the particular strains of working as a police officer, for enduring the work life of a 'marked man'.

Every policeman lives two lives. Off-duty he dresses like everybody else and prefers to be thought of as one more representative of John Q. Public. But once he puts on the authority and the obligations of a police job he becomes a marked man. In uniform or out of it he must learn to live and work under pressures few people outside his profession know or understand. This is a film about these pressures as they are experienced by four men.

Tracing the pains and 'pressures' of police work compels the narrator to dissolve the line between on- and off-duty. As he states: 'In uniform or out', the burden of policing never goes away and it ultimately leaves the officer alienated from others who don't share similar responsibilities.' Nevertheless, the film insists that this burden is worthwhile and maybe even desirable if one has the right kind of personality. For instance, one of the four highlighted officers is Fred McPherson. Following an early introduction of McPherson, we see him with his partner cruising the Cleveland streets at night and apprehending a pair of white burglars. In a voiceover, McPherson underscores the likelihood of 'physical danger' when one works as a police officer. However, instead of bemoaning this fact or implying that this is a particular kind of pressure to be endured, McPherson insists that he was made for 'this sort of thing'. 'I'm like my favorite uncle,' he notes, 'who's town marshal where I grew up out west.' The 'physical risks' are worthwhile as these are part of the officer's overall endeavour to 'make the jigsaw puzzle fit together'.

Here the alienation described at the outset is subsumed by a particular lineage of masculinity that is primed and ready for the physicality of law enforcement. And this masculinity does more than suppress the alienation of police work. It is also credited with smoothing over the rough edges of the social order, or making the 'jigsaw puzzle fit'. McPherson's masculine stamina supposedly represses both the interior pressures of the job and the exterior ruptures of social discord. In this manner, *Under Pressure* steers attention away from particular social problems and towards a transcendent masculinity that polices within as well as without. And yet a precariousness continues to seep into the persona of the policeman as the film plays out, teetering between professional restraint and prejudicial frustration. Halfway through the film, voiceover commentary from a police officer confesses that he's 'got prejudices' over footage of a protest over racial segregation. Picking up where the previous scene left off, he notes that a policeman's personal ties to a neighbourhood may ultimately thwart his capacity to be an objective arbiter: 'But if you own property in a neighborhood like this the way my mom and dad do, then it's a lot harder to take an impartial attitude.' This acknowledgement of a crack in the officer's professional demeanour and his assumed distanciation coincides with footage from the Civil Rights rally. Specifically, we open with a shot of an officer from behind and filmed from the waist down. The fixity of his stance, including a double grip on his baton, contrasts with the mobility of the protestors' legs as they march past the officer. The sequence proceeds with a deep focus shot of police officers stoically overseeing the protest from a lineup linking foreground to background. Again, the relative immobility of the officers is framed by the movement of the protestors, whose shadows can be seen on the wall beyond the police. A third shot highlights the signs wielded by the protestors, and hence the particular issue of racial inequality which galvanises them. Those most visible feature such slogans as 'Capitalism Feeds on Racism' and 'Black and White Unite against Wallace'.

Facing this scene compels the aforementioned admission from the policeman's voiceover narration: 'I'll admit, I've got prejudices. And it's a real strain trying to handle a situation impartially when you feel one side or the other is 100 [per cent] wrong.' In this brief sequence, Stoney highlights the 'strain' of history and the delicate veil of impartiality. While the film is charged with a certain ambivalence, Stoney's next police film is far more direct in its call for social change.

The Man in the Middle was Stoney's final police training film. And in many ways it is his boldest and most stylistically adventurous. Like *Under Pressure*, *The Man in the Middle* sets out to characterise the specific stresses and responsibilities that accrue for all police. However, its critique of contemporary policing practices and habits are more pointed and direct. The primary reason for this has to do with the film's focus on the work of a particular police department and its efforts at community outreach and collaboration. While Stoney's previous police films are staged in particular cities – Chicago and Cleveland, for instance – they nevertheless sought to speak universally about police work in urban areas. This universal address inhibited Stoney's films to a certain extent, forcing his point of view to the stylistic subtleties previously noted in this chapter. But with *The Man in the Middle* Stoney directs the viewer's attention to the police work in the 103rd Precinct in South Jamaica, Queens. By explicitly featuring 'intelligent police work' at a local level, this film is empowered to embrace a more overtly critical stance even as it praises the work of the featured precinct. Therefore, the content of *The Man in the Middle* allows for a discursive shift in address, pushing Stoney's critique of police work in the 1960s to the surface. But this doesn't tell the whole story. While channeling the film's exposition towards a particular precinct leads to a more politically charged aesthetic, Stoney also embraces a formal departure from his previous films by lacing his expository approach with observational techniques drawn from the direct cinema movement. Here, the camera crew's direct observation as events unfold displaces Stoney's use of reenactments.

In many ways, what we see in Stoney's *The Man in the Middle* is a dense intermingling of expository, observational and participatory modes of documentary filmmaking. The neutral observer is married to the filmmaker-diver and confronts viewers with an active portrait of contemporary policing – its problems, perils and possibilities – as well as a broader historical frame in which it operates. Stoney, then, marshals his use of the expository mode and its correspondent Voice of God narration to supply a sense of history. If the recording of history is important to Stoney, than it cuts both ways. On the one hand, Stoney was keenly aware of history happening in the moment. As we have seen, he desperately wanted to record what was happening in the streets, especially in the

Figure 10. Recording history in *The Man in the Middle*.

context of the struggle for civil rights and racial equality. But the recording of history also implies – to state the obvious – the past: what has already happened and how past events continue to echo in the present. For this, the expository mode continues to exude a unique power that escapes the quotidian focus of the observational and participatory modes. It is for this reason that propagandistic documentary filmmaking often insists on the need to be explicit and to harness the traits of expository documentary to mobilise an intervention into public discourse to change the way people perceive the world. *The Man in the Middle*, then, represents a concentration of post-war documentary techniques and a swelling of the Griersonian tradition to incorporate new modes that may otherwise appear oppositional. And this skillful coordination of competing modes is fueled by a focus on race relations and the responsibilities of community policing.

The Man in the Middle addresses history almost immediately. The first shot of the film centres on hands linked in protest. Protesters march and chant, but our view is limited to a procession of clasped hands signifying collective resistance to the state. Over chants of 'Now!' we can also make out an amplified voice (likely an organiser of the rally) reminding protesters to stay in line. 'Those who are with us, get into the line and keep behind,' exhorts the voice. 'The line is beautiful,' it continues, 'The line is orderly [and] let's keep it that way.' Subsequent shots of the march reveal this to be a protest against the Vietnam War with signs and banners echoing the sentiment of the crowd with calls to 'Get out of Vietnam'. The soundtrack also mixes excerpts of protestors singing 'Go with Me to that Land' and 'We Shall Overcome' with the faint static of policemen commenting over the radio. In a few minutes the film produces a dense audiovisual collage of the 1960s while also reminding us that making history and recording history are inextricably bound to one another.

Soon our envelopment in the present-ness of the 1960s shifts to accommodate a larger historical perspective. In doing so, the filmic image gives way to photographic and illustrated stills as the voiceover opens with an insistence on the history of social change in the United States.

> Public demonstration as a means of effecting social change has become a familiar feature of American life in the 1960s. And a major problem for the police. But policemen have been handling this kind of thing for generations. In fact, the right to peaceful assembly is as old as the constitution itself. Throughout our history people of every social, political and religious persuasion have used public assembly as a means of winning public support. Violence has also been a part of our social history. Police action is, of course, only one factor in determining how much violence accompanies these demonstrations.

The narrator's opening comments about social upheaval in the 1960s are paired with photographic stills of protestors marching for civil rights. We see shots of Catholic priests, activists marching in the fields and, finally, a close-up of a young African American male whose face is cast in both shadow and sunlight. As the narrator's address turns to our country's long history of protest and our constitutional 'right to peaceful assembly', illustrated stills are paired with particular decades. For the 1850s a newspaper illustration features an African American man standing and declaring as an upper-class white man seeks to restrain him from behind. A swarm of raised fists flesh out the depicted space triggering recollections of the abolitionist movement, particularly in the wake of the heinous Fugitive Slave Act of 1850. Additional imagery feature graphic illustrations of immigration rallies (1870s), the reform movement (1880s), as well as protests against Wall Street and economic inequality (1920s, 1930s). Our return to the 1960s – or the present tense of the film – marks a return to film footage, but it is equally diverse in its depiction of a variety of protest movements, including both for and against the Vietnam War.

The narrator seizes on this range of progressive and reactionary protest movements to stress that 'it is the duty of the police to maintain order and to protect all factions in their right to speak out whatever an officer's own private beliefs'. Here the footage presented of police standing stoically as the flow of protesters passes by works in tandem with the narrator's insistence on thwarting the view that protests are intrinsic social disturbances to be suppressed. Rather, as the film's brief historical survey is meant to imply, protests should be seen as an essential feature of our historical and social life. And police work should be seen as an enabler of protests rather than an inhibitor, if minimising violent outbreaks is a desired goal. For instance, the narrator notes that 'working with organised demonstrations is the surest way to reduce the likelihood of spontaneous violence'. Here the narrator advocates for 'intelligent police work' in order to nurture a productive 'tradition of peaceful protest'. No doubt the film can be rightly critiqued for its role as an instrument of the state, as a force for the attenuation of a protest's propensity to disturb, unsettle and derail everyday life to call attention to a neglected cause. However, as a *training* film for an audience of police, *The Man in the Middle* starts to pry open an internal critique of policing mindsets and habits. In many ways, it resonates thematically with an idea Stoney had for a film from a few years earlier. For instance, in 1963, Stoney wrote to Elizabeth 'Betty' Marchant: 'The film I have in mind (centered in Auburn, *Alabama*) can't wait until 1965' (1963; emphasis in original). In his film, members of the church would endure a 'situation in which their attitudes put them into actual physical conflict with people in their locality' (ibid.). A similar dynamic is at work here, where Stoney targets a particular attitude on the part of the police and how this manifests itself in terms of 'conflict ... in their locality'. To smooth over the tendency to view protests as eruptive events to be directly disciplined, the narrator intones that, for the most part, what matters in such instances are the 'weeks and months that precede and follow protests [and] this is a film about those weeks and months'.

Two of the key features that differentiate this film from Stoney's previous police films are highlighted at this point. From the interior of a police car during a daytime drive the narrator immerses the viewer into a particular community and the workings of a specific police precinct:

This is South Jamaica, New York. Like many communities it suffers from growing pains and racial tensions. Competent observers have predicted that South Jamaica will explode into violence on a massive scale before these problems are resolved. In recent years there have been a number of demonstrations which have aroused antagonisms that still linger. But the police of this precinct are determined that they will keep the peace and have allowed our cameras to record their efforts.

South Jamaica is positioned as a community that reflects a national sense of crisis, one that is rippling through American cities in the mid-1960s. The dramatic language deployed here – 'explode into violence on a massive scale' – reverberates more broadly around the country and speaks to an affective state unique to this moment in time. By 1966, American cities are torn asunder by entrenched inequalities around race and class. The narrow reach of the Civil Rights Act of 1964 left many racial minorities bereft of redress as the realities of structural racism and the stubborn persistence of white supremacist attitudes saturated everyday life for most minorities and especially for African Americans.

In addition to orienting the audience in terms of place, the narration also indirectly comments on the style of the film. The direct acknowledgement of the presence of the cameras reconfigures the cinematographer as an active observer on the scene, filming events as they unfold. As mentioned above, this marks a point of departure for Stoney as it more fully embraces the observational approach made famous by practitioners such as D. A. Pennebaker and Frederick Wiseman. Stoney's use of pedagogical reenactments in his earlier work necessarily entailed the disavowal of the camera's presence on the scene, in the tradition of classical narrative cinema. But these reenactments, in light of their educational purpose, were still ensconced in the documentary endeavour, retroactively and critically labelled 'expository' by Bill Nichols (1991: 34). While the incorporation of the observational mode does not necessarily transform Stoney's aesthetic – it enhances what is already a modally mixed approach – it does provoke subtle epistemological changes to the nature of the reality represented. Previously, Stoney sought to stage 'ideal' police behaviour within conditions that emulated the messy complications of real life. The distinction is crucial to the politics of Stoney's police films because these films were intended as a corrective to actual police performance in the real world. Rather than imply that this is how policing is actually done, Stoney – as an educational filmmaker – is reversing standard documentary discourse and suggesting that the behaviour shown onscreen is how policing *should* be done. This empowers Stoney to nudge police behaviour from within the institution, to show a different vision of community policing than is generally practiced in the historical world.

This mix of real and ideal fits well with, and is practically defined by, Stoney's use of reenactments. The move away from reenactments does not necessarily alter the basic thrust of Stoney's aims, but the shift to the observational mode of documentary filmmaking reworks our notion of the ideal. Now the film frames model behaviour in terms of spontaneity and improvisational cinematography, catching interactions as they occur in the shadow of the camera. This approach compels the film to specify the historical actors documented: who they are, where they work, and what are the specific circumstances at hand. But it also – at times – modulates the representation of reality by moving it away from the ideal and towards the ambiguity of the decisive moment. The narrator openly states that the policemen featured in the film 'are not always models of textbook police behavior [although] they hope that others will profit by their experience'. This clearly shifts the conversation away from the idealistic mirroring of Stoney's earlier police films. Although in many ways the idealistic has been repackaged. While the policemen in the film are not models, they nevertheless stage for the camera a mode of policing that dialectically speaks to prevailing policing attitudes in the streets *and* the possibilities of working towards a new era of community policing. The former aspect is underscored by the ubiquity of the handheld camera in this film which produces the feeling of being on the scene. The shakiness of the frame releases a sense of reality unfolding outside of the parameters of reenactment. It also emulates the view of a subject in which the camera metaphorically stages not *the* view of a scene, but *a* view. Not just a view of the camera, but the limited view of a metaphorical subject who watches without necessarily being noticed. The retention of transcendent narration problematises this particular affect, but narration was similarly used in direct cinema classics such as *Crisis: Behind a Presidential Commitment*. Although the voiceover was more restrained and reactive in *Crisis*, Stoney's film – particularly once it focuses on the 103rd Precinct – allows key moments of observation and participation to silence the narrator and open up space for discussion among the audience of police.

Two such moments stand out and taken together they paint a picture of racial discord and particular traumas incurred by African Americans at the hands of the police. About halfway through the film the work of 'neighbourhood leaders' is highlighted, specifically the efforts of an African American youth organiser named Stan Hamilton. Hamilton worked for the South Jamaican chapter of the Committee for Racial Equality (CORE) and his introduction features a two-shot of him with James Wren, previously introduced as the 103rd Precinct's Youth Outreach and Community Officer. Filming the two men speaking eye-to-eye in a congenial manner (while the music and narration drown them out) elevates Hamilton and sends a message that here is someone to be taken seriously. This use of the two-shot foreshadows the work of Colin Low and Julian Biggs discussed in chapters six and seven of this book. Quickly, though, the film cuts to a scene in which Hamilton is actively advocating in a medium shot to an off-screen audience at a local school:

> The young people have been doing a fine job. They've pledged themselves to
> do a better job and they asked the faculty of this school and the people of the

Figure 11. Stan Hamilton in *The Man in the Middle.*

community, civic organisations, to sit and listen to them. Let them tell you
… what may be the underlying causes…

After hearing Hamilton publicly advocate, the film transitions to a series of shots featuring Hamilton working with young people seated at a table and subsequently outside in the streets. As the film compels its audience of policemen to listen and view Hamilton at work, the narrator reinforces the necessity of having open communication and collaboration with 'street level leaders':

> Hamilton's program and those initiated by the 103rd are designed to keep the channels of communication open between citizens and police. Without this communication, demonstrations when they do come are much less likely to be peaceful. Working with such street level leaders is difficult at first for many patrolmen. But everyone soon learns that what these leaders have to say is extremely useful in uncovering and resolving differences that might otherwise lead to violence.

The narrator's acknowledgement of the 'difficulty' of such collaboration is an instance of the film addressing the audience of police where they reside, attitudinally speaking. And it does so in order to set up the most crucial scene in the film, where Hamilton addresses the camera crew and the police directly and attempts to give them access to – as the narrator puts it – a 'wider background of bitterness and tension'. Seated in his office, surrounded by several young African Americans, Hamilton addresses the camera crew and insists on the importance of seeing the police department through the eyes of young African Americans in South Jamaica. And, in doing so, Hamilton draws attention not only to a perspective that is otherwise ignored, but also to the broader epidemic of police violence towards people of colour. As he speaks, he directs our attention to a series of photographs published in *Life* magazine:

> Now when you speak of a police department here in Jamaica, you must look at it as young folks would. [...] For example, here you have scenes in a magazine and just about every daily paper of police attitude and action done unto black folk throughout or somewhere in the United States. Now we're not going to identify where in the United States, why in the United States, because this is no different – you understand? – to the viewer who sees this in South Jamaica. He isn't going to worry whether it's in Selma, Alabama or wherever. All he sees is [pointing at photos of riot police] there is a policeman, there is a dog and there is abuse.

Hamilton's use of the photograph accomplishes three tasks. First, it compels the viewer to see a reality s/he might not otherwise see, through the eyes of

Figure 12. "There is a policeman, there is a dog, and there is abuse," in *The Man in the Middle*.

a young African American in South Jamaica. If showing us the photograph weren't enough in and of itself, Hamilton specifically guides our look by pointing ('there is a policeman, there is a dog and there is abuse'). Second, the national scale of police violence and its inescapable racial inflections is both acknowledged and implicated at the local level of South Jamaica. For minority youth in Queens the events of Bloody Sunday in Selma are not bound by a particular geography. Rather, the 'actions and attitudes' exhibited by police in Selma traverse the country and constitute a national problem that links South Jamaica to other American cities. Third, the photographic spread draws our attention to mediation and the stakes of recording history as it happens. While this could be interpreted as a move to minimise the problem of police brutality towards people of colour – implying that the problem is one of media hype – the photographic stills work in concert with the opening of the film and its historical deployment of still imagery. The imagery here retains its indexical power and documents a crisis in process, one unfolding and overtaking the country at the moment of filming. And this is a hybridic moment, stylistically speaking. The film footage documents an interaction, a testimony from Hamilton to the camera crew and to the absent but present audience of policemen. From this vantage point it is a participatory scene, one in which Stoney enacts the role of *filmmaker-diver*. But at the same time the photograph featured in the magazine resonates with that of the observer, of the 'plain picture' – as Bob Dylan states in *Dont Look Back* (1967) – sought for by Pennebaker and other direct cinema documentarians. The two modes collide in this particular scene and remind us that the plain picture is not enough, that the mere recording of history is not enough. Staging the affective reality of 'bitterness and tension' that permeates race relations at this time and since necessitates a dense coordination of documentary techniques, allowing Hamilton to be heard and for the violence to be seen.

Stoney may have felt as if he was 'failing in [his] basic responsibility to record history as it is made', but a film like *The Man in the Middle* establishes a broad historical field in order to rewire police perceptions of protest movements while also tapping into the history unfolding in the streets, in direct confrontation with the police. Hamilton gives voice to that history-in-the-present and speaks for those who are otherwise silenced by the police. The police in South Jamaica, the narrator insists, are forced to reckon with the 'feeling' that Hamilton articulates and in this sense an aesthetic that is both real and ideal persists. It continues to speak to the film's broad intent to critique the institution of policing from within, however much it may be compromised by couching the issues in ways that would appeal to the audience of police. If classic Griersonian documentary is charged by broader modern liberal currents of regulation and stabilisation, Stoney's work both fits within that tradition while also absorbing new documentary epistemologies to capture the flow of quotidian time and nudge the documentary project away from closure and towards aperture. The films discussed in this chapter, then, call for a nuanced history of documentary form that registers the persistence of classical documentary traits and Griersonian priorities not only within the explicitly managerial arena of the state and the corporate workplace, but also from within post-war observational or participatory modes of documentary film.

CHAPTER FIVE

TRAINING DAYS: LIBERAL ADVOCACY AND SELF-IMPROVEMENT IN WAR ON POVERTY FILMS

In 1962 Michael Harrington's seminal work, *The Other America*, observed that the poor are always 'off the beaten track' (1962: 3), out of sight and hidden from the middle- and upper-classes. Reflecting on this 'invisible land', the author continues to note that modernity and post-war developments have exacerbated this trend, leaving the poor 'increasingly isolated from contact with, or sight of, anybody else' (1962: 3–4). The expansion of the American middle-class meant an increasing lack of proximity between the poor and beneficiaries of post-war economic growth. Dwight MacDonald's 1963 review of *The Other America*, entitled 'Our Invisible Poor', dramatically escalated the mainstream consciousness of Harrington's thesis and countered the more ingrained narrative of affluence so common during the 1950s and early 1960s. This line of thinking was continued by policymakers and journalists alike in the push for a war on poverty, in the lead-up to the establishment of the Office of Economic Opportunity in August 1964.

A year later Alex Poinsett argued in *Ebony* that the circumstances of poverty had substantially changed since the Great Depression and the problem most certainly was one of visibility:

> [The poor of the 1960s] are not as 'visible' as the poor of the 1930s' Great Depression when hordes of people camped at employment offices and apple sellers traded on Wall Street. They are hidden inside ghettos, behind catch phrases and between impersonal statistics. Yet the sufferings of the poor elude charts, graphs and percentages, which neither gauge a man's needs nor his longings. Poverty, ultimately, is a very personal matter. (1965: 104).

Here the author reinforces Harrington's belief that the experience of poverty has become increasingly sidelined and removed from the American imaginary. But Poinsett insists on the racialisation of American poverty in the 1960s, a sense that this 'invisibility' is bound up with racial difference and the hesitancy of a largely white middle-class to commit to a programme of poverty alleviation that would benefit people of colour. While Harrington insists that the approximately fifty million Americans living in poverty include 'skid-row whites, Negroes, Puerto Ricans' – participants in what the author calls 'an interracial misery' (1962: 17, 20) – MacDonald notes the disproportionate share of such misery by minorities: 'The most obvious citizens of the Other America,' he writes, 'are those whose skins are the wrong color. The folk slogans are realistic: "Last to be hired, first to be fired" and "If you're black, stay back"' (1963).

This chapter aims to chart the gradual incorporation of new documentary techniques into educational and training films produced by the Office of Economic Opportunity (OEO) between 1965 and 1967 as part of the agency's efforts to promote programmes affiliated with the War on Poverty. As we will see, the OEO's films during this period quickly evolve from a classic Griersonian approach to the incorporation of more contemporary documentary techniques. Our focus here is on this initial trajectory and will conclude with a close analysis of two understudied films produced for the OEO, *With No One to Help Us* (1967) and *Another Way* (1967). These films present us with an opportunity to map the politics that emerge from a mix of different documentary approaches to the subjects of race and poverty. While *Another Way* perpetuates the theme of liberal advocacy promoted by other OEO films, it also activates a different racial look on the part of the state. The observational mode wields a racial look that is self-conscious, content to downplay its own power as an active presence, and yet is still as foundational as ever precisely because of its apparent retreat from more overt forms of filmic expression. This tension plays out at a time when the economic conditions of minorities constituted an 'other America', one that remains out of view from the mainstream. The observational approach promises visibility without questioning the terms of this broader invisibility.

Other Americas: War on Poverty and the Dialectic of Liberal Advocacy

Changing the American public's perception of poverty was a prominent feature of policy discourse in the middle 1960s. In 1964, President Johnson insisted to a reporter that 'before I'm through, no community in America will be able to ignore the poverty in its midst' (qtd. in Gillette 2010: xi). This comment on the part of the president reflects a new consensus that poverty had gotten short shrift. It is no surprise, then, that – in addition to the very real economic accomplishments of the War on Poverty – there was a concerted effort to mobilise a variety of media in order to both highlight the problem of poverty as well as tout the efforts of federal programmes to combat it. The Public Affairs Office of the OEO, the agency's public relations and informational centre, was designed to serve these aims. Its origins stem from the Economic Opportunity Act of 1964 and its specific empowerment of the Director of the OEO to communicate 'data and information, in such form as he shall deem appropriate, to public agencies, private organizations, and the general public' (qtd. in Reiley 1969: 28–9). The Public Affairs Office took this authorisation as a starting point and sought to broaden its mandate to include the active solicitation of public support for OEO programs (see Reiley 1969: 29). In doing so, the importance of public outreach was recognised as crucial. Herbert Kramer, the head of public affairs from 1965 to 1968, recalled that Sargent Shriver – in recruiting Kramer to work at the OEO – described the agency as the 'hottest spot of its kind in Washington – except perhaps for the Defense Department and the guy who was trying to justify the Vietnamese war' (Anon. 1975).

In doing so, the Public Affairs Office was structurally arranged around four 'divisions' representing different types of media: Publications Liaison Division, Speakers Division, Graphic Arts Division and the Media Services/Audio-Visual Division (see Reiley 1969: 32). The last of these was responsible for the production of material for radio, television and film, all of which were designed in collaboration with the prevalent programme administrators for the Community Action Program (CAP), Volunteers in Service to America (VISTA) and Job Corps (see Reiley 1969: 42–3). Filmmaking was prominent in the activities of the Public Affairs Office from the outset. Under the guidance of Kramer the OEO produced several documentaries in the Griersonian tradition. Kramer, in response to a general question about the agency's use of promotional materials, specifically singled out film as a medium that was at the heart of the OEO's educational efforts. He insisted that the coordination of public relations activities was in service to a specific purpose:

> For example, we began in 1966 to make first-quality motion pictures which were shown on television and before various organizational groups throughout the country, and which were not promotional films. They were not in any sense 'PR' films; they were training; they were recruiting; they had an educational function. (Anon. 1975)

These 'first-quality motion pictures' were expository in design and relied on

Voice of God narration as well as poetic reenactments to romanticise the figure of the liberal advocate – typically young and white – whose heroic arrival on the scene promised uplift for downtrodden minorities. In fact, these films are most notable for the manner in which they manage the liberal advocate's agency as simultaneously aggressive and subservient in what I characterise here as the dialectic of liberal advocacy. The liberal advocate in these films registers both a transformative power as his or her knowledge base and organising skill set are deployed to remake subjects on the ground, calling forth new ways of seeing oneself and one's community. On the other hand, this advocate is also positioned as an outsider who functions as a refractive presence enabling poor subjects to grow into themselves, to become *closer* to who they are. From this perspective, the advocate triggers an internal identification rather than external one. The outsider prompts an interior searching that brings poor subjects into a state of renewal, shedding behaviours and attitudes that had previously impeded a full flourishing of their selves. In a sense, the white therapist from *The Quiet One* is made over as a young liberal activist.

This tension between transformation and refraction is evident throughout these films' depiction of the liberal advocate. In many ways the figure of the advocate serves as an expression of managerial liberalism's ambivalence towards the state and its role in managing social affairs. As an agent of reform, the advocate personifies the role of the state as both active and passive. In these films, the state is on the case – in the form of the advocate – and yet its role is to disseminate skills and to instill profound feelings of self-confidence among the poor so that they can improve their living conditions on their own. As we will see, a core ethos of the War on Poverty was self-reliance: the liberal advocate disseminates new skills so that the poor can better weather the ups and downs of the job market, more definitively meshing with the demands of a post-war economy. This particular discourse of liberal advocacy and its contradictions are manifest in the OEO's educational documentaries, produced throughout the 1960s.

With *The First Thirty* (1965) the Public Affairs Office of the OEO defines the War on Poverty for a new generation of advocates. The film opens with an omniscient narrator's determined announcement:

This is about a war our country has made up its mind to fight: a war on poverty. As someone who has been enlisted to play a role in that fight, you are about to see a skirmish. It takes place here, in the Catoctin Mountains not far from Washington. Mind you, it's just a skirmish, just one part of one battle on one front in a war that's going to be fought on many fronts, against an enemy that is cruel and big and elusive and has been around for a long,

long time. And one place where we're going after it is here: at a Job Corps camp. Poverty isn't something that happens in a vacuum, it's something that happens to people, so that's where we have to start: with the raw material of poverty. Young people like these – from Kentucky, West Virginia, Maryland – who come from poor families and who have no skills and no prospect for being anything but poor themselves, until this day … until January 15th, 1965, when, as the first thirty men to enroll in the Job Corps, they arrived at Camp Catoctin.

From the outset the narrator makes the stakes clear to the audience of new recruits. While falling short of referring to advocates as 'soldiers', this opening address doubles down on the militaristic metaphors as this opening of a Job Corps camp is referred to as a 'skirmish' and a 'battle on one front in a war [with] many fronts'. But more than this, what becomes clear is the particular relationship between the absent but present advocates and the poor people themselves.

Characterised as the 'raw material of poverty,' the young people featured in the opening scenes are depicted as both objects and subjects. As objects, as 'raw material', the youthful poor are to be – in a sense – made over and reconstituted

Figure 13. Making over the "raw material of poverty" in *The First Thirty* (Office of Economic Opportunity/Public Affairs Dept., 1965).

PROJECTING RACE

as renewed workers thanks to the efforts of the 'skilled men who came to teach their skills to others'. And yet the 'first thirty' will also be reborn as self-reliant and dynamic individuals with the newfound ability to 'break the vicious cycle of poverty'. The narrator goes on to insist that these young men 'are poor – not only in money – but in terms of spirit and confidence'. Bolstering the spirits of the first thirty so that they can navigate the job market on their own is at least as important as the specific skills instilled in them by the volunteers. The tension between the state's active role in remaking these young people and its eventual passive stance as the graduates make their way in the world is present from the outset and is at the heart of this film's pitch to future volunteers, a pitch supplemented by an outgoing barrage of celebrity endorsements from the likes of Danny Kaye, Jackie Gleason and Dick Van Dyke.

At stake here is a particular form of managerial liberalism that was perhaps best expressed by the Council of Economic Advisors (CEA), enlisted by President John F. Kennedy to explore the roots of American poverty (see Kearns 1976: 188). Their conclusions established the ideological backdrop for the OEO films, one that insists on the imbrication of federal intervention with self-help by 'favor[ing] human services over income transfers, reform of individuals rather than economic equality' (Brauer 1982: 108–9). The CEA focused on the benefits of 'investing' (1982: 107, 114) in young people as a potential approach to redressing poverty. Influenced by an overriding 'faith in society's ability to train, educate, and reform individuals' – an overarching 'human-capital theory' – the CEA preferred to locate the substance of the problem of poverty at the level of the poor person him or herself (1982: 108). By directing attention to the lack of 'productivity of the poor' and away from the 'paying them not to work' model, the CEA kept structural economic conditions off the table for consideration and preferred to emphasise 'reform of individuals rather than economic equality' (1982: 108, 109). After the assassination of Kennedy, President Johnson set out to underscore the continuity as well as the contrast between his administration and the one prior. By implementing the recommendations of the CEA under Kennedy, Johnson could signal to some that he was moving ahead with the priorities of the Kennedy White House and at the same time – since Kennedy had not had the chance to officially announce and implement these anti-poverty initiatives – Johnson could claim ownership of the 'War on Poverty' in the public arena. This was his chance to get out of the shadow of the 'Kennedy legacy' and forge a programme that would be 'his creation, his gift, and monument to his leadership' (Kearns 1976: 210). In the process, Johnson supported the findings of the CEA by stating publicly that the chief cause of poverty was the need for 'better schools' as well as 'better training' (qtd. in Brauer 1982: 117). His thought process followed an anti-welfare line of reasoning premised on what John A. Andrew described as 'managerial liberalism': a political ideology that held fast to the notion that the poor should be given the proper instruments for bettering their conditions so that the middle-class would only need to contribute on a minimal basis (1998: 9).

This logic not only gave shape to government efforts that sought to prioritise 'preparing people for jobs' (1998: 117) over generating new jobs, but it also was reflected in the educational films produced by the Public Affairs Office. A year after *The First Thirty*, another OEO film – *A Year Towards Tomorrow* (1966) – won an Academy Award for Best Documentary Short Subject. Conceived as a 'recruiting film', this work specifically recreates the experiences of three VISTA volunteers in two different locales: Atlanta, Georgia and Lukachukai, Arizona (see Anon. 1975). Building off of the initial pitch of *The First Thirty*, *A Year Towards Tomorrow* aims to demonstrate more concretely what life looks like in the field and resorts to staged re-enactments as the advocates play themselves alongside members of the impacted communities. While the film explicitly endorses the work of VISTA and its representatives, it also straddles the fine line between transformation and refraction in overt terms and even at times underscores the impossibility of the liberal advocate's position. While moments of self-doubt in the film's narrative arc are easily recuperated into its optimistic frame, singular displays of tension, frustration and conflict testify to the precariousness of the liberal advocate's aims. Furthermore, the status of the liberal advocates as the central protagonists in the unfolding drama onscreen is never challenged or problematised, resulting in a nagging residue of hypocrisy as the film claims over and over that the role of the advocates is to empower others.

The film opens with a passage to reassure the viewer as to the veracity of the experiences depicted onscreen: 'The events in this film actually happened and have been re-enacted by the VISTAs themselves.' An unseen narrator – voiced by Paul Newman – inaugurates the narrative by linking the first imagery of young advocates arriving on the scene to the broader VISTA mission:

> Some of the first VISTAs have been assigned here to the Navajo reservation. Karen ... has a recent degree in elementary education. Laurie ... left her studies in art. Their job? To form a bridge between poverty and opportunity. The obstacles? Numerous. All over the country, in Appalachia and Alaska, on Indian reservations and in migrant camps, in the shacks of rural America and the tenements of big cities, VISTA volunteers from 18 to 85 are serving in the War on Poverty. Here in Atlanta, Eric ... is driven by his supervisor to one of the highest delinquency areas in Georgia. It will be his home for a year.

As Eric and his supervisor pull into town – both of whom are white – two African American boys strategically roll a garbage bin down a hill in the direction of the outsiders and their car. The scene, roughly edited according to continuity principles, continues as Eric engages in some introductory banter with one of the youths. This exchange between the white outsider and the young African American 'delinquent' seems designed to establish a romantic narrative of white sacrifice ('You gonna live here mister?' – 'Yep.' – 'Any other friends?' – 'No, just me.' – 'Don't you know this is a coloured neighborhood?' – 'I know.' – 'Well, I guess you know what you're doing.'). Early on, then, the film establishes the VISTA volunteer – and, by extension, the liberal state – as the true transgressor, the one who is the first to challenge ingrained geographies of segregation. The pattern here is familiar as it reproduces a common Hollywood template for narratives of social change in which white protagonists confront racism and inequality on behalf of persons of colour. The effect of Paul Newman's voiceover – cast in Voice of God fashion – functions to flesh out the characterisation of Eric, whose performance is otherwise flat, and reinforces this rendition of the VISTA venture as a form of redemption.

The film cross-cuts between scenes of Eric's work in Atlanta and the efforts of Karen and Laurie in Lukachukai, and in the process constructs a dramatic narrative out of the volunteers' evolving self-image. Initially frustrated by the failure of locals to support their work, all three volunteers eventually settle into the recognition that their job, as VISTAs, chiefly consists of instigating change on terms established by the cultural environment in which they are ensconced. 'One of the first lessons a VISTA learns,' states the narrator, 'is that the poor are not waiting to be helped. They are reluctant to give up their accustomed ways.' Exasperated by rejections from her Navajo neighbours, Laurie is shown violently chopping wood to vent her frustration. Her partner, Karen, reminds her of the absurdity of the situation when she asks, 'How would you like it if a Chinese lady came into your house and – in very broken English, in front of your whole family – told you you didn't know how to cook?' To which Laurie replies, 'I'd throw her out!' Annoyed at the snail's pace of community organisation, Eric opens a youth recreation centre, only to have it beset by vandals and burglars. The narrator scolds Eric for taking a 'calculated risk': 'Only the people who live in the neighborhood can deal with the hazards to such a project.' And yet – the narrator admits – 'if he waited for adult interest to become active, he would've neglected what seemed a pressing need of the children for a place to play. [...] Eric took a chance and lost.' The specific tension at work here, then, represents the push and pull between transformation and refraction, or between seeing the advocate as a vanguard or as a medium, a facilitator for others. The admixture of these two impulses is resonant as the narrator concludes:

> The job of a VISTA is to become accepted and needed by the people he serves. But the final stage of service is to become unnecessary, to let the community take over completely. What Laurie began, Mrs Sole continues. What Karen taught, her pupils will also teach. What Eric started, others will build upon. VISTAs work with those who have painfully learned to expect very little from the world. But at times the volunteers supply the missing element which can liberate talent and redeem lost opportunities. That element is hope.

The passive aggressive goal of the advocate – to 'liberate talent' – is underscored here at the conclusion of the film. A VISTA volunteer takes on the role of being the 'missing element' that can prompt the poor to both change and grow into themselves, to become who they ought to be.

And yet the film struggles to uphold this rather arrogant charge, in spite of its best attempts to conclude with perfect confidence. If the role of the VISTA volunteer – like other liberal advocates – is to engage in the quixotic task of smoothing over the inconsistencies of the social system from the grassroots up (setting up a recreation centre, teaching job skills) as well as preparing poor persons of colour with the ways of the modern world, it is inevitable that the visceral absurdity of the task will rear its head. To be clear, this is most manifest when we grasp a fundamental affinity between the two poles of transformation and refraction: whether we see the advocate as a vanguard (creating the change him or herself) or as a medium (serving as a prompt for others to create change), the figure of the advocate still remains at the centre of the drama. In its very conception, this *narrative* of social change ostracises and marginalises those it purports to be helping. Even in the context of a training film such as *A Year Towards Tomorrow*, instances of chaotic absurdity temporarily derail the paternal project of the volunteers. For instance, at one point, Eric takes a group of African American children to visit a local airport ('A tour of an airport,' the narrator insists, 'can give a hint of what the world is like outside the ghetto'). The scene opens with a medium shot of Eric blowing a whistle while the children line up to get a tour of an airplane. A quick cut takes us to the plane's interior as the children – screaming at the top of their lungs – scramble to claim a seat. Shots of children playfully tussling are punctuated by the helpless figure of Eric in the centre of the frame frantically blowing his whistle. The advocate tries to restrain wild impulses in order to compel the children to sit quietly as the flight attendant describes air travel over the plane's public address system ('Welcome

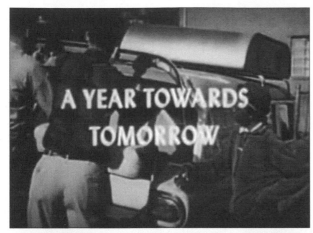

Figure 14.
Eric, a VISTA
volunteer, arrives in
Atlanta, in *A Year
Towards Tomorrow*
(d. Edmund A. Levy,
1967).

Figure 15.
The VISTA
volunteer's charge is
to 'liberate talent',
in *A Year Towards
Tomorrow.*

aboard … our aircraft is designed for an altitude of 15,000 feet and for a cruising speed of 250 miles per hour. Here are the restaurants that cater these flights…'). The absurd juxtaposition of the flight attendant's lifeless exposition – and Eric's hapless whistle-blowing – with the children's anarchic but brief takeover of the airplane provides relief that is both comedic and substantive. While the aim here is a form of uplift – to tame the ghetto mentality and introduce the children to a middle-class way of life – the condescension implied by this action is temporarily mocked by these 'juveniles' who refuse to be easily harnessed by well-meaning authorities.

While many films produced by the Public Affairs Office assumed a similar mode of address as *The First Thirty* and *A Year Towards Tomorrow*, other films embraced different documentary approaches that were more in line with the state of filmmaking in the 1960s. By 1967, the OEO's films began to look different.

Essentially, the classical expository form yields to the 'new approach' of observational documentary. Ideologically, the liberal advocate recedes as the camera acts as a witness to the state's efforts towards fighting poverty. Laborious and awkward exposition was now avoided in favour of conveying the texture of everyday life as it expresses the real work of the state on the ground. Bolstered by new modes of documentary filmmaking, these educational works marginalise the figure of the liberal advocate in order to bolster the voices and experiences of the subjects impacted by War on Poverty programmes. As we would expect, these films eschew reenactment in favour of eliciting direct expressions to the camera or filming events as they happen, to convey the feeling of witnessing actions in real time. *With No One to Help Us*, for instance, documents the deliberations of the Welfare Committee of the People's Action Group in Newark, New Jersey to form a food-buying cooperative to support low-income families. Filmmakers Eugene and Carole Marner privilege the voices and actions of black women engaged in self-governance, creatively debating and considering new strategies to mobilise the collective purchasing power of poor families in Newark. In this film – as the title suggests – the figure of the liberal advocate, the white outsider, is entirely absent and the work of the poor themselves assumes centre stage. It is as if the contradictions of films like *A Year Towards Tomorrow* melt away as the white liberal advocate is no longer a central protagonist in someone else's unfolding drama.

The film opens on a close-up of an African American woman testifying at a meeting about her experience with a local vendor who had 'made a mistake on my check so therefore they're making me pay back money to them for the mistake they made'. She and other African American women are seen sharing similar frustrations with unfair business practices in Newark. For instance, a dissolve transitions us to the tail end of another testimony in which a woman notes that a vendor 'didn't believe that I had purchased what I purchased'. A brief anonymous voice on the soundtrack states: 'This is Newark, New Jersey. These women are on welfare and have formed this committee to protect their rights. Their chairman is Mrs Marion Kidd.' This opening sets up Kidd as the protagonist in the film and, to a substantial degree, *With No One to Help Us* can be seen as a work of portraiture that highlights the work of Kidd as a community leader. From this point on, any voiceover narration in the film is Kidd's and her words both explain the actions recorded on camera as well as envelop them with political context and emotional depth. Over shots of her life at home, including footage of her children playing indoors, we hear Kidd describe the mindset of a community organiser.

> When you're volunteering in the community and you're really doing it – I
> say with all sincerity – sometimes you forget about time and you really forget

Figure 16.
Building a consumer
buying club in *With
No One to Help Us* (d.
Eugene and Carole
Marner, 1967).

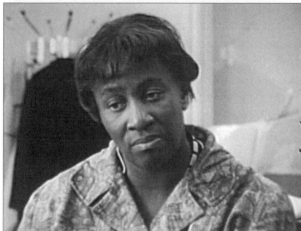

Figure 17.
Marion Kidd in *With
No One to Help Us*.

about some things that surround you otherwise. You're only thinking at that moment of things that you have dreamed about [and] now they're beginning to happen and you're part of that. You're one of the persons that's making it happen.

Kidd continues to describe the main project of the welfare committee: a bulk food-purchasing operation that would help welfare families save money and avoid getting gouged by unethical lending practices. For instance, in a medium shot of Kidd speaking on the phone, we overhear her insist that the committee 'found ... a client [who] went and bought food for ten dollars; when she went to pay her bill, the bill had gone up five dollars'. Over a series of shots featuring Kidd and another community organiser, Dorothy Jones, visiting stores in

Newark, Kidd's narration concludes that the next step is to get 'enough people interested' in joining their new 'consumer buying club'.

The welfare committee's meeting, chaired by Kidd, to set up the buying club is the main event of the film. In this sequence, *With No One to Help Us* actually foregrounds political tensions between the welfare committee and the United Community Corporation (UCC) of Newark, the 'official War on Poverty agency of the city' (Rabig 2010: 62). As the designated community action programme for Newark, UCC and its nine Area Boards 'became pawns in the political struggle between the Democratic party and the African American community' (Quadagno 1994: 48). As Jill Quadagno notes in *The Color of Welfare*:

> In the program's first year in operation, [Mayor Hugh] Addonizio used the community action agency to 'buy off all potential insurgency. [...] The slightest sign of influence used against the regime will put a Negro into a patronage job, an effective gag.' Instead of using federal funds to solve problems, they were used 'to get people to shut up about them.' (Ibid.)

The film crew observes an incident that underscores this gap between promise and fulfillment. The scene opens with footage of Jones explaining to a room of twenty African American women, many of whom are mothers, the mission of the food-buying club. Once she is able to calm the room down and explain the project ('Can I have a little bit of peace and quiet, please?'), the group settles in to listen as another woman reads aloud the list of items to be purchased wholesale ('soap powders ... canned peas, pork and beans, dry cereals, canned fruit...'). To be clear, the handheld cinematography in conjunction with the editing is frenzied and observational as speakers and listeners hash out their differences. For the first few minutes of the scene, the cooperative is messy and democratic with no accompanying commentary on the soundtrack.

However, as the women debate the appropriate cost of a monthly membership (Jones' suggestion is ten dollars), an African American man in a blazer and tie is seen entering the room in the background. The film cuts to a medium shot of the man addressing the room authoritatively from directly in front of Kidd. As he begins to speak, several of the women intervene and the film captures the following exchange:

> *Man*: There's a lot of business going on and perhaps this is the wrong time to say what I have to say. Because what I do have to say I'm quite sure you're not going to be pleased at it. This committee in the past month has raised to my knowledge several thousand dollars to provide free food for

the welfare recipients…

Kidd: Wait … we have a bank account and all money that was given to me haven't come to [that], not even. No, no. Check yourself.

Man: Well, I won't say several thousand dollars, but this committee has dedicated itself to raising funds to provide food. [The film edits out the end of this statement and cuts to…]

Woman: [Did you] come down to congratulate us or pat us on the back or what?

Man: I came down to congratulate you. I came down to tell you … what is needed to start a buying club and what kind of commitment is necessary to make it work.

Woman: Do you think twenty people is enough to start a buying club?

Man: I think twenty people is a start.

Woman: And that's what we've done.

Man: It's not enough. I think if the next meeting comes along and there's not forty people it's not enough.

At this point Kidd intervenes into the discussion, challenging the man's authority and by extension the legitimacy of the UCC:

Kidd: For a whole eighteen months I have been struggling to get this committee together. And I didn't have nobody, UCC, to come and help…

Man: And I will tell you in response to that: UCC is never going to do anything until the people make the demand, the people demand that UCC do something.

The scene unravels further as additional women join the debate and insist on challenging the man's condescension and obsession with numbers. 'I'm enough,' one woman exclaims, 'I'll go to Washington by myself.' The comments from both Kidd and the male outsider paint a portrait of UCC's political passivity and abdication of its responsibilities as an anti-poverty agency. Here, then, the observational documentary approach records disenchantment with the OEO's local anti-poverty efforts, as local African American welfare mothers join together to challenge the managerial indifference of the War on Poverty. Filmmakers Eugene and Carole Marner get out of the way and allow the grassroots to speak for itself, letting the film absorb the contradictions of the moment. The hapless Eric, the white liberal advocate in *A Year Towards Tomorrow*, is to some extent displaced here by the African American male outsider who arrives a bit late on the scene, only to reproach the welfare mothers. And yet he also speaks a truth, insisting on the power of numbers, even as he overlooks the power of the *process* that these women have initiated. Eric is also displaced by the filmmakers themselves. The Marners play the role of observant outsiders, performing a racial look that perceives on behalf of the OEO (the film was specifically produced by Project Head Start) while adopting a deferential posture. As a *documentary from below*, *With No One* captures a scene from everyday life in Newark that is historically dense and reflects Stoney's urgent need to record history as it is made.[1]

Another Way persists along these lines and charts a more defined narrative arc as the film documents the election of new officers, President and Vice-President, at a Job Corps centre. Unlike *With No One to Help Us*, this film utilises a Voice of God narration to establish the terms of the unfolding drama to draw the audience into the events captured onscreen. And yet, as is the case with *With No One to Help Us*, *Another Way* directly embraces a spontaneous documentary approach focused on the recording of everyday life as it happens, drawing on both participatory and observational modes in the process. While moments of subjective expression are initiated by the presence of the camera, others are filmed by an observant film crew assuming a fly-on-the-wall posture. In contrast to *A Year Towards Tomorrow*, *Another Way* opens with the testimony of a Job Corps enrollee and his testimony establishes the tone of the film as the narrator appropriates the enrollee's turn-of-phrase for the title of the piece. Jerry Young, a nineteen-year-old African American 'Corps-man', articulates his reasons for applying over shots of African American men in the streets and a vandalised brick wall reading, 'The Danger Boys'. 'They may not know it,' Jerry says, 'but people are looking down on them.' He continues to highlight his own discontent and willingness to imagine a different life for himself and the opportunity to participate in Job Corps is presented as an outlet for Jerry to find a new path, 'another way'. This theme is repeated by the narrator as he positions Jerry as an emblem for the 'thousands of boys and girls around the country [who are] working at a Job Corps center, learning a trade, going to school, becoming a responsible citizen'. As this opening narration underscores, more is at stake than the simple acquisition of job skills. Rather, Job Corps aims to instill feelings of 'self-confidence, self-respect, and hope'. The film, in this regard, underscores the managerial liberal insistence that training young people is tethered to a project of moral uplift and not simply a means of lowering unemployment statistics. This conventional dimension of *Another Way*, however, shouldn't diminish its significant difference as a film that privileges the voices of the poor people involved in Job Corps and in its spontaneous documentary pedigree. Produced by Drew Associates, the style of the film mirrors that of their other – better known – documentaries, including *Primary* (1960) and *Crisis: Behind a Presidential Commitment*. For us, the hybridic style of *Another Way* – its direct engagement with and observation of its subjects – situates the film within the style of documentary prevalent in the 1960s and within the overall corpus of Drew Associates.

While the film is organised around the events of the campaign, this narrative structure is more or less secondary to the film's reassurance of an outsider audience that the work of Job Corps is worthwhile. From this vantage point, the film fulfills one of Jerry's ideas for improving life on the Job Corps campus: to give outsiders a chance to see what life is like on the campus, to show them – in the words of one visitor in the film – 'how [their] tax money is being spent'. Like *With No One to Help Us*, this film documents the War on Poverty as an unfolding endeavour. Whereas the former film underscores the realities of political conflict and discord when the War on Poverty engages a specific social terrain, *Another Way* portrays the Job Corps campus as a safe haven. The historical world of the film is overtly insular as if to reassure the viewers that these young men are effectively reconstituted and made over as the last vestiges of a chaotic upbringing are cast aside. Frank Estrada, a Mexican American Corps-man and one of the featured candidates in the film, praises Job Corps for bringing people from so many different races together to correct the reality of ongoing segregation beyond the confines of the campus.

> I was so surprised [at] how many races were in the Job Corps. I was sorta scared like everybody is when you first come into Job Corps, but you get adjusted. Because I do come from a community [where] all Mexican Americans live: no Caucasians, no Negroes, no Indians, nothing. You're just with your race all the time. And this is wrong, this is real bad, because you don't know people, you don't know what they feel, their ideas or different views. And when I came in here you eventually start talking to everybody. You get adjusted to it, like I said. It's just like a home to me. Everybody's been real good. I should say the Lord's been real good to me while I've been here.

Estrada's testimony upholds the social value of Job Corps above and beyond the vocational skills imparted. As a managerial refuge, the Job Corps campus is positioned as a multicultural space that heals the wounds of a segregated country. This aspect also soothes the anxieties of white middle-class Americans who are less inclined to support social programmes for minorities. The insularity of the film is strategic in order to imply that what is happening 'in here' will transform what is taking place 'out there'. The entire space of the campus transforms these young men and bolsters their spirits and confidence.

Figure 18. 'They may not know it, but people are looking down on them', from *Another Way* (Produced by Gregory Shuker/Drew Associates, 1967).

Figure 19. Jerry Young addresses his fellow 'Corpsmen', from *Another Way*.

Figure 20. Frank Estrada is paired with Sargent Shriver in *Another Way*.

In this sense, *Another Way* is an observational counterpart to *The First Thirty*. Both films underscore the spiritual transformation of young men over and above the vocational education provided. Although given the historical gap between the films, *Another Way* speaks to the audience in the present tense while *The First Thirty* is aligned with a future tense as it overtly promotes the beginning of a campaign. From this vantage point, *Another Way* picks up where *The First Thirty* left off and deflects the critique generated by *With No One to Help Us*. While *With No One to Help Us* unsettles, *Another Way* reassures as the Job Corps campus reproduces hundreds of new, well-behaved liberal subjects. Even though the film is ostensibly about a campaign, there are very few scenes featuring debates about real issues facing the Corps men. All of the candidates featured are polite and soft-spoken, and most are mildly disappointed when the results are announced. The transformation feels complete at the end of the film when Estrada is paired with Sargent Shriver, the managerial father figure of the OEO. Estrada is clearly made over here as both an agent and product of the War on Poverty.

As we can see, the politics of observational documentary are bifurcated between the anxious critique of *With No One* and the promotional dimensions of *Another Way*. The latter film's blend of new documentary technique with expository purpose is a kind of precursor to the new communicative experiments on the horizon for the OEO. These experiments, reviewed in chapters six and seven, nudge the documentary project closer to the 'decisive moments' of subjective expression and performance and away from the heavy burden of exposition and reenactment. The work that would shortly begin in Farmersville, California would take these efforts in an even more dramatic direction by re-imagining the communicative edifice of filmmaking and its potential for conflict and even *crisis* mediation.

Note

1 The early history of the UCC is complicated and this film does not and was not intended to present a complete view of UCC in the mid-to-late 1960s. While the appropriation of the agency by Mayor Addonizio, as noted by Quadagno, is accurate, she nevertheless continues to note that several of UCC's boards were subject to political takeovers by activists. For instance, she writes that the 'Newark Community Union Project (NCUP), a coalition of three civil rights groups – Students for a Democratic Society (SDS), CORE, and SNCC ... decided to take over the UCC [specifically Areas 2 and 3]' (1994: 49).

CHAPTER SIX

THE WORLD IS QUIET HERE: WAR ON POVERTY, PARTICIPATORY FILMMAKING AND *THE FARMERSVILLE PROJECT* (1968)[1]

In a post-Civil Rights America, the liberal documentary project intersects with a particular politics of crisis. The documentary activities discussed in this chapter take place during the mid-to-late 1960s, a period in which the federal government is coping with enough domestic strife to rival its concerns abroad. Urban rebellions in Detroit, Watts, Hartford, Chicago and elsewhere speak to the intensification of racial and class-based frustrations in the wake of ongoing social and economic inequalities. During this time, Lyndon Johnson's 'War on Poverty' programmes are forced to compete with the cost of the Vietnam War as well as manage increasingly hostile and polarised communities at home. Our particular focus here will be on a relatively unknown use of documentary filmmaking by the OEO, one that involved an experiment in pedagogical and communicative media through a collaboration with Canada. In 1968 and 1969 – a period of utmost frustration and uncertainty for the embattled federal agency – the OEO Public Affairs Office renewed ties with its counterparts in Canada at the National Film Board and hired Canadian filmmakers to attempt a new form of filmic communication designed to alleviate and temper social conflict. The agency's aim was to test the applicability of a new kind of documentary filmmaking in communities struggling with deep divisions along racial and economic lines. The 'Fogo process', as this technique was called, rewired traditional expectations of nonfiction film and the role it can play in mediating conflict at the local level. This approach recast films as something other than discrete objects, not to be seen as events in and of themselves. Instead, the aim of the Fogo process was to imbed films produced about a community within a broader process of communication, within a framework of staged screenings coupled with moderated discussions. In fact, reactions to the films themselves were frequently filmed and incorporated back into the discourse. The end result was a continuous circuit of inter-subjective exchange, or what Colin Low – one of the architects of this approach – described as 'communication loops' (n.d.).

The final two chapters of this book will look at two separate but interrelated instances of this collaboration. Our focus here will be on *The Farmersville Project* (1968), the first of many applications of the Fogo process within the United States. As is consistent with the previous chapter, we shall continue to look at educational documentaries that incorporate new techniques in documentary filmmaking that relegate the position of the filmmaker to that of observer and/or participant. As we will see, Low viewed his Fogo films as *vertical* films that deviated from the classical or *horizontal* imposition of the expository documentary. He perceived his role as a kind of facilitator whose films could help a community learn more about itself from itself. As a result, the relatively short films that were produced in Farmersville, California, as well as in Hartford, Connecticut, reflect both observational and participatory styles as a way to encourage audiences to see themselves and their neighbours differently or in a new light. The films are truly in the moment as their address focuses on the present tense and are often devoid of historical or social context given that their circulation was limited to locals or audiences from the featured community. While the films are often poetic and compelling, these experiments were limited by the managerial liberal imagination of the agency as a whole. As was noted in the previous chapter, the War on Poverty was based on findings from the Council of Economic Advisors that argued for a more modest form of federal intervention, ultimately 'favor[ing] human services over income transfers, reform of individuals rather than economic equality' (Brauer 1982: 108–9). This core preference for individualistic reform sets the stage for the OEO's adaptation of the Fogo process, or what I describe as the OEO Communication Experiments (OEOCE). These experiments are compelling in hindsight for their partial success and inevitable failure as they struggle to balance an acknowledgement of racial inequality and tense social relations with a therapeutic or 'self-help' brand of idealism.

'Challenge for Change' / *Société nouvelle*

The OEOCE speak to the influence of the National Film Board of Canada's historic experiment in media and social change, 'Challenge for Change'/*Société nouvelle*. In fact, this programme impacted the United States two years before George Stoney and Red Burns established the Alternate Media Center in New York in 1972. Founded in 1967, 'Challenge for Change' 'gained almost instant international recognition [consolidating] the image of Canada as an advanced democratic nation' (Marchessault 1995: 134). This event cannot be disentangled from a broader shift in governance towards volunteerism and managerial liberalism. Gary Evans notes that both the United States and Canada had, by the mid-1960s, declared their own wars on poverty and launched volunteer initiatives to put young people to work assisting the poor (such as VISTA, Job Corps and the Company of Young Canadians) (1991: 157). Within this atmosphere, the National Film Board supported new approaches to filmmaking. Short films such as Arthur Lipsett's *Trip down Memory Lane* (1965) and Derek May's *Angel* (1966) reflected a more experimental turn that questioned professionalisation and 'rigorous standards' (ibid.). But more significantly, filmmakers were also influenced by the desire to uncover an otherwise repressed poverty.

'Challenge for Change' was officially established in February 1967; two and a half years later the programme was renewed through 1974 and expanded to include French-language production (ibid.). In the process, 'Challenge for Change' was bundled with *Société nouvelle*, a parallel Francophone production unit. The project's primary purpose was to enhance the expressivity of the poor and downtrodden in Canada through media. A key word was 'access', which entailed giving individuals access to the means of moving image production as a way to initiate a dialogue between polarised sides on a contentious issue. In the process, the goal was to bring social problems – in particular poverty – into the limelight and to incite new ways of thinking about them. To be avoided was the experience of *The Things I Cannot Change*, where the subjects of the film were reduced to caricature. Memories of reactions to this film stayed with Colin Low who advocated a participatory approach to film production in order to 'counter both the objectification of earlier ethnographic approaches and the aestheticism of an emerging auteurist tendency at the National Film Board' (Marchessault 1995: 135).

The Newfoundland Project (1967–69) inaugurated the 'Challenge for Change' programme for the NFB while also serving as the catalyst and template for the OEOCE. Over the last few decades, a relatively clear narrative has been adopted to explain how this project came about. Nevertheless, scholars have also begun to challenge this narrative as new perspectives attained through archival research and oral histories have added greater nuance and clarification. The commonly held view of *The Newfoundland Project* is as follows. Fogo Island, near the north-eastern coast of Newfoundland, was in the throes of a crisis with social, political and economic implications. Specifically, Stephen Crocker notes, 'more than 1,000 communities had been moved' in the wake of Premier Joey Smallwood's commitment to 'resettle as many as 50,000 people from remote settlements that had, as he put it, "no great future"' (2008: 62). Crocker continues:

A powerful set of photographs from that time shows villagers floating their homes across the inlets and ocean channels to their new destinations. In one especially poignant picture a house sinks as it is floated from Deep Bay to 'Fogo proper', giving us a powerful metaphor for the villagers' attempts to integrate their existing lives into the new industrial future that they were being directed toward. (ibid.)

The growing controversy around these resettlement policies set the stage for the National Film Board's work on Fogo Island. This 'experiment in the role of communications in social change' – as described by the narrator in one of the original Fogo films, *An Introduction to Fogo Island* – was the inaugural project of the NFB's 'Challenge for Change'. This initiative was designed to deploy film production as a way to 'help eradicate the causes of poverty by provoking basic social change'. With the crisis growing on Fogo Island and pressures mounting on the Newfoundland government, producers at the NFB saw an opportunity to use film as a communicative tool to help find a solution. Colin Low – the head filmmaker on the project – initially assumed that the crew would produce a traditional documentary about the issue of modernisation and the concerns of the islanders. However, the producers wound up embracing a different kind of approach, one more participatory in nature. Specifically, in collaboration with Memorial University of Newfoundland's Extension Service (MUN Extension), the film crew produced twenty-seven short films and used the exhibition of these

Figure 21. Provoking social change, a still from *The Children of Fogo Island* (directed by Colin Low, 1967). National Film Board of Canada.

works as incitements to discussion among the locals and as a means of communicating with bureaucrats in Ottawa. In this sense, the films were perceived as elements of a broader process of communication, of opening up new channels of communication both internally – between various factions – and externally – between Fogo Islanders and the state.

Screenings were also held for government officials and academics – the 'power people', as Snowden referred to them (n.d.) – whose reactions were themselves filmed and exhibited to Fogo Islanders. This exchange of films and the dialogue achieved is what Stephen Crocker has called the 'hallmark of the Fogo Process' (2008: 66), a methodology that would be frequently adapted and exported to foreign locales. Crocker insists that this process empowered Fogo Islanders to overcome their pluralism, their heterogeneity, and 'imagine themselves as a part of a single common community. Thus [he continues], the films created an external "virtual community" that could act as a reference point for people to give them an image of themselves' (2008: 69). The Fogo films, then, supposedly helped constitute a collective identity that otherwise would have failed to take root. In this regard, Crocker suggests that the films temporarily dissolve or diminish those elements that were resistant to the forging of a common Fogo narrative. Snowden later wrote that the Fogo process enables this new common identity by facilitating a 'continuous flow of ... filmed materials between areas of deprivation' (n.d.). In the end, resettlement was successfully resisted and a new fishing cooperative was formed. While it is generally acknowledged that the Fogo process played a role in facilitating this end result – 'opening channels of communication both among island communities and between the island and the government' – it is difficult to say how significant this role was.

Scholars such as Susan Newhook have helped bring sharper clarity to the events that transpired on Fogo Island, and such corrections are crucial for understanding where the filmmakers' attempts to bring the Fogo process to the United States went awry. In the narrative above, the active protagonists of this historical episode tends to be the National Film Board and the filmmakers themselves. However, Newhook's research has shown that *The Newfoundland Project* was just as much the result of local efforts to bring about social change:

> I want to emphasize that the project was not generated by people from 'away' who arrived in a community which had lost all hope, as has often been suggested. The project is not only about the National Film Board doing good by using film well. The Newfoundlanders involved were not the passive recipients of an intellectual transfer payment from Montreal; rather, the NFB was recruited to participate in a project which had already begun, and

it contributed its considerable talents toward the success of that project. The results worked to the benefit of all concerned: MUN Extension, the NFB and the people of Fogo Island. (2009: 172–3)

Newhook's contribution here is to reclaim local efforts as part of the story of *The Newfoundland Project*. Of course, Low qualified his contributions as an NFB filmmaker by insisting that the Fogo process only 'intensified' community dynamics which were already in place. Nevertheless, casting the filmmakers in the spotlight suppresses the experiment's 'importance to the history of post-Confederation society and culture in Newfoundland and Labrador' (2009: 173). The whole enterprise, Newhook insists, was indicative of a broader 'independent counterpoint to the government's centralization and industrialization strategies' (ibid.). For a number of years, the possibility of setting up a cooperative was talked about as a possible solution for the economic problems facing Fogo Islanders (see Newhook 2009: 174). Nevertheless, synopses of what transpired on Fogo Island and the role of the National Film Board tend to obscure this bigger picture (ibid.). Specifically, Newhook notes that MUN Extension has been marginalised in historical accounts of *The Newfoundland Project*: 'The impression is usually left that the film project prompted Fogo Islanders to think about starting a co-operative; however, Extension and others had been trying to encourage interest in starting a co-op for several years before the NFB arrived' (ibid.). What Newhook correctly targets is this foggy 'impression', which contributes to a particular mythology around *The Newfoundland Project* with the NFB and its representatives propped up as a vanguard for social change.

Nevertheless, the life of this particular impression is not limited to the arena of scholarship. Even in the immediate aftermath of the events on Fogo Island, this specific narrative attracted the attention of Ann Michaels at the OEO. And, to some extent, this impression contributed to the adaptation of the Fogo process to California and Connecticut. Understanding the potency of this askew narrative also helps us understand the crucial differences between Fogo Island and the subsequent applications of the Fogo process in Farmersville and Hartford. The years of organising that took place in Fogo Island – in short, the work of MUN Extension – constituted a structuring absence in the 'success' of the Fogo process and the dearth of comparable efforts in the United States dogged the OEOCE.

Crisis and Communication in the United States

It was the Fogo process that the American government – specifically, the OEO – sought to import. And there was precedent for collaboration of this sort. A memorandum written for Bertrand Harding, the head of the OEO, by Public Affairs Officer Anne Michaels makes special note of the 'sporadic cooperation between this office and the Canadian Government' (1968). She writes:

> For example ... film crews have produced motion pictures on OEO programs for telecast over Canadian broadcasting. The last one produced by a Canadian crew was, for example, made by Romeo LeBlanc who is now Press Secretary to Prime Minister Trudeau. Also we have provided Canadian outlets with our films and have on occasion used their product. (Ibid.)

Michaels herself was inspired to adapt the Fogo process in the United States through her visit to a joint workshop held by Memorial University of Newfoundland and the NFB in 1968 (see Pennybacker 2001a). The workshop's theme was 'The Role of Film in Community Development' and it lasted nearly a month, from 31 May to 28 June. The aim of the workshop, as described in a brochure, was as follows:

> The course has been designed to equip those attending with an understanding of the processes and techniques which can be applied in the successful use of film in encouraging and guiding change. The techniques are equally applicable in rural and urban areas. Students will also be given opportunity for private consultations on the production, distribution, and administration of film and on the costs and types of equipment and facilities which can be used, ranging from simple still cameras and tape recorders to elaborate and well-equipped film units. Technical experts from the National Film Board and from the University will be available for these consultations.
>
> The course will consist of lectures, film screenings and analyses, group discussions, field observations of community reactions to film already produced for community development work, and field work centered around the making of film and the use of film as an agent in change. Students will also be required to assemble and discuss their own film material based on the field assignment. (National Film Board of Canada, n.d.)

This, then, was an in-depth course on the Fogo process and the utility of film and audio production in the promotion of social change and communitarian identity. The particular emphasis on this methodology's pertinence to community building in both 'rural and urban areas' prefigures Michaels' institution of the OEOCE in Farmersville, California and Hartford, Connecticut. Such an initiation inaugurated a new chapter in the recent history of Canadian and

American cooperation around the use of media and their respective wars on poverty. Michaels herself underscored this point in her memo to Harding when she noted that, in spite of a prior history of collaboration between the OEO and the Canadian government, 'there has ... never been any in-depth cooperative effort until now although the [National] Film Board, particularly in view of their "Challenge for a Change" [sic] program has long sought some kind of liaison' (1968). Donald Snowden, in a report to the OEO, made special note of Michaels' affinity for their project, stating that 'Miss Michaels shared [my] conviction that the processes which were being developed with film to help overcome the problems of the deprived and the ignored in Newfoundland might well have application elsewhere' (n.d.: 1). Michaels visit later prompted Snowden to travel to Washington to develop uses of the Fogo process for the 'OEO and other interested agencies' (ibid.).

This exposure to the use of film as an agent in social change, mired in struggles at the grassroots, fostered a different outlook on the medium for the federal agency Michaels represented. Commenting on the OEOCE, Michaels underscores the significance of this shift in understanding how film could be deployed by the federal agency:

> I never saw these as films. I saw them as communication community development projects. I never thought of them in the same way as films. There were a lot of filmmakers that got involved in it ... but I never viewed it in that way. (Qtd. in Pennybacker 2001a)

Michaels, then, was – in this case – looking at filmmaking from a different vantage point. The films did not have value in and of themselves, but were contributors to 'community development' as vessels of communication. They were designed to mobilise new ways of coping with internal communal strife and, therefore, would serve no purpose outside of that context. This was a significant departure from how the Public Affairs Office had used film and reflected a mindset that would come to be more familiar as video technology became more pervasive in the coming years. But Michaels was compelled to see film in this light by a broader atmosphere of frustration prevalent at the time in the agency. Her particular attraction to the Fogo process was buttressed by a deep sense of fatigue stemming from community meetings in which local conflicts were addressed:

> We were so tired of community meetings where spokesmen would get up and they would talk whether it was establishment spokesmen or black spokesmen or whoever they were, they would talk for their 'people.' And it was ...

as if the people had nothing to say. I don't care how good these guys are that were talking. But ... the people seemed intimidated and let the people who would shout the loudest talk for them. (Ibid.)

Here Michaels describes a feeling – her own and likely shared with others at the OEO – that the way in which such community meetings were proceeding was possibly hindering progress as much as advancing it. She recognises a tension – albeit a familiar one – between the 'spokesmen' and the 'people' they claim to represent or speak for. There's an assumption or suspicion here that the speech from the representative, no matter 'how good' it was, was not synonymous with the feelings of the community at large from which the speaker hails. Another element registered here but undeveloped is Michaels' implication that the predominant conflict at hand is racial, occurring between 'establishment spokesmen' and 'black spokesmen'. Kramer, the head of the Public Affairs Office at the time, repeatedly emphasised in his oral history testimony to the Lyndon Baines Johnson Library that a core concern for OEO staffers was a new climate of 'militancy and separatism between black and white in this country, of violence, and of the new attempts to gain power by means other than simply the opening of representative doors for participation' (Anon. 1975). The inflamed circumstances following the passage of civil rights in the United States thwarted efforts to bolster stable liberal modes of engagement. Profound feelings of frustration with liberal institutions, local services and the limited reach of civil rights legislation contributed to an intensified atmosphere of social and class conflict in community meetings as well as in the streets all over the country.

Michaels, then, appears to have been drawn to the use of film as a communicative utility by way of a different frustration. Her frustration is that of the liberal advocate, whose efforts to advance social change are undermined by the militancy of those she wishes to help. Cinema, from this vantage point, becomes a kind of managerial pressure release. A novel and participatory approach to documentary filmmaking – energised by the reflexive principles of *cinema vérité* – was seen as a kind of coping mechanism, as a way to deal with internal lines of division within the community (based on class and race) as well as alienation between the state and the subjects of its programs. As Snowden put it: 'This is an attempt to lead the deprived out of some of the shadows of their lives through helping them ... by replacing bitterness and apathy with ways for hope' (n.d.: 3). In other words – to a substantial degree – this was a qualitatively different venture than had been undertaken in the past. Here we have a fissure, or a break, that cannot be easily explained through a simple historical narrative or recourse to the psychological dispositions of administrators such as Michaels.

In order to fully understand why the American state hired Canadian film-makers to stage this participatory film practice in the cities of Farmersville, California and Hartford, Connecticut, we have to set our critical aperture at the level of the broader social horizon in which this work took place. Specifically, 1968 was a year filled with turmoil and uncertainty. The nation was experiencing a multi-faceted social crisis encompassing the assassinations of Martin Luther King, Jr. and Robert F. Kennedy as well as the Vietnam War and race riots in various cities. The reminiscences of Herbert Kramer, former Head of Public Affairs for the OEO, register awareness on the part of OEO staff that their work needed to account for a new climate of radicalism and frustration in black communities. The agency's impression of the Fogo process in 1968 spoke to its investment in new communicative procedures and practices in light of the racial turmoil and urban uprisings gripping the nation throughout the 1960s, as well as a degree of anxiety about its increasingly marginalised status. Having just been reauthorised in 1967, the OEO was no longer under the tutelage of Sargent Shriver. In place of Shriver, Bertrand Harding, a more reserved and 'traditional federal manager' (Clark 2002: 59), became the new head of the OEO. Harding oversaw the OEO at a time when President Johnson was preoccupied by the Vietnam War, and the guidance and funding of his anti-poverty initiatives were increasingly seen as secondary (see Clark 2002: 13). The year of 1968, then, was one marked by uncertainty and a sense of declining support. Making matters worse, the likelihood of a Nixon administration loomed and the fate of the OEO under new Republican leadership appeared grim.

While the agency had deployed film as a public relations instrument for years, institutional and societal pressures converged to carve out a space at the agency to consider its utility of film outside of training or as a source of skilled labour, as a vocational pursuit. These traditional applications of film fell short in light of the severity of the racial and class-based conflicts developing around the country. With its confidence rattled, seeing film as a possible means toward enhancing the visibility and expressivity of the poor no doubt held some appeal to the agency. To reiterate, this was not part of an effort to inform well-off Americans what was happening in the 'other America' in a manner akin to the use of film and photography during the Great Depression. Rather, the American adaptation of the Fogo process reflects a desire to utilise film production as a means of bridging gaps of communication across racial and class divisions as well as between the distant state and isolated poor communities. A participatory documentary approach appealed to a managerial desire for information on the ground as well as for a 'communications bridge' between the poor and policy-makers in Washington (see Snowden, n.d.: 3).

The factors are numerous, but the circumstances of 1968 are to a significant degree different than previous years, primarily due to pent-up frustration in a post-Civil Rights America. Such frustration – powerfully felt in communities of colour – was eminently visible in the form of protests, urban uprisings and Black Nationalism, an increasingly radical emancipatory politics that took aim at the persistence of structural indignities and inequalities after desegregation. In fact, the perception of Black Nationalism among the OEO staff was particularly contradictory. On the one hand, there was recognition that the increasingly radical political climate was an impediment to the OEO's managerial programmes. But by the same token, many felt there was a bond of sorts between the work of the OEO and black radicals. Herbert Kramer, rather condescendingly, insists that the OEO 'stimulated black power. We [the OEO] gave black people in this country more power, more opportunity to get on a platform, more opportunity to take positions of leadership, than any other program in the government. Consequently, we both bred this and brought it down upon us' (Anon. 1975).

These developments frame the OEO's endorsement of the Fogo process and help us see this act as contingent upon an experience of national crisis. Such a feeling of crisis compelled the federal agency to consider the use of the motion picture in a new way. Circumstances seem to have compelled the agency to think outside of the box and to develop a particular infatuation with film and its presumed potential to re-constitute a community's sense of its collective self. Snowden wrote to the OEO that films produced as part of the Fogo process are meant to 'serve' a troubled community – or 'problem zone' – by creating 'an effective linkage point for mutual discussion and action, where this does not already exist' (n.d.: 5). Dealing with problem zones would require 'participation at all screenings by community development workers, social and behavioral scientists involved in the project, and the filmmaker' (ibid.). To a large extent, the crises of the late 1960s and a myriad of 'problem zones' challenged the prevailing managerial liberal mindset of administrators and – as we will see below – the embrace of the Fogo process by the OEO speaks to the managerial liberal's limited response to such circumstances. This response retreats to the comfortable position of a belief in the power of communication, in the power of intersubjective exchanges to ground disputes in an immutable human essence. From this perspective the prevailing attitude insists that the more communication there is the better, nudging individuals away from 'bitterness' towards 'hope'. The work of the filmmakers in Farmersville and, later on, Hartford can therefore be rightly critiqued for a particular kind of idealism that resonates with the liberal framework of the state at the time. But – nevertheless – a utopian kernel persists that advances a discourse that is, in part, elusive and outside of the domain of right-minded experts and steeped in the messy social fabric of community politics.

For instance, the work of Low and Biggs in California and Connecticut materialises a participatory and inductive posture that challenges the managerial style of the federal government and its programmes. The beginning of the Fogo process itself was rooted in the notion of coordinated resistance to top-down policies imposed on a community from above. Furthermore, the filmmakers' willingness to – in a sense – reconstitute film as a small part of a larger process of communication introduces an admirable degree of uncertainty into their work. As we will see later on, the filmmakers struggled to convey their definition of success for their work, especially in Farmersville. Articulating their aims for the film project was an elusive task at best, often resulting in vague platitudes or rhetorical stretches. This work of explanation was also endless and mutable as the rationale for the Fogo process in the United States traversed the various stages of written proposals, conversations with administrators, planning with local community action agencies and interactions with Farmersville residents. The nature of *The Farmersville Project* – like Hartford – was fundamentally odd as it necessitated a kind of blind leap of faith as well as openness to the vicissitudes of the dialogues instigated by the camera and crew with the locals. The trajectory here was uncertain and dependent upon the attitudes and feelings of the people filmed as well as those in attendance at screenings. In a way, then, failure was sort of built into the endeavour: measurable success beyond promoting 'communication' slipped through the filmmakers' fingers and positively reflected a resistant participatory core.

At the same time, however, this inductive approach casts the state and – by extension – the filmmakers as neutral players, and such neutrality should be treated sceptically. Representing *The Farmersville Project*, and – by extension – the OEO, as a dispassionate medium for the airing out of grievances obscures the subtle undercurrent of legitimisation at work here. *The Farmersville Project* invited testimonies from a number of vantage points: farm workers, teachers, foremen, farmers, students, politicians, reporters, etc. But the participatory dimensions reviewed above are short-circuited by a number of factors. The endeavour unfortunately was the product of decision-making from the top, from policymakers in Washington invested in developing new techniques in communication. As a result, *The Farmersville Project* – from the outset – is faced with the daunting task of overcoming a double-dose of outsider credentials as a Canadian film team is funded by Washington to assist in facilitating communication in an agrarian Californian town. Complementing this top-down form of decision-making is *The Farmersville Project*'s fetish for communication as an essential step forward in managing social conflict and coping with poverty. Here the project fits easily within the managerial zone of balancing competing claims and mitigating militancy.

Evidence of these traits can be found in the language of the contract between the OEO and the filmmakers. For instance, the primary duties of the 'Contractor' – Low and Biggs – include the following: an evaluation of 'current communications … approaches to Community Action'; the development of 'communications systems involving the entire community'; and measuring the

> effectiveness of these new communications systems, especially films and film production as well as other audio-visual materials as the basis for developing a national program in this area. (Office of Economic Opportunity, n.d.: 1)

And, in doing so, the film crew should heed the following stipulation:

> In all instances, the contractor shall involve the poor in the planning and implementation of this effort. (Office of Economic Opportunity, n.d.: 2)

Here the agency sets forth the core aims of *The Farmersville Project* and, later on, *The Hartford Project*. The focus is on shoring up networks of communication by assessing 'current … approaches' and – as a result of this assessment – generating novel forms of communication utilising the moving image. This insistence on refining the means of communication – on the one hand – explicitly opens up channels for bottom-up participation through the reminder to involve the poor in both the 'planning and implementation' stages. But – on the other hand – this overview places limits on these possibilities by positioning the 'entire community' as objects of 'new communications systems,' rather than subjects. Additionally, highlighting the importance of communication systems without acknowledging the ways in which these are enmeshed in specific social conditions – indeed, before *even knowing* which particular community would be filmed – speaks to the liberal manager's constitution of the rational outsider, one who's very outsider status enables s/he to become the ultimate insider. Precisely because the rational outsider comes from elsewhere, s/he is able to assess the core of a community's communication problems in an objective manner. But, as much as this, the contract betrays a submerged belief in the power of communication to solve problems so long as it involves the 'entire community'. This posture frames social conflict as the result of a communication deficit, to be overcome by compelling all sides to participate in a face-to-face dialogue.

As the contract continues, its summary of the film crew's responsibilities increasingly synchronise with the 'human capital' theory of the CEA in its initial recommendations to President Kennedy for a new anti-poverty programme. In addition to the work of research and ethnographic surveying, the crew is tasked with the production of a 'Self-Help Mini Film project' (ibid.). This project will consist of a 'series of films and the development and activation of systems for their distribution'. Furthermore, the films produced

> shall be between three to fifteen minutes duration in edited form and provide visual self-analysis, self-appraisal, self-correction. They will provide insights into community problems designed to engage subject groups in solving community difficulties. Groups to be covered will include all segments of the community including educators, business and health officials, industrialists, media representatives, government and political officials, civic groups and the poor. [...] Prior to their completion mini films will be taken back to the communities where they were made for local audience evaluation, and trial use in community problem-solving. (Office of Economic Opportunity, n.d.: 2–3)

Here the contract acknowledges this project's indebtedness to the work of the National Film Board of Canada in Fogo Island, Newfoundland ('This Phase shall be based upon the National Film Board of Canada and Memorial University of Newfoundland's Film and Community Development project.'; OEO, n.d.: 2). The production and exhibition of short films to facilitate new lines of communication is at the heart of what was considered to be the Fogo process. But, more than this, the therapeutic roots of the agency's efforts here are laid bare. The work in Farmersville will be – at its best – thoroughly pluralistic (to 'include all segments of the community') and democratic by accommodating *inside* voices, with analysis and appraisal emanating from the site of the 'self' rather than from the outsider. Again, there is a remarkable insistence on facilitating expression from the grassroots, from below rather than above. While the phrase 'self-help' triggers contemporary associations of individual betterment, its usage in this context – as a continuation of the Fogo process begun in Canada – should denote a communal image of the 'self', more in line with auto-ethnographic values. When the contract uses terms such as 'self-analysis' and 'self-appraisal' the implication is that the community – as a mosaic of individual voices – diagnoses its own problems and enacts its own solutions. As other scholars have pointed out, the work originally conducted on Fogo Island set out to buttress a new 'self-image' of the community, one that coordinated an alignment of competing internal interests into an imaginary cohesion better prepared to resist the modernising policies of the state.

However, this participatory disposition is couched within a managerial liberal belief in the rational nature of communication and in the insistence upon 'self-help', on framing social problems within the romantic field of communitarian intentionality. From this perspective, this contract continues the line of thinking endorsed by the CEA in its recommendations to Kennedy. Within this paradigm of managerial liberalism – to repeat – the focus is on 'human services' and 'reform of individuals rather than economic equality' (Brauer 1982: 108–109). The state addresses itself to a perceived gap in the psyches, dispositions and skill levels of subjects caught up in troubled socio-economic circumstances. Hoping to leave subjects changed and better equipped to navigate the world, governing in such instances entails reading social conflict and poverty as expressions of depleted job skills and poor communication. Herbert Kramer insisted that OEO programs were always seen as 'self-help programs', first and foremost (Anon. 1975). The Farmersville and Hartford projects, in spite of the admirable participatory intent, affirms this retreat to the betterment of individuals while casting a blind eye to the material circumstances in which individuals, groups and communities are situated. As Donald Snowden put it in a report to the OEO, where the Fogo process is concerned, film 'is shot around personalities – not around issues' ('Film and...': 5). The 'Self-Help Mini Film project' legitimates the state as a vessel for 'self-analysis' and as an arena where a diverse set of interest groups can encounter one another and overcome entrenched social conflicts. Indeed, conflict in the agency's address here is understood as a kind of distortion in need of smoothing over to restore a sense of balance and equality. The notion that conflict is constitutive of the various groups' identities is lost in the wake of the agency's distinct managerial stance.

The film practices undertaken by Low and Biggs in the United States are, as I've demonstrated, caught betwixt and between participatory and managerial discourses. And, rather than read this fact as an indication of a simple transition from one paradigm to another in the late 1960s, this schizophrenic character of the OEOCE reflect a crisis point in governance, in an agency's attempt to grapple with the profound depth of the crises facing the nation in 1968. The constitutive powers of the state in the case of the Farmersville and Hartford projects call out subjects to testify and to undertake a program of *self-evaluation* in order to discern the ineffable roots of socio-economic discord. But of course this outreach upholds a vision of these communities that leaves out as much as it includes. While coping with poverty is explicitly addressed in the contract, racial tension is not. And what the liberal manager is struggling with at this moment in time is the entrenchment of racial conflict in a post-Civil Rights America and – in the case of Farmersville at least – the emergence of a pluralistic and majoritarian Mexican-American community.

The Farmersville Project: Production Overview

A handwritten note to Bertrand Harding from an anonymous author informally reminds the OEO director that

> There will be some Canadians visiting us on Tuesday [24 September 1968]. Anne Michaels says they have been extremely cooperative and helpful in connection with the project mentioned in attached material – with which you may be vaguely familiar. […] I told Anne that – if you were free at time of their arrival – you would meet with them briefly as courtesy. (Anon.: 1968b)

Attached to the note is a memorandum that provides brief biographical sketches of three prominent figures in Canadian film. The first listed is Julian Biggs, a senior producer at the National Film Board of Canada and a former Director of Production of the Board. Next up is John Kemeny who is listed as the Director of 'Challenge for a Change' [sic] and finally Colin Low, a 'Senior-Director-Producer' who was 'responsible … for execution of the Fogo-Newfoundland experiment on which our project is patterned' (ibid.). Rounding out the party is Donald Snowden, Director of Extension at Memorial University; and Richard O'Hagen, 'Minister-Counsellor of the Canadian Embassy in Washington, D. C.' (ibid.). Biggs and Low, the memo notes, are expected to be 'active on our project' (ibid.).

The Canadian film team launched the project – soon to be known as *The Farmersville Project* – around the same time as their meeting with OEO officials. As the memo states, the two key figures responsible for steering the adaptation of the Fogo process in the United States were Julian Biggs and Colin Low. Through consultation with the OEO and Ann Michaels, the decision was made to focus on a southern Californian farm town where race and class-based relations were particularly strained. Work began in late October and the production team would eventually come to include: Dr Joseph G. Colmen from the Washington-based Public Affairs Communications, Inc. as 'Project Director'; Julian Biggs as a co-producer; Colin Low as a co-producer/director; Harold 'Casey' Case as the sound technician; Harry Keramidas as 'Editor/Director'; Verna Fields as supervising editor and advisor; and, finally, both Baylis Glascock and Stan Lazan would go on to serve as cinematographers in Farmersville (see Anon. 1968a). Case and Keramidas were recruited by Julian Biggs from the University of California, Los Angeles, where they were graduate students in film production. Both had spent time together as volunteers for the Peace Corps in the Dominican Republic and were bilingual in Spanish and English (see Charbonneau 2012).

The most in-depth account of what happened during production in California can be found in the diary of Henry Lanford. His official title on *The Farmersville Project* was 'Production Research Assistant', although he is sometimes also described as a 'community development specialist' for *The Farmersville Project*. He was attracted to the work of the National Film Board when – as a graduate student at the University of Oregon in the winter of 1968 – he attended a presentation by John Kemeny on the NFB's *Challenge for Change* and saw 'several' of the agency's films (see Lanford n.d.: 2). Lanford later wrote in an application to the aforementioned workshop on 'Film and Community Development' that he was 'struck … with stunning force that here were people with the right attitude toward the change process' (ibid.). 'It was,' he continued, 'exciting to see such promising techniques for letting people come together and develop directions to improve their circumstances' (ibid.). The connections Lanford made in Canada at the 'Film and Community Development' workshop led to a job in short order as a member of the main film unit in Farmersville. Lanford assisted with all levels of the production, including pre-production work such as location scouting and interviewing locals; 'As a trained observer of people and political processes [Lanford] spent time in the community attempting to discern issues that hindered economic progress' (Glascock 1997: 1). Lanford's 'observations informed the filmmakers' choices' and he was instrumental in leading the exhibition of the 'edited films in public meetings as a catalyst for discussion and the airing of differing points of view' (ibid.). In the end, Lanford's involvement was multifaceted and – as the project's community development specialist – he was in the best position to assess the project's overall impact on Farmersville. Nevertheless, Lanford was an outsider to Farmersville and this posed a significant challenge for the production team. In fact, the lack of an equivalent to Fred Earle – the community development officer based in Fogo Island who assisted Colin Low with *The Newfoundland Project* – was their 'one real handicap' in Farmersville, according to Low (qtd. in Wiesner 2010: 94).

On 8 October 1968 – two weeks after Biggs, Low and Kemeny met with OEO officials – the news went public. A Newfoundland newspaper – *The Evening Telegram* – announced American interest in some 'highly dramatic' filmmaking endeavours, proclaiming 'U.S. Adopts Plan from Newfoundland' (MacKenzie 1968). The article opens by noting that the American government 'has reached into Newfoundland's Fogo Island for a process it hopes will broaden communications into and out of low-income communities' (ibid.). The OEO, the article continued, was 'deeply impressed and [plans] to launch the same technique shortly in California [in a community] that mixes Mexican-Americans, some "Anglos" – whites – and Negroes in a rural setting' (ibid.). Moreover, the American adaptation of this particular film 'process' is just the beginning as the article hints at a ripple effect which is expected to resonate not just south of the border, but transnationally as the 'Food and Agriculture Organization of the United Nations has also expressed interest' (ibid.).

As the article indicates, it was not initially clear which town would be the focus for the filmmakers' application of the Fogo process. The first several days of the project – between 21 and 24 October – were spent deciding on the community to be filmed; initially there was some debate about whether to focus on one town or to spread the filmmaking process across several communities. Location scouting by Biggs and Lanford centred on the communities of Richgrove, Porterville, North Visalia and Farmersville, among others (approximately nine were considered). Overall, the filmmakers had the support not just of the Public Affairs Office in Washington, but also of the local Tulare County Community Action Agency (TCCAA), headed by Everet Krackoff. The TCCAA's enthusiasm for the filmmakers was equaled by the Tulare County Board of Supervisors, who gave their full support to the project (see Lanford 1968).

By 24 October, a consensus on which town to film was reached at a meeting attended by the staff of TCCAA as well as several production crew – including Donald Snowden, Julian Biggs and Henry Lanford. Farmersville fulfilled the filmmakers' and organisers' chief requirements pertaining to size and diversity. Of utmost importance was achieving an 'in-depth profile on a small enough community with adequate intimacy' (ibid.). What exactly was meant by 'intimacy' is not entirely clear. Lanford himself linked the term to the process of personal testimony or 'self-examination', implying a mode of interaction between filmmaker and subject that supports the latter's self-expression above all else (ibid.). The city of Farmersville could, it was determined, best accommodate the Fogo process and its drive towards intimacy by virtue of its small population (approximately 3,000 people at the time; see Glascock 1997: 1). The result, the filmmakers hoped, would be an in-depth portrait of a community with opportunities for 'self-examination', for a film project that prioritises self-awareness and expression over a more objectifying social problem-solving discourse (see Lanford 1968). In spite of Farmersville's size, the filmmakers and the organisers felt that the town was significantly stratified in terms of race and class to reflect the social unrest experienced elsewhere around the country. Lanford noted a 'striking degree of segregation between classes', between working-class and middle-class residents, and a population that was 'largely Chicano' (ibid.). In spite of the fact that fifty percent of the population was Mexican American, all the leadership positions were held by whites (see Glascock 1968). Pressure was building in the San Joaquin Valley in the late 1960s where a national grape boycott was headquartered, led by Cesar Chavez (ibid.). With much of the labour force – largely Mexican American – working on farms or in food-processing plants, the push for unionisation was strong in farm-worker enclaves like Farmersville and it was amplified by a general atmosphere of reform as the disconnect between the town's encroaching majoritarian Mexican American status and the white power structure became too obvious to ignore. This fundamental imbalance predictably contributed to marginalisation of Mexican American voices in other organisations such as the PTA, Lions Club and the Chamber of Commerce (ibid.). Neither 'did the schools address the cultural needs of children of Mexican ancestry' (ibid.).

Following Farmersville's selection the production team had a little over two weeks before filming would commence on 10 November. As a result, the crew had to work diligently to familiarise themselves with the political landscape of the town as well as to find and build relationships with the most representative voices of Farmersville's various constituencies. Based on Lanford's diary, a group of personalities were immediately drawn to the crew's attention as references ricocheted over the course of several meetings, interviews and surveys. These included Irma Gutierrez, a community worker active in the local Gathering Teens Organization (GTO). Lanford met with her on 28 October in order to get a fuller picture of the politics of Farmersville and its leaders (see Lanford 1968). While the failure to recruit and hire a local community worker was an unfortunate 'handicap' for the production team, Gutierrez's perspective on Farmersville had a significant influence on the filming.

For instance, she gave Lanford additional information about Martin Fuentes, 'an important leader in the Mexican American community' whom Biggs and Lanford had briefly met a few days earlier (ibid.). At the time, Fuentes was serving as the chair of the Bi-Lingual Advisory Committee for the Farmersville Unified School District while also assisting Self-Help Enterprises (SHE), a rural housing programme founded in 1965 and awarded grant money by the OEO shortly thereafter. In addition to these civic responsibilities, Fuentes ran a 'fairly successful Mexican food factory and store' after having worked 'in the real estate business in Texas' (ibid.). Fuentes' prime motivation was – according to Lanford – 'education [or getting] parents, especially Mexican-Americans, to realize how crucial education is for any real solution to the problem of Mexican-Americans today' (ibid.). Lanford added a note suggesting that Fuentes may be 'seen as an "Uncle Tom" by many [given that he] doesn't believe "rabble-rousing" is of any help; he thinks the Mexican-American must operate on the Anglo-American's terms, which he sees as the only fair terms' (ibid.). Shortly after, both Lanford and Biggs agreed that Fuentes should be the subject of a film for *The Farmersville Project* (ibid.). This particular passage from Lanford's diary is worth quoting in full:

> I felt that [Fuentes] represented an extremely important point of view. He was very much concerned with the problems of Mexican-Americans in Farmersville, and very concerned about the future. He was an unusually open and articulate person, and I felt confident he would come across well on film. He was especially interested in talking about the needs for parents to fully support the work of the schools in educating their children. He struck me as very responsible. He would speak against militancy and disruptive attitudes. I suspected also that he would be well received by the Anglo-American community. (Ibid.)

While we cannot be certain about how the other filmmakers felt, Lanford's rationale for filming Fuentes resonates with some of the broader managerial principles that compelled the OEO to adapt the Fogo process in the first place. If we recall, Michaels' attraction to *The Newfoundland Project* was energised by a fatigue from militancy and the liberal manager's desire for cohesion and conflict resolution. The turmoil and rebellion of the late 1960s was agitating the OEO's programmatic work and the Fogo process appealed to a weary manager's longing for communication and distrust of radical politics. Lanford's dwelling on Fuentes' 'dislike for rabble-rousing' as well as the latter's perception by Anglos in Farmersville as a 'good Chicano' underscores the degree to which Fuentes' persona fits the bill. He represents the disenfranchised, but is also invested in the status quo and speaks the 'responsible' language of the state and the white establishment. Fuentes, in other words, is a Mexican American voice who will be perceived as safe by a white audience and address the Anglos on 'their terms'. This preference for Fuentes demonstrates the degree to which the crew had internalised the managerial liberal ethos of the OEO as well as how their outsider status – appearing 'above the fray' – to a substantial degree reproduced the status quo. A few weeks of acclimation was clearly not enough time to move past ingrained narratives and empower otherwise marginalised voices.

Nevertheless, the crew pursued as many preliminary interviews as they could, given the limited time frame. During this research phase, the filmmakers also spoke with the Mayor of Farmersville, Jay Kemp, who expressed his own concerns about the organising efforts of Chavez and the encroachment of the OEO. They also met with Marion Cundiff, a six-year resident and the only reporter for the *Farmersville Herald* (ibid.). Like Gutierrez, Cundiff was an important source of information for the crew. Her perspective guided the filmmakers as they tried to grasp the broader social and economic dynamics of Farmersville. It was Cundiff's view that Farmersville was the perfect subject for the Fogo process since it presented – by virtue of its racial makeup and poverty – 'a perfect specimen of what is wrong with the United States today' (ibid.). She reiterated the clear disconnect between the town's soon-to-be majoritarian Mexican American population and a more traditional white male leadership. The white mayor was in her view a 'dictator … and a two-faced person' (ibid.). Her observations reinforced Kemp's own admission that he views the War on Poverty with suspicion and unease (ibid.). Cundiff also made special note of the role of religion in Farmersville. At the time, there were seventeen churches in the town, but the most vocal in opposing co-educational activities for youth – 'dancing, card playing, swimming' – was the Free Holiness Church, a church 'invented in Farmersville' (ibid.). 'Women are to be seen and not heard,' as Lanford succinctly summarised in his notes. And, Cundiff insisted, racially integrated youth activities outside of school were particularly 'controversial'. According to Lanford, Cundiff maintained that parents 'get very upset at any togetherness of young Anglos and Mexican Americans which might be sexual' (ibid.). This anxiety was directed specifically at the GTO from the City Council, as the former served mostly Mexican American youth and the latter represented the traditional white status quo – although at this time 'things are beginning to quiver' (ibid.). In response to these and other testimonies recorded during this research phase, Lanford wrote: 'Racism does, at this time, seem to me to be the dominant thing about Farmersville' (ibid.). Lanford recognised that the 'racism is camflouged [sic] in religious [terms] … [the Anglos' largely Pentecostal] religion' is being used to attack 'all things the Mexican-Americans are and do' (ibid.).

While local politics were not surprisingly bogged down by in-fighting, the hot topic of the day in 1968 was the disincorporation of the city of Farmersville – leaving citizens to be governed by the county – and its chief advocate was a man named Tom Bray. This campaign was bolstered by a desire to dissolve the community just as the status quo was feeling the most threatened by Farmersville's growing Mexican American population. The GTO and *Illusion y Progresso* both opposed disincorporation of Farmersville as 'they felt they were more likely to progress with the potential help of the city than they would be under county jurisdiction' (ibid.), according to Gutierrez. As an indication of his compromised status as a prominent voice for Mexican Americans, Fuentes was also an advocate for disincorporation, a position which Gutierrez felt was 'surpris[ing]' and was largely the result of 'some sort of business connection' (ibid.) Fuentes had with Bray. The subject went on to be covered by several films as part of *The Farmersville Project*, including *The Chamber of Commerce* (45 minutes) and *County Supervisor Don Hillman on Disincorporation* (12 minutes). The former documented a 'public meeting called by the Chamber of Commerce president, Chuck Jackson, to discuss disincorporation petitions ... by citizens who wished to see Farmersville revert to county control' (Anon. n.d.). From Gutierrez's point of view, the push for the disincorporation of the city was largely sour grapes, motivated in part by individuals who were 'defeated in election for [city] council' (see Lanford 1968).

The Farmersville Project was announced locally by a headline in the *Tulare Advance-Register* on 2 November 1968: 'U.S. Pays the Bill: Farmersville, a Movie Star' (Crawford 1968). Biggs and his credentials are featured as the article notes his status as a film producer who has been twice nominated for Academy Awards:

> Biggs hopes to capture his first Oscar for his Farmersville job, which also just might win the small city a place alongside other western towns immortalized on the screen, such as Dodge City and Virginia City. Actually Biggs is making a documentary type production, a related battery of short films, but the message is highly original. Citizens, by appearing in the movies, can and are likely to make Farmersville a more dynamic community, Biggs said. (Ibid.)

Noting that this venture would be 'the first of its kind in the United States', Biggs emphasised citizen control over what ends up onscreen ('Whether anyone except Farmersville residents will see the 15 to 30 individual films to be shot there will be a decision of those persons photographed'; ibid.). This deferral to the townspeople is further underscored by one of the hallmarks of the Fogo process, the 'self-editing process', in which those filmed will be allowed to 'rul[e] on what parts, if any, should be cut' (ibid.). The managerial ethos rears its head when Biggs insists in the article that *The Farmersville Project* is 'expected to be sort of a sensitivity session, leading to better relations between individuals and groups' (ibid.). The desire to smooth over social discord through improved communication is fully evident in the following blurb from Biggs:

> People seldom realize how they sometimes discuss their problems coming face to face with their lack of definition, they realize the difficulties others

have in understanding them and become more appreciative of other points of view. (Qtd. in ibid.)

Biggs' idealism here reflects the OEO's grasp for a communicative transcendence that can solve problems through more effective modes of speaking and listening. The communication loop of which Low spoke is seen here as a fetishisation of 'face to face' interaction, losing sight of the more intractable realities of class struggle and institutionalised racism.

With the exception of some initial filming at a dance sponsored by *Illusion y Progresso* on 2 November, production officially commenced on the morning of 10 November 1968 with Biggs at the helm and in the absence of Low who wouldn't arrive in Farmersville until three days later. Over the next six weeks the crew would produce nearly three-dozen films adding up to over six hours of completed film. As the *Tulare Advance-Register* article noted, the team shot on '16-millimeter film, black and white for faster processing', which will allow the footage 'to be ready for editing ... six days from the time of shooting' (ibid.). The schedule was relentless as the crew filmed daily from 12 to 21 November and from 23 to 27 November. Thanksgiving weekend was essentially a break with only one evening of filming scheduled (a teenage dance). The production picked up again on 2 December and continued daily until 14 December. Most days involved two or three scheduled shoots. On the busiest days, the crew might have four different shoots lined up (see Anon. 1968d: 4). For instance, the schedule for 25 November reads:

> 10:00am: orange packing plant (Naranjo Packing House)
> 11:00am: orange picking (orchard)
> 1:30pm: various shots around town
> 7:30pm: School Board meeting (new Library and Kindegarten Room, Snowden School) (Ibid.)

A few shoots in December also took place at the house rented by the crew for the duration of the production, located at 737 E. Costner Street. The resulting films were *Hector & Ruben* (15 minutes; discussed below), *An Anglo-American Teenagers' Discussion* (14 minutes), *Mexican-American Teenager Discussion* (19 minutes) and *Our Film* (12 minutes; ibid.). In the end, *The Farmersville Project* yielded thirty-four sound films shot on black and white, 16-millimeter.

Exhibitions began while filming was still taking place. The first film screenings were held on 18 and 19 November with an additional ten during the month of December. Screenings continued into the New Year with a total of fifteen in

January and a final screening in February 1969 (see Anon. 1968c: 1–4). Attendance wavered between a low of eight on 18 January 1969 and high of 170 on 30 January 1969. Overall, the screenings enjoyed an average turnout of about eighty attendees (1968c: 3–4). Not surprisingly, the early screenings tended to feature fewer films as the team was still in the midst of production. A film of the *Illusion y Progreso*-sponsored dance was complete and ready for screening on 18 November (a mere sixteen days after it had been shot). The following three screenings – two of which took place on 19 November and the third on 3 December – included uncut footage from the crew's coverage of a turkey shoot sponsored by the Veterans of Foreign Wars (VFW). Screenings held later in December and January generally included anywhere from three to six different titles. A little less than half of the total screenings – thirteen out of twenty-nine – were presented to a 'general public'. The other screenings were aimed specifically at Spanish-speaking audiences, particular age groups – such as 'teenagers' – or organisations, including *Illusion y Progreso*, the VFW, the Sportsmen's Club, 'Church members' and the Lion's Club.

Fortunately, the archival record and the testimony of the still surviving participants allow us to reconstruct more than a simple calendar of the production. We can – for instance – access a thicker account of what it was like for the crew as they began the process of filming and introducing themselves to the community of Farmersville. For instance, the second event to be filmed was the aforementioned VFW turkey shoot on 10 November (see *Turkeyshoot* – 10 minutes). The aim during these early stages of filmmaking was, first and foremost, to 'make ourselves visible' (see Lanford 1968) and to win the support of community leaders for the film project. This strategy was enacted at other sites as well, in particular at schools as well as at events such as a local auction (ibid.). Becoming 'known' to the community was a prime motivator in these early days. This entailed, for instance, an exhibition of Fogo Island films to VIPs in Farmersville (including county supervisors, journalists and the mayor) in order to give these leaders a sense of the project's goals. And while footage of students walking to school and citizens mingling at the turkey shoot would be incorporated in subsequent films, being seen was the most important thing for the film crew. The dynamic at work here entailed a delicate dance of acknowledging their outsider status, even of creating a spectacle of themselves as a film crew, while also performing as passive observers not invested in imposing a predetermined agenda. Engendering a perception of themselves as safe outsiders included using the footage shot to develop what Harold Case called 'safe films', works that could be shown to Farmersville audiences that would promote the filmmakers as an inductive and anti-propagandistic force (1969). Such films – ideally constituted – would also seek to foster a space of communal self-identification, a transparent process where the hand of the filmmakers would disappear in favour of audiences bearing witness to themselves and their neighbours. This ideological manoeuvre was essential for a managerial liberal ethos of information gathering and communication. If the films were to create an imaginary space of an 'encounter' between groups within Farmersville as well as between Farmersville and Washington, then they could not embrace a reflexive approach which would draw audiences' attention to the work of the filmmakers. Following the line of reasoning behind the Fogo process, the films were intended to serve as a forum for communal re-constitution where prior lines of alliances and oppositions might be disturbed, opening the way for dialogue. Towards this end, the filmmakers' presentation of themselves as a visible entity during the production phase had to be overturned and obscured during exhibition. In getting to know the filmmakers early on, the crew's mixed status as both local and foreign could, to some degree, be exploited in order to uphold their preferred identity as friendly outsiders and passive observers.

Nevertheless, this approach would ultimately prove to be untenable. Contradictory impulses to be both visible and invisible, depending on the stage of the Fogo process at hand, imploded in practice. Case notes that, in spite of the filmmakers' intent, their presence was inevitably the main attraction. Even during screenings – where the intent was to facilitate discussion among residents of Farmersville about politics, economics and race – focus inevitably turned to the filmmakers and their agenda. The fundamental point of the whole enterprise was ambiguous, even to members of the film crew. Drawing parallels between his work with Low and Biggs and his time as a Peace Corps Volunteer, Case notes that engaging in community development work entails a balance between broad ambitions (promoting a sense of community) and specific material projects (such as 'organizing co-operatives': ibid.). The former can be difficult for the liberal advocate to articulate to him or herself, much less to locals. While the latter can serve to galvanise residents around a concrete proposal that is easily visualised and communicated. In the case of *The Farmersville Project*, the broad managerial aims of igniting 'community awareness' and creating 'new channels of communication' were found to be confusing and opaque (ibid.). It didn't help that the concrete activities of the group, the production of the films and their exhibition to an array of audiences, did little to clarify the point of the project. Case observes that even local participants who had had the project described to them 'several times' could not turn around and explain the filmmakers' purpose to neighbours; the result, according to Case, was poor 'integration of the project into the community' (ibid.). Discussions following screenings of the Farmersville films inevitably revealed a distrust of the filmmakers and scepticism as to the value of what they were doing. We might revise Case's observation that audiences 'did respond, but not to the films; it seemed rather that they were reacting to us. They saw our films and wondered what we were trying to do to them, the suffering innocents of Farmersville' (ibid.). In this case, the spectators were refusing to see the films transparently, as frames prompting a new way of seeing themselves and their community as a whole. Rather – turning Case's observation on its head – the spectators precisely responded to the films *as films*, as impositions on them from outsiders funded by the state.

It is helpful to pause for a moment and to consider the significance of the confusion felt by both the crew and Farmersville residents. Case's records suggest that the production process was contradictory to its core, demonstrating the difficulty of extracting an exportable model from the Fogo Island experience. Furthermore, much of the confusion expressed in these surviving records can be attributed to the fact that the filmmakers find themselves torn between two horizons. On the one hand, the filmmakers exhibit a participatory consciousness as their words reflect desire for a democratic and inductive film practice in hopes of nurturing more 'community awareness'. On the other hand, the primary reason for the project's failed 'integration' into the community has to do with the lack of community involvement from the outset. The initiation, preparation, planning and filming of the project was undertaken by outsiders – by a crew of Canadians and Americans, funded by the federal government. These documents suggest that – while the films produced as part of the Farmersville experiment denote a significant degree of openness between filmmaker and subject – the fact that *The Farmersville Project* was conceptualised with minimal input from the residents themselves short-circuits many of the project's community development ambitions. This contradiction between intent and practice amounts to friction between the project's managerial and participatory elements noted earlier. The crew's inability to retool and/or rethink their film practice to allow for more community input in the earlier stages – to let the film series respond to the needs of the grassroots – suggests their work was still largely determined by a managerial ethos with themselves unwittingly lodged at the centre of the project's implementation. The idea here seems to have been that the outsider-status of the crew can be overcome through good intentions, rather than devising a wholly different form of film production. As with the experiment in Fogo Island, the crew was caught between managerial confidence and a desire for a new participatory practice that was often hard to articulate.

Safe Vertical Films

As stated earlier, the films produced were – to some extent – not necessarily the point. What mattered most was the process within which the films were situated: promoting the expressivity of subjects through an active but at times observational camera, and also employing the films' exhibition as an opportunity to energise new lines of communication across racial and class barriers. Nevertheless, the films persist as material objects which reflect some elements of the Farmersville experience while also expressing their own unique-ness. Jerry White has made the argument that the original Fogo films should be seen precisely as *discrete* objects – or as 'an aesthetically sophisticated form of non-narrative, poetic cinema' (2009: 57) – against the tendency to treat them as subordinate to the whole edifice of the communicative process. The inevitable appearance of gaps and ambiguities within production notes and personal testimonies are rarely filled by the films. Yet the films can complement and contradict our knowledge of the Farmersville experience through their ability to register ephemeral fragments of everyday life in Farmersville. A significant amount of effort is made to document the material labour performed by Mexican American farm workers in an observational manner. Therefore, a chief aim of the film crew was to elevate the stature of the labour performed by the workers to a plane of equivalency with the town's white power structure. To this end, exhibition programmes would intentionally juxtapose – for instance – an interview with the white mayor of Farmersville and testimonies from Mexican American workers on their increasingly hazardous working conditions (see Charbonneau 2012).

An example of this emphasis on the labour performed by the Mexican American citizens of Farmersville is the film *Orange Pickers*. This is described in production notes as a documentation of 'pickers picking oranges, packers packing and loaders loading' (Anon. n.d.). Nevertheless, *Orange Pickers* opens poetically with a montage of life in the orange groves, including shots of a foreman walking amongst the workers, women workers warming themselves around a campfire and two young boys cavorting.

To appreciate the significance of this opening, it is critical to recall the filmmakers' intended use for the film. Specifically – as Case has testified – the aim was to reconstitute the town's self-image in such a way that the contribution of Mexican Americans is truly 'seen' and appreciated as integral to the prosperity of Farmersville. The film mixes imagery of labour with those of play, camaraderie and community. While not ignorant of the physical cost and the material toil of the labour involved, this opening montage prioritises scenes that might recall memories of Okie experiences in the fields from previous decades. In the process, through the presentation of relatively generic scenes of life in the groves, the film suggests that the Mexican American working class is participating in a broader history of the town and mirroring the experience of migratory Okies who came to Farmersville during the Great Depression.

The film would have been characterised as 'lyrical', following the specific methodology associated with the Fogo process. Back when Low was filming in Fogo Island he had divided the twenty-eight films produced into one of two categories: those that were focused more rigorously on social problems (*Discussion of Welfare, Citizens' Discussion*) and those that were 'lyrical', less invested in an argumentative logic and more intent on conveying a sense of Fogo culture and experience (*Jim Decker's Party, The Children of Fogo*). This dichotomy was strategic on the filmmakers' part, having learned that alternating films from these two groups would 'help initiate community discussion and dialogue after the films were shown', and that 'too much serious material … might deaden the atmosphere' (Crocker 2008: 66). *Orange Pickers*, then, with its investment in a more observational or experiential aesthetic is clearly intended to disturb the contentious discourse between Mexican Americans and Anglos in the audience by putting aside specific controversies and wallowing in the humanity of life in the fields.

Another way of differentiating 'lyrical' films – and *Orange Pickers* in particular – is to emphasise their observational approach and their distrust of language. If the 'social problem' films are relentless in their incitement to speech on topics such as racial prejudice, working conditions and small town life, the 'lyrical' films prefer to assume a more inductive posture, content to hang back and assume the clichéd 'fly-on-the-wall' stance that we associate with direct cinema. A counterpart to *Orange Pickers* and another example of this 'lyrical' approach is *Gathering Sounds*. The title alone conveys the 'safe' posture of the crew as merely collecting footage. Disavowing direct interaction with the subjects, *Gathering Sounds* presents scenes of Anglo teenagers engrossed in extracurricular activities. Specifically, the structure of the film is arranged around the performance of two songs by an all-white, mostly male, teenage rock band. The opening shot of the film is of the band's reflection in a studio mirror, presenting an image of the cinematographer alongside his subjects. As the teens launch into the song, the camera surveys the scene zooming in and out of close-ups on faces singing and hands playing. Punctuating the footage of the band are masculine scenes of high school wrestling matches and football games. In keeping with the title of the film, the sound of the live music from the studio is interwoven with ambient sounds from the athletic activities. One of the most striking sounds in the film is that of a high school football coach calling out the last names of his players in the locker room during a pre-game meeting ('Young, Miller, Newsom … and Johnson will start!'). This particular scene marks a break from the music and is situated between the two songs performed. As with *Orange Pickers*, this film serves as a passive snapshot of cultural life in Farmersville although the emphasis placed on leisure activities here contrasts with the work space of the orange groves.

Low argued that the Fogo process yields what he calls 'vertical' films: a style of documentary filmmaking whose stylistic traits fundamentally 'distinguished [it] from most documentary images' (ibid.). From Low's perspective, documentaries traditionally adhered to a 'horizontal' structure, which characterised the intervention of the filmmaker, arranging and organising interviews, found footage and other shots into an over-arching exposition (through montage, for instance; ibid.). 'Horizontal' documentaries supposedly closed down discussion, privileging the filmmaker's point of view and burying the singular voices of subjects under the layers of the film's argument. In a more theoretical context, Vivian Sobchack makes a similar point when she writes of an expository documentary's 'lateral consciousness' whereby meaning accrues through a linear 'temporal progression that usually entails a causal logic as well as a teleological movement' (1992: 250). 'Vertical' films, on the other hand, functioned like portraits: prioritising single points of view and individual stories. These were more amenable to the initiation of discussion and assumed a more inductive aesthetic on the filmmaker's part. Low himself commented on how this approach developed: 'When I went to Fogo I thought that I would make one, or perhaps two or more films. But as the project developed, I found that people were much freer when I made short vertical films: each one the record of a single interview, or a single occasion' (qtd. in Crocker 2008: 67). Vertical films, from this perspective, represent a release from the pressure of horizontal exposition, from the constraints of argumentation and linear presentation. Low is expressing a transition in his thinking as a documentarian from closure to aperture, thus paving the way for more expressive and 'freer' subjects whose voices are not made to serve an impervious narrational framework.

Low's articulation of verticality is – again – echoed by Sobchack as a 'longitudinal consciousness' (1992: 250). Here documentary imagery such as home movies refuse the horizontal or syntagmatic imposition of meaning that takes place in expository documentary films. When we screen home movies, Sobchack notes, 'we do not usually retrospect on the film's past screen images and scenes, nor do we usually project forward to future ones so as to create meaning and value from a syntagmatic enchaining' (1992: 248). Instead, our look homes in on the '*present* presence of each set of images and scenes that both catalyze our general memory of existentially known persons and events and exist as fragments of a whole experience we never fully remember' (ibid.). The application of the Fogo process to Farmersville was premised on a unique application of filmmaking as a form of community development, one that embraced a fractured vertical or longitudinal aesthetic so as to prompt dialogue and discussion within an audience that represents the community at large. The Farmersville films – especially the lyrical ones – are quasi-longitudinal in style with the hope of having a lateral or progressive effect on the community depicted.

A final example of both the lyrical and vertical style in the Farmersville films is *Los bailes de Farmersville/Dances of Farmersville*. Of the thirty-six films produced by the production team, this is one of the most cited and discussed in project summaries and reports. The production team filmed two different dances in the same venue, Memorial Hall. The first dance is hosted by the Mexican American *Illusion y Progreso* club and the second by the *Swinging Stars Square Dance Club* of Farmersville. At nine minutes and thirty seconds long, there are no interviews and there is very little attempt to frame the phenomena filmed from any particular perspective. The film was, then, seen as 'safe'. With the expectation that the crew would 'introduce ourselves and the project over the loud speaker' (Lanford 1968) during the dances, the production was as much an opportunity to establish a relationship between the crew and the community as it was to document an important cultural event. In fact, this shoot occurred on 2 November 1968, and it was the crew's first.

The film was shot by Stan Lazan with Lanford recording the sound. Lanford notes that Lazan was particularly adept at 'disappear[ing] in candid work. His "secret" ... is to be direct and not to try to hide or be inconspicuous, which arouses suspicion' (ibid.). Lazan's talent registers the crew's desire to manage their visibility in such a way that they establish a *passive presence*, a production stance that invites recognition on the part of the subjects being filmed while also reassuring them that the crew is an agenda-free, inductive force; 'he is an object of attention,' Lanford writes of Lazan, 'but he moves about with no hesitation or nervousness, and soon people seem to forget about him' (ibid.). This description of Lazan animates a certain contradictory discourse associated with direct cinema or the observational mode (see Nichols 2001: 109–15). Documentarians such as D. A. Pennebaker, Richard Leacock, Robert Drew, Frederick Wiseman and the Maysles Brothers frequently positioned themselves as passive observers while also receiving praise for the skills they displayed in capturing a particular reality. This tension is manifest in a famous publicity still taken for *Dont Look Back*, in which Pennebaker, the director-cinematographer, is depicted in the middle plane of the image – waiting in the wings – while filming Bob

Dylan in the foreground. Even though observational documentaries purport to minimise the authorial hand of the filmmaker, assuming a passive stance in relation to the pro-filmic action, they are inevitably bound up with an extra-filmic discourse that draws attention to the physical performance of the cameraperson. Fascination with pro-filmic reality is intertwined with an admiration for a kind of athletic handheld cinematography that navigates the action, presumably improvising compositions on the fly. This publicity still from *Dont Look Back* illustrates this dynamic as Dylan's gaze is directed forward and avoids any peripheral acknowledgement of Pennebaker's presence to his immediate left. In this regard, Pennebaker is shown to be upholding a central observational ethos, that the filmmaker shall not interfere with or disturb actions occurring in front of the camera. At the same time, we admire Pennebaker's foresight and spatial position demonstrating a physical mobility and keen awareness on his part of the subject's actions and peripheral visual field (the hat also reinforces the director's status as a kind of master of ceremonies). This tension is also evident textually as the ubiquitous handheld camera in the film reminds us both of the unfolding nature of the action depicted while also underscoring the physical labour and skill of the cameraperson, registered in the shaky status of the image.

Figure 22.
D. A. Pennebaker
actively observes in this
publicity still from
Dont Look Back
(d. D. A. Pennebaker,
1967).

Lazan's cinematographic talent for being seen but forgotten synchronises with this discourse of observational documentary. His camerawork – via his unassuming posture – settles into the pro-filmic environment, supposedly blending in as the subjects accept the camera as part of their experience. Visibility, in this case, facilitates acceptance, particularly since the nature of the event is a dance where people are already assuming an exhibitionist posture, entering a space where being seen is part of the experience. As stated earlier, *Los bailes de Farmersville/Dances of Farmersville* is a 'lyrical' film, one primarily interested in conveying the atmosphere and texture of a cultural experience through observational techniques. Handheld shots of both the *Illusion y Progresso* and *Swinging Stars Square Dance Club* events consist of crowded frames of dancers, musicians and families enjoying themselves. While the filmmakers don't make an appearance in the film, playful glances at the camera indicate the passive presence of which Lanford writes. More than once, attendees – a young girl at the *Illusion y Progresso* dance, for instance – look and smile directly at the camera lens. Throughout the film, a lack of synchronisation or syntagmatic coordination between image and sound contributes to its reception as a longitudinal document, as an unrefined record of the two dances. The coverage of both dances includes a soundtrack consisting of the live music performed interwoven with ambient noises from the attendees laughing, singing and talking with one another. That the sound does not directly align with the images presented only serves to reinforce the fragmented nature of the cuts. While linked by a contiguous space – that of Memorial Hall – and a contiguous soundtrack, the shots themselves accrue into a sloppy montage effect in a series of disparate shots of dancers, musicians and spectators. This 'spotty' editing – as Lanford describes it – has the effect of feeling amateurish but also underscores the film's safety to an audience of nervous Farmersville residents who have been or potentially could be subjects of the films produced. The relatively unstructured presentation of shots gives the film that home movie feel, with the effect of reassuring spectators that the crew is on their side despite their outsider status and funding from Washington. In this sense, the crew is engaged in a strategic or performative longitudinality.

Los bailes de Farmersville/Dances of Farmersville was actually screened in a truncated form. Specifically, the first half – the portion presenting the *Illusion y Progresso* dance – was screened as its own film without the subsequent segment on the square dancers. In fact, this segment – shown on 18 November in the cafeteria at Snowden Elementary to a meeting of *Illusion y Progresso* and an audience of 85 – was the first film to be screened as part of *The Farmersville Project*. Lanford makes special note of this screening, observing that the film's warm reception 'made a striking impression on me' (1968). The film, he writes, was met with 'applause and a short speech of real gratitude and well wishes' (ibid.). By popular demand the film was played twice and – in a move that echoes the film's longitudinal posturing – Lanford notes that one woman in the audience broke out into tears upon seeing her mother in the film who had been visiting from Mexico at the time (ibid.). The *Illusion y Progresso* portion of the film was also screened the following night to a general audience. With two hundred locals present, the first half of the dance film was coupled with rushes from the filming of *Turkeyshoot* on 10 November. Lanford writes that the reception was warm, but there was no 'opportunity for any discussion' (ibid.). Furthermore, the clash between the footage of Mexican Americans 'beautifully enjoying themselves at a dance, and a somewhat nasty [series of scenes] about Okies shooting and loading their guns' made for a number of 'tensions' (ibid.).

Given that there was no formal discussion at this particular screening, it is hard to be sure what these 'tensions' were and how they were made manifest. But clearly Lanford felt a sense of discomfort over both the quality of the rushes shown for *Turkeyshoot* – supposedly the crew was later 'resolved never to have public screenings of uncut materials' – as well as the discordant effect of the exhibition's double bill, juxtaposing a Mexican American dance with an Anglo hunt. The gap between Lanford's expectations in this instance and the reality of the audience's reception speaks to the slippery nature of these vertical films' horizontal impact. The hermeneutic aperture sought by the Fogo process – or the films' longitudinality, in Sobchack's terms – leads to unexpected interpretations at the moment of presentation to the audience. We also saw this in the case of *Los bailes de Farmersville/Dances of Farmersville* where an audience member reacted to the film precisely as a home movie, as an archival record of her mother's visit from Mexico. While these elements of surprise are to some degree embraced by the filmmakers, the resulting tensions call into question the 'safety' of their endeavour. Here – in the instance of these 'lyrical' films, at least – the crew's liberal advocacy gets unsettled to some degree as the managerial dimension of their work encounters friction with its distinct participatory stance, a reminder of their status as presumptuous outsiders.

Contentious Vertical Films

The films just discussed – *Orange Pickers, Gathering Sounds* and *Los bailes de Farmersville/Dances of Farmersville* – exemplify Low's 'lyrical' approach. At every level of these films' production – planning, shooting, cutting, screening – the makers were mindful of mitigating their outsider status. Insistent on making films that were 'safe' – that in some sense demonstrated the crew's credentials as friendly observers – Low, Biggs and the rest of the crew also recognised that difficult social issues needed to be addressed. The longitudinality of films such as *Orange Pickers* had to be supplemented by films that would compel discourse, prompting subjects to stage their feelings and attitudes for the camera. The filmmakers' use of the observational mode was only realised in conjunction with the more contentious and interactive stance of gauging the views of locals on topics such as the working conditions of farm workers, the roots of racial animosity between Anglos and Mexican Americans and the question of cultural and social segregation within Farmersville. In other words, Low and Biggs realised that their embrace of observational filmmaking represented only one of two primary modes of engaging the citizens of Farmersville. The other approach eschewed the stance of the passive observer and embraced a participatory modality, focusing on interviews filmed in long takes with minimal editing.

The range of documentary styles implied by the label, 'participatory', is indeed broad. To some extent, the renown of the Fogo process has to do with the way in which a participatory ethos infuses the whole mode of production, from the moment of interactive filming to the editing process (in which the subjects of the film may give feedback) and finally to the films' exhibition in which post-screening discussions are a key feature. The 'social problem' films of the *The Farmersville Project* are participatory in the most basic sense as documents of an interaction. The result is that these films are received as portraits of particular individuals, their personal lives as well as their views of the community of Farmersville more generally. The two films reviewed in this section – *Hector and Ruben* and *Danny and Leo* – are clear examples of this approach. In both films, the filmmakers query the locals on class and race in Farmersville and the respondents draw on their own personal experiences for the camera. The featured interviewees in *Hector and Ruben* are two Mexican-American veterans who have each completed a tour of duty in Vietnam and have returned to Farmersville changed men. In *Danny and Leo*, the filmmakers interview Daniel Ybarra – a Mexican American labour contractor – and Leo Fry – a white farm foreman – about their views on the plight of the farm worker and race relations in Farmersville. The relatively static frame and the minimal editing render these films less visually engaging than the lyrical films of *The Farmersville Project*. Nevertheless, the focus here is on the testimonies of the subjects and their expressivity to the camera. Only occasionally are the faces of the interviewers shown on camera, brought about by a quick pan or cut. Instead, these films tend to keep the interviewer out of frame even as we can hear him pose his question or comment. Most often we hear Colin Low's soft-spoken voice off-camera and the delicate ways in which he poses questions registers the crew's uneasiness with confrontation. These films feel intimate and conversational rather than forceful and polemical. In this regard, the relative *safety* of the lyrical films is not too far from one's mind when viewing these participatory portraits. Open-ended questions typically allow for a wide variety of responses from the participants and speak to the filmmakers' sensitivity to their own status as outsiders.

Like the lyrical/observational films discussed above, these films – in part – settle within a field of verticality and longitudinality. While the interactive features of the social problem films formally designate them as participatory films – as filmic records of interviews – their fragmentary status as 'community development' films whose discourse is decontextualised retains a feeling of verticality, a sense of wallowing in a moment of expressivity akin to Sobchack's *present* presence. Textually speaking, both *Hector and Ruben* and *Danny and Leo* leave the viewer with the impression of having seen a straight filmic document of an interview. Each film begins with a question from an off-screen speaker without any narrational or even imagistic context. The films present the interview in what feels like real time as the discussion flows from topic to topic. The visual style of these films is dry, largely consisting of medium close-ups of the interviewee with occasional pans to the questioner. Periodic cuts punctuate these films and are largely concealed by the continuity of the soundtrack. There are no voiceovers providing contextual or background information to the viewer. These films are meant to be seen as participatory portraits or as documents of encounters with minimal lateral or horizontal intervention. Again – in spite of the fact that the filmmakers are partially seen and heard as well as completely addressed – the vertical and longitudinal stance persists in the way that these films retain only the loosest of syntagmatic momentum, leaving the overall signification of the film fragmented and ephemeral. In fact, a critique of the filmmaker's efforts to make meaning is directly targeted by these films as the respondents themselves take control of the interview, resisting or often redirecting the filmmakers' queries into poverty, race and culture.

However, in spite of the fact that these social problem films retain the vertical disposition of their lyrical counterparts, this was not enough to assuage concern about the effects of the whole endeavour. Henry Lanford describes a key moment in which an exchange between himself and a local reporter, Marion Cundiff, leaves him worried (ibid.). During the conversation Lanford attempts to 'find different ways' to explain the project, ultimately conveying the production team's mantra that 'any increase in honest communication is bound to be progress in the right direction', an assertion that 'turns out to be one of my most firm beliefs' (ibid.). This determined, almost 'missionary-like devotion' to expressivity through the filmmaking process fails to sway Cundiff who insists that the romantic premise of the project ignores the possibility – and, for Cundiff, the likelihood – of 'inflaming underlying tensions' in the community (ibid.).

This ambivalence eventually influences Lanford's thinking about the Fogo process. Specifically, he devotes space in his production diary to the airing out of his own misgivings about the crew's pursuit of interviews on controversial topics in their participatory or 'social problem' films. The Fogo process is needed, Lanford maintains, as a corrective to heightened alienation between 'individuals within … society' (or what he refers to as a growing 'lack of vital connection' between citizens; ibid.). Public discourse, he insists, needs to reflect 'a wider range of human experience' (ibid.). The assumption here is that a contracting and increasingly individualised public sphere is in need of community development processes – such as the Fogo process – to reconstitute the civic body. And yet, against the backdrop of this observation, Lanford admits that the Fogo process – in practice – necessitates far too many political and 'diplomatic' machinations for his taste (ibid.). He notes his discomfort with the filmmakers' efforts to dodge and redirect objections from community leaders in Farmersville. The end result, he claims, is narrow adherence to 'the idea' over the 'community and its people' (ibid.). More often than not, locals who resist the film crew inevitably concede in the face of 'our superior sense of missionary zeal' (ibid.). 'I would like to raise the question,' Lanford writes, 'as to just how strong a reaction would it take from an individual or from a community to overcome our zealous conviction that a certain subject should be discussed? How strong would that have to be?' (ibid.) In spite of Low and Biggs' insistence on submitting films to the interviewees for review in advance of any screenings, the concern here is that none of this truly mitigates the power of the state, which underpins the whole endeavour.

This returns us to the dialectic of liberal advocacy discussed earlier and its fundamentally passive-aggressive posture. The Fogo process as we have seen was deployed as a means of 'community development' or, put another way, as an embodiment of liberal advocacy that both intervenes into the community and seeks to reflect or amplify aspects of the community that preceded it. The lyrical or observational approach can only go so far as a form of 'self-help' – to quote the OEO contract with the filmmakers. Eventually, the filmmakers needed to address and film the residents of Farmersville more pointedly and directly, in the way that nudged the residents to speak out about the politics of class and race in their community. In this regard, the dialectic of liberal advocacy – the notion of the enlightened outsider who knows simultaneously everything and nothing – returns to us. A narrative discourse in the OEO's educational and training films re-emerges as a particular structure of feeling that defines the contours of the filmmakers' engagement with the citizens of Farmersville as well as the overall ethos of the Fogo process. The use of the participatory mode in this historical and social context reproduces the dialectic of liberal advocacy as the filmmakers and the federal agency which supports them insist on seeing these communication experiments as exercises in 'self-help'. The insistent but deferent film crew has come to Farmersville to serve as a medium for the townspeople to re-encounter each other, to see each other in a new light and become changed in a vague yet progressive way.

As examples of filmic self-help, *Hector and Ruben* and *Danny and Leo* commence in similar ways. *Danny and Leo* opens with an establishing shot of orange groves over which is shown a simple title identifying the names of the interviewees and their respective occupations: 'Danny Ibarra, Labor Contractor' and 'Leo Fry, Farm Foreman'. As this opening image zooms into a closer look of the groves, a quick dissolve transitions to a medium shot of Ibarra seated outside with orange trees in the background. A momentary voiceover flatly states, 'Interview with Daniel Ibarra in the Orange Grove', and the interview begins with a simple question: 'What time do you usually start in the morning?' *Hector and Ruben* opens more directly with a two-shot of the young men seated inside next to one another with cigarettes in hand. Following a brief title – 'Two Young Veterans … Hector and Ruben' – Low asks from off-screen: 'Have you always known each other?'

The starting point for these two films – and for the majority of the filmed interviews conducted for *The Farmersville Project* – is the subjects' everyday life. By opening the films with enquiries into relatively banal aspects of the interviewees' lives, the filmmakers establish these films as works of portraiture. In such instances, Ibarra, Hector and Ruben participate in their own constitution as authentic selves whose life experiences – addressed in this generic manner – are recognisable to an audience of Farmersville residents. To a certain extent, these participatory portraits are caught up in what Timothy Corrigan describes as the 'myths of portraiture' (2011: 88). The individuals featured are presented as coherent subjects constituted by an unproblematic expressivity. Characterised 'by spontaneity and depth, by direct expression/speech/language, and by signification of gesture and eye contact', these portraits present individuals whose delineation comes about through their improvisatory responses to the filmmakers' open-ended questions and enquiries into their daily lives (ibid.). The 'sociohistorical world' is accessed simultaneously as 'background' (2011: 89) and as a dissectible object rather than a dynamic field. The films in this regard represent a kind of sphere outside of the material forces of the real world or as a reprieve from the controversies of the day even as these are touched upon in the course of the conversation. Here we can see the persistence of a *safe* mode of engagement, carried over from the lyrical/observational films. The opening questions establish a tone and style that is conversational, friendly, and interested in accessing everyday feelings and experiences. The self-consciousness of the filmmakers compels this approach. They are deeply aware of the fact that they are outsiders and, to a certain extent, the myth of portraiture that prevails here is a byproduct of the filmmakers' desire to produce a means of communication that settles rather than unsettles, reassures rather than disturbs.

Furthermore, the relegation of the sociohistorical world to the realm of discursive pondering rather than engagement synchronises with the therapeutic frame established at the outset by the filmmakers' contract with the federal government. Bear in mind that the aim was to create a series of self-help films. As quoted earlier, these were to be films that 'provide visual self-analysis, self-appraisal, self-correction' while also offering 'insights into community problems'. The film frame, then, becomes a discordant therapeutic space or a kind of safe zone where the interviewees intimately respond to questions from a soft-spoken interlocutor while also submitting to a public visibility, a broader projection of their testimonies to an audience of Farmersville residents as well as community development officers. The *self* is what gets emphasised at the outset of the 'social problem' films as well as at the outset of the whole endeavour – in the language of the inaugural contract. The application of the Fogo process here gets caught up in an inertia in which the myth of portraiture is harnessed as way to mitigate and navigate through social conflict. As limited as this approach may have been, there nevertheless was a sense that these films represented a real intervention into Farmersville as an imagined community caught between the legacy of its Okie past and its clear future as a majoritarian Mexican American town.

From this vantage point, the drawbacks as well as the accomplishments of these films come into sharper focus. The drawbacks are clearly to be found in these films' infatuation with a romantic mythos of portraiture and their insistence on reading reality within a therapeutic frame. At the same time, however, this hindrance accrues political significance within a particular sociohistorical time and space where the racial makeup has radically changed and yet the power structure is slow to reflect this fact. Here the projection of 'authentic' Mexican American selves through the 'signification of gesture and eye contact' as well as verbal expression crucially intervenes into the imagined community of Farmersville, into the town's collective understanding of itself. Both *Hector and Ruben* and *Danny and Leo* compel this realisation in different ways.

To begin with, we cannot ignore the fact that both of these films are portraits of relationships, rather than individuals. Their respective titles make this clear from the outset. However, the nature of the two films' relationships could not be more at odds. In the case of *Hector and Ruben*, the relationship depicted is one of close kinship or long-term friendship. Both are young Mexican American veterans who served in the Vietnam War and grew up together in Farmersville. In *Danny and Leo*, the relationship is a structural one; Danny works for Leo. As the farm foreman, Leo is responsible for managing and supervising the labour on the orange groves. Danny – as the labour contractor – recruits and hires seasonal workers for Leo. The basis for their interactions or transactions is largely economic. Danny ensures that Leo has enough manual labour to harvest and process the oranges in a timely and efficient manner so as to maximise the return on the farmer's investment. Danny, of course, is Mexican American and Leo is white. While Leo – at least in this film – is positioned as representative of a white power structure, Danny is caught within this power structure as well as between it and the workers it exploits.

Taking these elements into account underscores the political potency of these films. With *Hector and Ruben*, *The Farmersville Project* counters stereotypes by devoting screen time to two Mexican American men whose lives and views defy easy categorisation. Both Hector and Ruben are – as mentioned earlier – veterans of the Vietnam War and their service is clearly the prevailing backdrop for their interaction with the film crew. Their time in the army is characterised as a kind of reprieve from the racism and alienation both experienced as students in Farmersville. Early in the film, Hector speaks about the difficulties he and Ruben encountered in school:

> *Hector:* Well, the situation was … there was a lot of prejudice in school. And, I don't know, I guess other people could take it. I know I couldn't, speaking for myself. The way things turned out, Ruben couldn't either.

Low inquires further at this point, asking Hector open-ended questions about life in the Farmersville schools as a Mexican American:

> *Low:* Were you razzed or teased?
> *Hector:* All the time.
> *Low:* What was that like? Being called what? Wetback?
> *Hector:* Yeah. Or maybe it was said in a joking manner, but it couldn't be taken that way. Not by myself anyway. It just got to a situation where we got in a fight in our senior year and we were kicked out for it. And Ruben and another friend of ours never returned, but I went back. And then in the gym you weren't supposed to have glass of any kind but I broke a

cologne bottle accidentally and the coach jumped all over me. He started calling me all sorts of names so I just told him where he could go and what they could do with their school and I walked out. And the principal said he'd fix it so that I could go to any school or graduate that year so I guess I just forgot about it. But I got my diploma in the army. I worked extra in the army and nights so I could get it.

For Hector, the racism in the schools compelled him to seek his diploma elsewhere. The army functions, in this instance, as a haven from abuse. Ruben, while disliking the army, feels similarly:

> *Ruben:* Well, I don't like the army. I can't say too much about it. But like you said it is a better school in the army. Seems like you get more attention, they treat you nicer. Because they want you to get your high school diploma, they wanted me to get it real bad, because they know it's about the last chance you'll get. Because most of the people, well, they don't go back to school after they get out of the army unless they're real strongminded. So they try to give them all the schooling they can in the service, depending upon your company commander, whether he needs you or if he's just the way he is and doesn't want to let you go.
>
> *Low:* You volunteered for the service?
>
> *Ruben:* Yes. And I regretted it at the time, but now I don't.

Hector and Ruben, then, have a shared experience with racial discrimination in Farmersville, one that prompts them to enlist in the military. The military, by comparison with their hometown, is more egalitarian and supportive of their aspirations; it's a 'better school', following Ruben's characterisation. While this story of racial discrimination in the Farmersville schools would probably not have been surprising to Farmersville audiences, both Hector and Ruben's conciliatory and casual tone while discussing such experiences ('maybe it was said in a joking manner') shuns any sense of bitterness. Furthermore, their qualified embrace of the military – especially given Ruben's admission that he willingly chose to join as opposed to being drafted – cements their status as citizens who have served at a time of great crisis. While feeling rejected by the public institutions of their hometown, they felt acceptance at the national level within the military, an institution of public service.

The juxtaposition of alienation from Farmersville with a sense of belonging in the United States Army accomplishes two feats. On the one hand, this narrative mars the town of Farmersville as the true haven of outsiders, as a community out of step with a nation whose institutions are inching closer toward a prevailing racial equality. On the other hand, this schism is breached by a sense of kinship across generations as Hector and Ruben's testimonies about their service in Vietnam dovetails with the experience of veterans from wars past, such as the Korean War and World War II. Clearly, one of the most powerful signifiers of one's participation in the life of the nation is military service. And Hector and Ruben's service bolsters their claims of belonging in the present tense even as it maps an affinity between their own experience and white veterans of the VFW like those featured in *Turkeyshoot*.

At this point, the filmmakers further enquire into Hector and Ruben's experience in Vietnam. Ruben, the quieter of the two in the film, shares a particular harrowing anecdote. Following a commentary from Hector on the question of homesickness – and how the 'responsibilities of command' temper this feeling over time – the film quickly fades out to black and fades in to a medium close-up on Ruben. This transition is a punctuating moment in the film, setting up Ruben's story. Ruben notes that he had been sleeping in his bunker when his platoon came under attack.

> *Ruben:* I don't know what got me to wake up, but all of a sudden I stood up out of bed and I could hear the bullets. It seemed like they were coming through the window and hitting the wall right in front of me. And the next thing I knew I was on the floor, some concussion … knocked me down or something. I started looking for my rifle. They told me later on that they had it on top of the bunker because I had a newer type of rifle. And it was pretty good up there on top of the bunker. So what I started doing was passing out my magazines to the fellows who were getting shorter because the battle had been going for ten, fifteen minutes. And that's a lot of time.
>
> *Low:* You must sleep pretty well?
>
> *Ruben:* Yes, I'm a pretty heavy sleeper. And the rest of the things just blurred. […] We were just trying to keep them away from coming into our bunker and throwing grenades in there. They did throw one grenade in there, but we were lucky and it landed on the radio. So we didn't get nothing but concussion.
>
> *Low:* Anybody hurt?
>
> *Ruben:* Yes. Three guys. One … our platoon sergeant got a little piece torn out of his leg and one of the members of my squad got some shrapnel in the back. And the other one got a little bit in the face. Not serious, though. And the next thing I know the Viet Cong are going down the

hill and they've taken off. The artillery's coming in, starting to clean them out, I guess. They were getting pretty close to us – I thought I was a goner for a minute. But after they started leaving, the reinforcements started coming in and well they got it pretty well under control … started to run them off the hill. They managed to get about eleven of us, out of the 29 that were up there. Ten or eleven, before we could get them away from the area.

Low: What was your feeling at the time?

Ruben: Well, I thought I was going to be dead, pretty soon. It's a funny feeling, so many things run through your mind. But I thought I was going to be dead just like everyone else did.

While the military served as an alternative educational experience for Hector and Ruben, the perils of serving – particularly during the Vietnam War – are not glossed over. Ruben's story here is both unique and generic in that it simultaneously conveys that sense of shock which the Viet Cong deployed so effectively (most famously during the Tet Offensive on 30 January 1968) while also resonating with a more generalised soldier narrative, accessible to other veterans of foreign wars in the audience.

The film might easily have been made as a simple portrait of one of these two young men, rather than both. By highlighting their experience as shared to some degree, the film frames Hector and Ruben's individual stories as indicative of a broader Mexican American experience in Farmersville. Low might have intended this film to follow his schema of verticality. But clearly the vertical ethos does not completely take hold in a film such as *Hector and Ruben*. While the lyrical films fit the bill more easily, the social problem films of *The Farmersville Project* seek to compel discourse and narratives of the self. In this regard, *Hector and Ruben* is more lateral than longitudinal as it sets out to explicitly 'create meaning and value from a syntagmatic enchaining' driven by their distinct yet shared experiences. This accrual of meaning from Hector and Ruben's personal narratives bears the hopes of the filmmakers for a new collective vision of Farmersville, one where the Mexican American experience is not seen as an intrusion from the outside but – rather – already part of the social fabric of the town. While de-contextualised and fragmented on its own, the film is explicitly positioned as a component of a broader effort to reconfigure Farmersville's sense of itself, to engineer a new encounter between Anglos and Mexican Americans. In the case of *Hector and Ruben*, the encounter desired by the filmmakers – between Mexican Americans and Anglos – is to be found off-screen in the circumstances of projection and exhibition. In *Danny and Leo*, however, the encounter is arranged entirely onscreen. This is evidenced by the visual framing of the two participants side-by-side throughout the latter half of the filmed conversation. Here Danny, a Mexican American, and Leo, Anglo American, are addressed directly by the filmmakers at the same time and drawn into a broad – and often awkward – discussion about economics as well as the segregated cultural and social life of Farmersville. While they are, to some extent, posed as representatives from different cultural and economic spheres, the two men are also bound to one another through their work association and figuratively positioned as equals in the film. In this regard, the framing of the film's primary two-shot is critical. The side-by-side positioning of the two men works to undermine the presumed hierarchy of the Anglo American who oversees the Mexican American and instead frames them as peers. Their respective one-shots parallel each other and further reinforce the film's egalitarian posture. Here, depictions of Danny and Leo listening carefully to – and often reiterating – each other's comments can also be seen as an extension of the film crew's overall communicative ethos, or an aesthetic reflection of their managerial liberal insistence on the power of dialogue.

This theme of equality is touched on fairly early in the film when Danny speaks about farm labour's denigration in the United States, specifically bemoaning the fact that farm workers are denied unemployment insurance:

> *Danny*: I think that farm labor should be equal to any kind of labor in the United States whatsoever. Everybody, mostly everybody gets unemployment compensation. I don't know why they [are] rooting out the farm laborer.

This leads to an exchange between Danny and the crew about the distinction between welfare and unemployment insurance from the view of the farm worker:

> *Question:* Well, if he could just as easily get it in welfare now, what difference does it make whether it's unemployment compensation or welfare?
> *Danny:* Oh it makes a lot of difference. To me it makes a lot of difference. Because when a person goes up to stand in a welfare line he doesn't feel too good, anyway I wouldn't. And I know a lot of them said the same thing. They're trying to hide their face when they go up there. And you show me one fellow that's went up to the unemployment line and hide his face, no … he figures he's got that thing coming. Because he paid for it. This other way, no, he feels like he's going up there and ask for charity. He doesn't like it, but he has to because his kids need it. And I would and you would and anybody else would if his kids got hungry.

At this point in the film Danny is making the case for the farm worker to be treated like other workers. This core indignity – denial of unemployment benefits – speaks directly to a post-Civil Rights sensibility as farm workers – who are disproportionately Latino and Filipino – grapple with the feeling of having their labour denigrated or devalued by an unequal allocation of benefits. Danny's advocacy here is addressed to the crew – who is off-screen, for the most part – in the apparent absence of Leo. The first half of the film features Danny being interviewed alone, allowing his expressivity to flow without the distraction of the foreman's presence in the frame as a fellow interviewee. As a result, Danny's articulation of a fundamental inequality facing farm workers is prioritised within the film and works to re-shape a public sphere where such advocacy could not be voiced so prominently.

Throughout this segment of the film, the visual staging of Danny's interview outdoors, in the orange groves, works to underscore Anne Michaels' insistence that these communication experiments would feature 'the people' not the 'spokesmen'. Danny is interviewed 'out there' in the real world. He is positioned as a kind of everyman speaking his mind rather than as a political leader. It is only at the end of the film – when Danny admits that many of his friends, Mexican American and Anglo, frequently ask him to 'run for councilman' – that Danny starts to appear to us as more than an everyman. Here the conversation turns on Low's suggestion that Mexican Americans in Farmersville might be hesitant to get involved in the town's more historically white institutions because it might be seen as 'putting on airs'. Leo initially concurs, prompting the following response from Danny:

Danny: I don't know, Leo. As far as I'm concerned, what you said there …
   that might be with other Mexican American people. But not with me. It's
   not the sense that I say well if I join the Lion's Club I'm going to step out
   of my class and people are going to think well he's getting [to be a] big
   shot. No. In fact, some of the Mexican American people in Farmersville
   have always said, 'Dan, why don't you run for councilman?' Not only the
   Mexican American people, I have had some Anglo-American people ask
   me, 'how come you don't try to run for councilman?'
Low: Why don't you?
Danny: Well, I've always told them this. I say, I haven't got enough education
   to try to help run a city. Maybe I have got the common sense. But still
   this is what always kept me back, I haven't got enough school.
Low: You said there aren't enough people who are potentially good leaders
   taking this kind of involvement and this kind of interest and that's what's

> wrong with Farmersville.
>
> *Danny:* Well, I think so...
>
> *Leo:* In a case like this I don't think education is the answer. Because if you've got good common sense I don't care if you've never went to school a day in your life, you can help. And this is the case with Danny. Danny's got good common sense about everything he does ... running this crew ... working for this rancher. Anything he does. Why couldn't he help in a city where half of the people are Mexican people?

This comment is the concluding one for the film and it marks a shift in our perception of Danny from that of everyman to potential leader. Leo's endorsement of Danny as an important and under-utilised voice in Farmersville is the film's dénouement. This climactic moment is the by-product of the crew's incitement to discourse – it's notable that Low is the first to ask, 'Why don't you?' and Leo repeats it nearly verbatim – and conveniently affirms Michaels' broader rationale for the experiment as a 'community development project' that generates dialogue and discourages violent confrontation. *Danny and Leo* is the perfect encapsulation of the driving impulse of the project, namely to compel conversations on camera grounded in rationality from individuals in communities in crisis.

Nevertheless, the elevation of Danny as a new leader for Farmersville and a spokesman for Mexican Americans has the effect of obfuscating or blunting the earlier conversations about economics. Initially, Danny makes the case for the unionisation of the farm worker and insists on this as the only way to ensure effective representation of farm workers' interests.

> *Danny:* The farm laborer is not organised so therefore you've got nobody to negotiate for you. You've got nobody like say for instance right now that boycott they're having. Well that's the only way they can go about it. There's no other means.

And yet in the very next sentence, Danny hedges and distances himself from the farm workers while still making the case for unionisation.

> *Danny:* I don't approve of it myself, really, but what else are they going to do? Sure I understand the farmers got a lot of problems too. I'm not just gonna go and say the farm laborers are the only ones hurting. Maybe some of the little farmers are hurting too.

Danny's dance between passionate advocate and sober realist speaks to his structural position within the farm industry as well as to the social relationship inaugurated by the – mostly – unseen camera crew. The 'personal' approach of the Fogo process – whatever its merits – tend to unwittingly place a heavy burden on the shoulders of those who testify. Danny's performance registers this burden through his rhetorical see-saw as he negotiates not just Leo's presence, but the presence of the state as well as the absent but present audience. This burden of representation is also felt by Hector in *Hector and Ruben* as he distances himself from the civil rights struggle and any semblance of 'militancy', bolstered by his US Army service record. To Low's query about the 'grievances' of 'black people' and 'brown people', Hector argues that 'patience and understanding' is in short supply 'with all the militants around'. The desire for social change among African American and Mexican American activists reflects – for Hector – a lack of 'patience': 'They want to change overnight and it's impossible.' Like Fuentes, Danny and Hector both appeal to the managerial attraction to subjects caught in the 'middle', or at the intersection of competing social zones. Both testify to the experience of discrimination and racial hardship while also couching their response in the language of moderation and noting their personal investment in the status quo. It is an investment also shared by the crew itself, whose very presence is made possible by a state agency fueled by a managerial liberal investment in 'self-help' as well as an anxiety triggered by the collective efforts of Mexican Americans and African Americans to close the gap between frustration and fulfillment.

Farmersville's motto is, 'The world is quiet here.' More than simply suggesting a community above the fray and free of conflict, the motto speaks to the methodology of the OEO film crew. The Fogo process – by its very design – is premised on the liberal manager's hope for reason, for attentive reception and careful expression. The mechanisms of documentation and projection are used here to pry loose entrenched positions by featuring 'thoughtful' works of portraiture and observational imagery. But underlying the impulse for a renewed communication 'loop' is the recognition of inequality, struggle and – inevitably – change. In spite of the moderate tone of the production and the subjects featured in the films of the *The Farmersville Project*, the most impactful element of the experiment was its imagery. Regardless of the statements articulated to the camera in the 'mini self-help' films, the significant reach of the films *within* Farmersville (recall an average audience size of eighty over the course of twenty-nine separate screenings) suggests that the imagery of the films represent their greatest impact. The totality of the visuals across these films elevates the presence of Mexican Americans in Farmersville who work, play and express themselves in tandem with white citizens or in isolation, in scenes of dynamic portraiture.

Nevertheless, this is a political and aesthetic contribution that resists the liberal manager's comprehension. It isn't easily measured or documented in any report. While it is felt by some of the crew – Case notes that juxtaposing a film of the white mayor (*Mayor Jay Kemp*, 1968) with that of farm workers (*Orange Pickers*) implicitly equates the two and short-circuits the prevailing hierarchy of the town – this representational intervention was difficult to fully grasp and convey in the moment. Again, as we have seen, the managerial aspects of the Fogo process and its retreat to a faithful and idealised mode of communication appealed to an agency in crisis, deeply troubled by the intensification of racial and class conflict around the country. But, in the end, this particular goal – while its pursuit may sooth – was vacuous and what was left in its wake were the screenings themselves and their breadth of their reach within the town. And, with this in mind, perhaps the simplest films are the most notable in hindsight. *Our Film*, for instance, was a film shot at the crew's home and features Mexican American youth playing music in the backyard. In some ways it parallels the earlier film of white youth performing for the crew – *Gathering Sounds* – but in other ways it demonstrates a warm connection between the crew of outsiders and the Mexican American teens. Unlike *Gathering Sounds*, *Our Film* is shot outdoors and feels more spontaneous and less closed off from the world than the Anglo teens' studio. The ambiguity of the title – *Our Film* – leaves us questioning the possessive adjective and to whom it refers. Is it the crew's film, since they are the handlers of the camera, microphone and editing bay? Or is it the teenagers' film, the ones who perform and are at the heart of the film's spectacle? This open-ended title reflects a close bond between these subjects and the crew, a bond further underscored by the fact that this is the temporary home of the filmmakers, a perceived safe space for the Mexican American teens.

This retroactive and ideological assessment of *The Farmersville Project* should also be juxtaposed with the significant material output of the film crew. When Low, Biggs and company were recruited by the OEO's Office of Public Affairs, the intent was to recreate the Fogo Island experience in Farmersville. To a large extent this was achieved. Approximately the same number of films was produced over a similar time period (thirty-four films in less than six weeks) and the films also adhered to the 'vertical' format preferred by Low. However, looking back upon his experiences, Lanford expresses strong reservations about both the Fogo process as an abstract method of filmmaking and its application to the community of Farmersville. Most critical is the 'very real danger that the work will develop into a terrible force in the world ... this could be the first stage of a development of a Big-Brother-Is-Watching-You situation – an ever present television eye making no distinctions between private and public' (Lanford 1968). This danger emerges from the Fogo process's obfuscation of the dividing line between private and public spheres, a tendency that he believes – while justified – could threaten to open the flood gates for an uninhibited media gaze.

Lanford's own scepticism and doubts – while dramatically stated – cannot be easily swept under the rug as they speak to the awkward paternalism of the endeavour. Here the process tends to fall into a different kind of loop where it becomes an end in itself, where the value of the filmmakers' gentle incitement to express accomplishes not much more than self-aggrandisement. Lanford's struggle with – and recognition of – an elitist trumpeting of the idea over the people on the part of the filmmakers registers a double bind. Specifically, he and – very likely – his colleagues are ensnared in a crisis or epistemic break which both empowers them to recognise the institutional and ideological inertia of their privileged position as filmmakers even as they fail to disentangle themselves from this logic, from the entrenched nature of a classic communicative and managerial posture. Lanford recognises that 'the power is all on our side'; he knows that despite the commitment to providing a platform for the unfettered expressivity of documentary subjects, the film crew's presumed entitlement to the words, imagery and experiences of Farmersville residents is a force that creates rather than discovers, incites rather than records. His noble desire to bridge otherwise disparate realms of the personal and the public in hopes of opening up public discourse to the experiences and voices of subjects who are otherwise ignored is overturned in practice. Specifically, his 'liberation' of the private sphere is simultaneously an objectification of it, a kind of reduction whose visibility elicits responses for which Lanford is unprepared. While Lanford insists on respecting the unique expressions of the subject, he hesitates to exhibit the footage to an audience that may greet the subject with derision or hostility. At the heart of Lanford's internal narrative – and perhaps at the heart of the whole endeavour – is a hesitation to offend or, put another way, a discomfort with politics and division.

From this vantage point the awkward and askew glances directed at Lazan's camera in *Los bailes de Farmersville/Dances of Farmersville* can be seen metonymically connected to a broader unease between the outsider crew and the subjects of their film practice. The looks back at the passive presence of the crew simultaneously suggest a desire to be seen and a hesitancy to submit to the needs of the project or – put another way – an inclination to largely withhold participation in a film practice under the purview of outsiders. It is appropriate, I believe, to read the crew's struggles and difficulties against the backdrop of a series of crises in documentary consciousness as well as in managerial governance as a federal agency fights for its life and navigates widespread social upheaval in the late

1960s. However, Lanford's anxiety is not unfamiliar in our particular historical, technological and cultural horizon of the early twenty-first century. No doubt, the stakes of being seen and being heard are as crucial now as they were in the late 1960s. And yet the failure of *The Farmersville Project* speaks to the crucial politics of withholding participation and resisting visibility.

Note

1 Excerpts from this chapter were previously published in Stephen Charbonneau (2014) 'Exporting Fogo: Participatory Filmmaking, War on Poverty, and the Politics of Visibility', *Framework*, 55, 2, 220–47. Reproduced with permission of Wayne State University Press.

CHAPTER SEVEN

AN URBAN SITUATION:
THE HARTFORD PROJECT (1969) AND
THE NORTH AMERICAN CHALLENGE

This 'crew' will be at the heart of the North American challenge. [...] What is happening (or not happening) in Hartford is a model of many global situations.

– Colin Low (1969)

The questions that haunted Julian Biggs' and Colin Low's production team persisted as the OEO transferred the crew from Farmersville to an urban environment, specifically Hartford, Connecticut. The circumstances of a city in the midst of an urban rebellion throughout the late 1960s raised new challenges, particularly as the crew became more aligned with the radical politics of their Black Panther cohorts just as Donald Rumsfeld took the helm of the state agency. As soon as the final screening in Farmersville had concluded, Low recognised that Hartford was the next site for the Fogo process. The enthusiasm exhibited by the last audience in Farmersville in late 1968, while remarkable in its own way, was partly illusory and had a distorting effect on the state's perception of the Fogo process and its application. First, the experience of the final screening in *Farmersville* predisposed policymakers to conclude that *The Farmersville Project* had succeeded, that it was – in essence – complete. In fact, most of the crew – including Low, Biggs, Lanford and Glascock – believed that it was premature to draw any such conclusions regarding the effects of their filmmaking on the community. While their purpose was always somewhat abstract, the team clung to the abiding notion that this was always a *process* that would necessitate an ongoing commitment on the part of the OEO to fund its activities for many more months, if not years. While Henry Lanford was retained and continued to work in Farmersville after the initial project was completed, momentum had truly shifted to Hartford as Biggs, Glascock, Fields and Keramidas prepared for the city (see Pennybacker 2001b).

But aside from cutting *The Farmersville Project* short, the transition from a small agrarian community in California's Central Valley to a major American city rocked by riots was, for Low at least, difficult to imagine. Low's analytic disposition struggled to cognitively map this unique and highly tenuous urban community, with all the various constituencies in play. Hartford at this time was a liberal northeastern city experiencing an extensive political awakening on the part of the city's African American and Puerto Rican communities. Issues of political representation, police brutality and failing schools were prominent and contributed to a pervasive sense of disenfranchisement in Hartford's North End. In two short years, the Fogo process had graduated from its inaugural application in Newfoundland – over the very specific political issue of resettlement – to Hartford and an urban space that was, Low suspected, metonymically tied to deeper structural problems. Low found the transition from a small fishing community to an agrarian one easier to manage and both suited his sensibility. However, Hartford represented a qualitative leap forward in political, social and economic terms. Low was 'startled' by the suggestion to take this next step:

> I thought we should have worked longer in Farmersville and finished it elegantly. And the urban situation worried me because I didn't think that I was up to it. I felt all right about going to Farmersville because I knew agriculture and I knew farmers and I could talk to them. I knew fishermen really. But the whole idea of going into anything [as] large and important as a major city … I couldn't feel it. (ibid.)

While Low was willing to participate as a consultant, he was clearly conscious of the boundaries of his personal experience and knowledge base (ibid.). Hartford represented something other, something outside his comfort zone. Low's feeling here is telling in hindsight. Biggs himself, by all accounts, was not as sceptical and enthusiastically embraced *The Hartford Project*, as did the other members of the crew and OEO staff. Nevertheless, the managerial posture of the Fogo process – already rife with contradiction and instability in Farmersville, as we have seen – reached a breaking point in Hartford as the crew on the ground increasingly allied themselves with the activists and reformers, to Anne Michaels' chagrin. The politics of crisis were, then, amplified by the social conditions of Hartford in the late 1960s and overwhelmed the *safe* mode of the Fogo process.

This final chapter continues our review of the OEO's flirtation with participatory educational filmmaking. As is consistent with the previous three chapters, the educational films discussed here are far removed from the neorealism of the early post-war period and, instead, reflect new approaches in documentary filmmaking. The verticality of *The Farmersville Project* soldiers on to Hartford where the production team struggles to complete the task at hand. Ensconced in an urban environment where social and economic inequalities are rampant, the racial look of the state-sponsored outsider is rattled and dispersed. The crew would no doubt have identified with Stoney's articulated desire to 'record history as it is made' (see chapter four). History was all around as Hartford – like other American cities at the time – was forced to reckon with the frustration felt by its African American and Puerto Rican communities. Like the other films discussed in this book, *The Hartford Project* is even more radically invested in the *documentary from below*, to chase down the *decisive moment* through its vertical posture. This was a documentary film series that was similar to *The Farmersville Project* in that it entailed the production of documentary shorts designed to compel discussion among the residents of the city as well as its political leadership. However, *The Hartford Project* – filmed in 1969 – was left somewhat incomplete and the total number of films produced remains ambiguous, although I was able to review a total of twenty-five completed films of varying lengths because of the work of the Hartford Studies Project at Trinity College.[1] This heightened sense of incompletion speaks to the troubled nature of the production, which included Julian Biggs' health struggles as well as the complexity of the urban environment. The production's tenuous rollout conjoined with the post-Fordist conditions of an American city undermined the stability of these films' liberal racial look and encouraged even further collaboration than was evident in Farmersville. One of the most notable aspects of *The Hartford Project* is the team's collaboration with Charles 'Butch' Lewis, a community leader in Hartford and founder of the city's chapter of the Black Panther Party. Lewis brought both an insider's access as well as a point of view that would have otherwise been absent from the production. Lewis's involvement ultimately rewires the look of the managerial liberal and opens it up to the realities of political and social conflict.

What follows is an overview of the team's work in Hartford as well as an analysis of the films produced as part of *The Hartford Project* and their specific brand of Fogo-inspired verticality, or in this case a *radical verticality*. These films retain the fragmentary or longitudinal structure of their counterparts from *The Farmersville Project*, while upholding the *safe* posture preferred by Low and Michaels. And yet the films did not elicit the same enthusiasm from Michaels and, by all accounts, Biggs and Verna Fields. As we will see, Michaels expressed disappointment over the politicised tone of the films produced for *The Hartford Project*. For her, the films were too anti-establishment. While my own readings of the films don't necessarily coincide, I can see how the voices and experiences they reflect would upset the managerial liberal perspective. The shift in reaction from OEO staffers is dialectically motivated by both the political orientation of the subjects interviewed as well as by the filmmakers' situation in an urban environment charged with a deep-seated sense of disenfranchisement on the part of the city's African American and Puerto Rican citizenry. The material conditions of Hartford in 1969 steep the Fogo process in a radical critique as the teachers, students, activists, political representatives and reformers featured in the films speak to the systemic neglect of the needs of the North End. From the vantage point of OEO administrators, the films were too aligned with the disenfranchised, with the malcontent, and ultimately undercut the Fogo ethos of rational communication. Of all the educational films reviewed in this book, *The Hartford Project* – for us – represents a sharp retreat of the liberal racial look through its collaborative and even failed attempt to map the spatial and temporal coordinates of an urban crisis. The suggestion of *failure* is not intended to be read negatively. Instead, the managerial 'failure' of *The Hartford Project* is tethered to its refusal to be above the fray, to truly share the means of production with a representative from the community.

The fractured and incomplete nature of the project also complicates what Paula J. Massood has characterised as a familiar *chronotope* in African American cinema. Following Mikhail Bakhtin's critical theory, Massood demonstrates the usefulness of the concept of the chronotope:

> It is, as the term suggests, a *topos* (a place, person, figure) that embodies (or is embodied by) *chronos* (time). Places as disparate as roads, castles, salons, thresholds, and trains function as 'materialized history,' where temporal relationships are literalized by the objects, spaces, or persons with which they intersect. [...] The chronotope's links to genre make it a salient theoretical construct for this study because particular African American genres are defined or enabled by certain spatiotemporal tropes, such as the antebellum South in black-cast musicals or the contemporary city in hood films. (2003: 4–5).

The Hartford Project's vertical engagement with the city, as well as its collaborative stance, reflects a concrete spatiotemporal fixture: Hartford in 1969. While the films themselves are like bits of 'materialized history' as well as time, their meaning and significance swells over the years as 'Hartford '69' grows both more distant and familiar in light of continued legacies of neglect and inequality in the American city. The films of *The Hartford Project* also complicate the more familiar *chronotope* noted by Massood, the 'contemporary city in hood films'.

Vertical portraiture of community leaders forges a civic space where typically stereotyped African American and Puerto Rican peoples are allowed to speak before a camera uninterrupted and, as a result, a new inflection of the familiar chronotope of the city is achieved. The result is a picture of 'Hartford '69' that refuses a clear narrative through its polyvocality and unease with managerial resolutions.

A Response of Conscience: Preparing for Production in Hartford

The public affairs staff at the OEO had been following the social and economic tensions in Hartford, most notably Herbert Kramer, who had a home in the city (see Pennybacker 2001a). Kramer was 'impressed' with the work of the Greater Hartford Corporation – a coalition of regional business leaders, led by F. Peter Libassi – on issues such as 'urban blight' (ibid.). This effort and others left Kramer with the impression that, as Michaels put it, there 'were good people that we could work with' (ibid.). But beyond the philanthropic efforts of Hartford's elites, the political uprisings in the city were no doubt a critical factor in any effort to engage Hartford in the late 1960s. Lewis later claimed that the riots in 1967 were particularly responsible for drawing the attention of OEO staff (see McFarland 2000).

The period between *The Farmersville Project* and *The Hartford Project* – a matter of months – was a turbulent one for the filmmakers. During this time Low was shuttling back and forth between Japan, Canada and the United States as he developed two very different film practices enacting two divergent uses of the adjective 'vertical': these included new innovations in large, vertical screen formats – what was to become IMAX – and participatory or 'vertical' filmmaking in the form of the Fogo process (see Pennybacker 2001b). Biggs had come down with pneumonia, but, once recovered, was still 'keen to go to Hartford' (ibid.) and continue his work for the OEO. Low informed Biggs that, while he would consult with the production team, he would remain in Montreal for the duration of any application of the Fogo process to a major American city (ibid.). Most of the crew on *The Farmersville Project* made the transition to Hartford in March 1969, including Baylis Glascock and Harry Keramidas. Richard Pearce, cinematographer, and Joseph Louw, sound recordist, also joined the production team (see Charbonneau 2015a, 2015b).

No doubt, the crew's intent as they transitioned from Farmersville to Hartford was to uphold the managerial liberal insistence on both remaining above the fray while also enhancing communication as a form of rational conflict mediation. In a handwritten outline on the core 'objectives' of *The Hartford Project*,

Low listed six essential aims articulating the basic principles of the Fogo process. The fourth is the most pivotal and substantive as it highlights the filmmakers' desire to enhance 'community dialogue' and 'communication loops' (n.d.). This stance was designed to keep the filmmakers entrenched in the OEO's ethos of self-help. Michaels underscores the OEO's managerial liberal ideology and its self-help predisposition quite explicitly in reflections on the legacy of the War on Poverty:

> OEO, I think was a great agency. I still do and a lot of it still exists today and I think it is probably the most misunderstood. We had nothing to do with welfare. We had nothing to do with the kinds of stuff that people talk about. Quite the contrary. It was an empowerment agency that believed that people should [be] empowered to do things for themselves and not hurt other people. And it wasn't an exclusionary agency. [...] Business and social agencies and poor folk ... and the politicos and you mix them all up in one big pot and you let them solve their own problems as they defined it. And I still think it is the only answer to these kinds of situations. What I liked about what I saw in the film, and which I think we showed we could do, was it removed the labels of who people were and it removed the business of this one had power and this one didn't have power and all that. And it leveled out the playing field so that ideas and attitudes can emerge rather than someone's social position. (Pennybacker 2001a).

This view of the agency as a neutral arbiter – dialectically positioned to somehow intervene without interfering – dovetails with Low's belief that the crew should film without advocating for any political point of view by replicating the passive presence pursued in Farmersville. The foundation for the Fogo process, according to Michaels, was an attentive silence designed to invite expressivity from subjects on the ground: if 'people ... are listened to in a certain way ... with interest [and] respect, then [they will] have something to say' (ibid.). The aim was always community development and to use film 'to get away from the violence and the stigmas and the labeling of people' (ibid.).

As a result of Low's distance from the *The Hartford Project*, he authored an overview of the Fogo process's applicability to an urban environment, entitled 'Notes on Hartford' (1969). In line with the crew's first few days on *The Farmersville Project*, Low insisted that the 'crew should be visible in as many parts of the community as possible (particularly ghetto)' (ibid.). He believed that the team in Hartford should avoid the temptation to focus exclusively on 'economic and political factors' (ibid.). Not unlike *The Farmersville Project*, Low maintained that 'the most important work that could be accomplished is that of creating dialogue at an *almost* horizontal level within the ghetto' (ibid.; emphasis in original). The supposed problem in Hartford, from this vantage point, becomes the lack of 'consensus' (ibid.). Low had hoped that the films produced in Hartford might 'subtly reveal the reasons for lack of unified front without increasing abrasion' (ibid.). For him, what was needed – above all – was 'cohesion', 'unity' and 'synthesis' in the face of an entrenched social and economic 'fragmentation' (ibid.). These problems should not be seen as exclusively the by-product of a devious 'establishment', but – rather – 'the result of the same kind of selfish divisions, inertia, [and] failure to communicate that exists at the grass roots' (ibid.). Both the 'establishment' and the 'ghetto' fail to see the full 'possibilities [both] human and economic' that are intrinsic to the city of Hartford (ibid.). Aware of the presumptuousness of his claim, Low acknowledged that it 'sounds like an idea that I'm imposing – actually, I simply have confidence that if the project attitude is essentially optimistic, *this idea* will emerge' (ibid.; emphasis in original).

Reflecting on all this more than three decades later, Michaels made special note of the 'many problems' facing Hartford in the late 1960s (see Pennybacker 2001a). The neglect of the city's North End, in particular, was the most prominent in her mind. Michaels bemoaned the conflict between 'the establishment and the people', which obscured what she felt was a genuine 'dependence' or necessary connection between these two sides (ibid.). 'And,' she insisted, 'if they didn't get themselves [the establishment and the people] together and work [with one another] they were going to have [additional] problems' (ibid.). The alienation between the supposed two sides is the underlying factor – from Michaels' point of view – for the riots, violence and general decline of the city. She also insisted that the violence was, ultimately, 'not important', just an expression of a deeper 'frustration'. Michaels put it simply: 'I forgot about the violence' (ibid.).

Low was emphatic that *The Hartford Project* should pursue a politics of optimism:

In many situations today, attitudes have become so negative that the expression of optimism is something of a shock. The expression of optimism coming from people who have chosen a political pose of pessimism to conform with the popular pessimism and cynacism [sic] can have a strong effect. This cannot be tricked – faked or rigged – but, it can be watched for. People who take a habitually negative response *cannot* look at themselves played back without feeling the need to modify the image. This *was* demonstrated in Farmersville. (1969; emphasis in original)

Low wanted to make sure that the crew never lost sight of the fact 'that they are essentially outsiders-strangers' (ibid.). Impassivity continued to be the preferred mode of interviewing: 'The technique of interview is essentially Socratic,' he wrote, 'anyone who *consistently advises, identifies or becomes* visibly emotionally involved does not belong in this activity' (ibid.; emphasis in original). Perhaps aware that the project could do more damage if not applied 'correctly' or in a manner that he envisions, Low insisted that 'if the Office of Economic Opportunity does not know what this project is all about, it should not finance it' (ibid.). In a similar vein, Low warns that 'if a member of this project feels that confrontation and attack are more valid or practical forms of precipitating social change than dialogue then he should have the integrity to stand aside and observe' (ibid.). Nevertheless, such a staunch insistence on observation was coupled with his recognition of the significance of expression on the part of the filmed subject. Low, then, sticks close to the managerial line by insisting on the '*power* in expression … if there is undeniable truth and integrity behind [it]' (ibid.; emphasis in original). Such earnestness 'is capable of generating a *response of conscience* in the observer' (ibid.; emphasis in original). Nevertheless, the issue of whether these films – 'this kind of social document' – are capable of inciting such a reaction 'is a question' (ibid.). He suggests that these films can, as long as they are 'recorded with sufficient sincerity, integrity and compassion and presented with simplicity' (ibid.).

Ultimately, in spite of his hesitance, *The Hartford Project* was worth pursuing for Low because of the significance of the American city and the historical moment of the late 1960s. He saw Hartford as an extension of 'many global situations', where the city materialises broader cultural and systemic clashes around the world: 'capitalism – socialism – black – white – wealth – poverty – individualism – collectivization – welfare – automation' (ibid.). The situation facing Hartford, Low insisted, exceeded his or anyone's cognitive frame: 'Little is really known about all the forces at work[:] economic, social and political [and as a result] the best attitude to take … is one of humility' (ibid.).

Finally, on 16 March, a story in *The Hartford Courant* announced a 'tentative plan to produce a movie showing life in Hartford's ghetto' (Anon. 1969b). The report noted that the plans for production 'were discussed with the Community Renewal Team and the Task Force on Neighborhood Services' (ibid.) and would move quickly to the City Council for consideration and approval. Herbert Kramer – now the former Head of Public Affairs for the OEO – was quoted emphasising how the 'film will be patterned after one produced in Farmersville' (ibid.). The article further solidified the view that *The Farmersville Project* was a success:

The film made in California points out attitudes toward the community and the people in it. When city officials later viewed the film, Kramer said, they were for the first time aware of the real turmoil in the community. (Ibid.)

After viewing forty-five minutes of footage from *The Farmersville Project*, Hartford's City Council voted to support *The Hartford Project*, whose budget of $80,000 would be drawn from the OEO's coffers (Anon. 1969a). The vote came about in spite of the expressed nervousness of the mayor, Antonina 'Ann' Uccello, who reportedly said that she was 'afraid of anything, frankly, that would rock the boat' (qtd. in ibid.). Kramer spoke to the council and emphasised the production team's plans to film 'people from all walks of life in the Hartford area' (ibid.) during the spring and summer (April through July). In keeping with the Fogo method, Kramer also announced plans to screen the resulting films 'at four or five places each week followed by a discussion period' (ibid.). Of the four councilpersons, George Levine and Allyn A. Martin both spoke favourably of the project, with the former expressing hope that it could 'remove the element of confrontation from communication' and the latter insisting on the project's potential to compel new perspectives or 'to see ourselves as others see us' (qtd. in ibid.). Kramer concurred with both and emphasised the crew's commitment to 'not film' any violence as well as their deep-rooted objectivity ('there is no point of view that the film maker takes to this'; qtd. in ibid.). It was Kramer's belief that *The Hartford Project* would 'give people a chance to feel they are being heard and seen and that their gripes are being listened to' (ibid.).

The OEO specifically sought out local collaborators for *The Hartford Project* in the North End. Michaels herself had heard that Lewis would likely support the OEO's work. Initially Low was concerned that working in African American neighbourhoods – or being able to 'operate in the black community' – would necessitate funds for bribery to accommodate unwanted 'white faces' with cameras (Pennybacker 2001a). But it was Lewis who insisted to Low that the crew would be able to film without the need 'to pay anybody off' (ibid.). According to Michaels, once they had Lewis's support and assurance, any lingering hesitation went away (ibid.). Lewis was a veteran of the Vietnam War and the 'head of the Black Panther Party at the time' (McFarland 2000). He was a natural ally partly due to his status in the African American community of Hartford, but also in light of his interest in filmmaking. As he later commented: 'I always wanted to learn about cameras and never had a chance' (ibid.). Lewis's involvement lent the production an aura of local credibility and, in return, he received training in 16-millimeter cinematography and sound recording (ibid.). In fact, Biggs 'was like a drill sergeant', as Lewis later recalled (ibid.). The skills Lewis acquired by working with the OEO crew later led him to New York where he worked for the American Film Council (ibid.). And yet, in the end, it was the prospects for work that initially appealed to Lewis. At first, he recalled, 'I thought it was a crock of bull … but it was money, and I had a job, and [it helped keep] the police off my ass' (ibid.).

The production team arrived in Hartford in the midst of urban turmoil. One of the goals was to take advantage of this timing and encourage 'people to come in [and] talk' (ibid.). They also seized on the opportunity to film a community meeting and this was quickly arranged – in part – thanks to Lewis's dual status as both a meeting participant and member of the film crew (ibid.). Lewis later claimed that – throughout the production – 'no one turned us down' (ibid.). His modesty leads him to largely attribute this fact to the 'charisma' of Biggs (ibid.). 'I think Julian could sit down and talk to the devil and convince him to come on camera,' he remarked (ibid.). But clearly another reason for the crew's success in this regard was the presence and participation of Lewis, helping to bridge the gap between insider and outsider at a very delicate time in the history of Hartford.

While much of the crew's experience remains unclear, what is evident from interviews conducted with the Hartford Studies Project at Trinity College is that Michaels was growing increasingly frustrated with the political posture of the production. In the early weeks of *The Hartford Project*, Michaels notes that the production team was by and large disinclined to engage those who represented the 'establishment' or the power structure in the city. This attitude was pervasive enough to leave Fields frustrated. 'She was fighting all the time,' Michaels noted (Pennybacker 2001a). The other filmmakers were becoming more politicised than was the case in Farmersville and Fields struggled to hold the line. As Michaels sums up, Fields 'got caught up in this … and didn't really know what to do about it' (ibid.). In fact, when Biggs finally returned to Hartford, he set out to mitigate the increasing alliance between the production team and the so-called radicals (ibid.). Of course, Michaels was relatively distant or uninvolved with *The Hartford Project* as the films were being produced. She later expressed regrets at not having 'steered' the endeavour enough, to ensure that the Fogo ethos was upheld by the production team. 'I am not, and I never was an administrator,' she insists (ibid.). Michaels also claims responsibility for continuing the supervisory work of Verna Fields on *The Hartford Project*. From her point of view, Fields encountered 'big problems' as the film crew became increasingly intent on moving away from the predominant *safe* mode of interaction pursued in Farmersville. In Michaels' words, the crew was 'trying to take over the project' through their pursuit of 'problem exposés' (ibid.). Fields had in fact articulated to Michaels a deep 'frustration about not being able to control the crew' in this regard (ibid.).

From Michaels' vantage point, the filmmakers lost perspective on the core values of the Fogo process. The critical violation, in her mind, is the crew's gravitation towards the critical issues of race and class in Hartford. While at first glance the critique strikes one as odd, it speaks to the precariousness of the film crew's *safe* mode of interaction in Farmersville. The crew's methodology was delicate to begin with and was fundamentally torn between an ethos of intervention and a commitment to observation, or an insistence on cultivating a *passive presence*. Clearly, this contradiction played out differently and perhaps more overtly in Hartford, in an urban environment embroiled in racial and class tensions (ibid.). Essentially, for Michaels, these were not Fogo films. Specifically, the filmmakers homed in on social problems at the expense of 'understanding the people' involved (ibid.). 'Problem oriented' and 'subject oriented', the films of *The Hartford Project* fell short of the Fogo standard to 'zero in on what was right' rather than 'what was wrong' (ibid.). Michaels is giving voice here to a broader managerial insistence on mitigating conflict through communication, by grounding discourse first in a presumably relatable human experience that is separate from the messy world of politics, conflict and frustration (ibid.).

In hindsight, Michaels believes everyone involved on the OEO side – including her – lacked 'a clear understanding of what we were doing' (ibid.). Her preference was to produce a series of films that would 'uncover' Hartford in a totalising way, 'not a particular block in the community' (ibid.). While the film crew was bogged down trying to document the 'social ills' of the city, Michaels felt they too readily assumed the perspective of the disenfranchised and failed to be fully 'inclusive', ultimately 'promoting more frustration' (ibid.). The activist stance of the film crew belied what Michaels' felt was the predominant aim of the Fogo process to facilitate communication and, in her words, 'that is a very intellectual … managerial and … academic' pursuit (ibid.). While she never saw herself as an administrator, Michaels, in retrospective, clearly articulates the appeal of the Fogo ethos and its animation of a managerial liberal ideal:

> I really believe … that most people are basically good and decent unless they are psychopaths. And that if you can find that aspect of people and identify it, it will make them more likely to do the kinds of things that will benefit other people. I think the Fogo technique, and it is a technique, makes this possible because of the removal of confrontation, of anger, of violence … and allowing people to deal with the problem. (Ibid.)

Michaels insists that the project failed to promote cooperation between the various sides of Hartford's racial and economic conflicts. The Fogo vision was intended to drive people 'to figure out the solutions to their own problems with the help of government … insurance … whatever you want … they have to work together.' What should have been avoided were approaches that prompted 'screaming and yelling' about abuse, whether such clamour emanates from the 'poor' or the 'establishment' (ibid.).

Radical Verticalities: The Films of *The Hartford Project*

To be clear, my claim is not that the films of *The Hartford Project* are more radical than their counterparts from Farmersville because the individuals and groups featured are somehow more sophisticated or articulate in their politics. Nor do I think that the other filmmakers necessarily intended to diverge from Low's vision and approach Hartford with a more politicised stance, shedding the familiarity of the Fogo process's *safe* mode of production. Rather, I would suggest that these films exhibit a radicalised verticality on the basis of their heightened historical consciousness given the events of Hartford in 1969. The filmmakers, perhaps, had a more concrete sense of bearing witness to real historical change. In Hartford, the filmmakers were confronted with a condensation of activities, people, classes and struggles and the resulting films more directly register frustration and confrontation than was represented by *The Farmersville Project*. From this point of view, Michaels is both right and wrong to point the finger at the crew for the films' heightened politicisation. She is correct that the tone in these films differs from *The Farmersville Project*, but this more radical posture is the result of the filmmakers' tangible historical conditions rather than a mere shift in attitude.

The films of *The Hartford Project* often refrain from directly addressing Hartford's urban disturbances, which were intensifying throughout the late 1960s. Instead, many of the films are works of portraiture – of individuals, families and groups – that waver in their focus on particular social problems. In some cases, concern with the 'Hartford disturbances' is woven into the expressions elicited by the crew. And in others they barely register as the production team records testimonies about everyday life from different residents of the city. As vertical films, they embrace the open-endedness of other educational films and seek to promote discussion. And, more specifically, the sounds and imagery recorded echo life in Hartford at a particular moment in time. Ultimately, Michaels' critique of the films speaks more to their social and historical surroundings then the substance of the films themselves. Taken together the films simultaneously leave the intensity of the moment out of frame while also addressing it by hinting at a broader backdrop of alienation and frustration.

One of the community profiles produced by the filmmakers includes a look at Hartford's 'street academy' founded by Lewis. Given Lewis's involvement in *The Hartford Project*, it was natural to start with one of his seminal contributions to the disenfranchised youth of the city. Lewis recognised that Hartford was facing a major crisis as significant numbers of students were simply 'not going to school' and were falling through the cracks of the educational system. He eventually visited Harlem and witnessed the success of the Black Panthers' street academy firsthand with the intent of replicating their experience in Hartford. Lewis later recruited Professor Oscar Walters, a faculty member of the Art Department at the University of Connecticut and one of the university's first African Americans to receive tenure, to serve as the street academy's first principal. Lewis himself served as the academy's vice principal (see McFarland 2000).

Entitled *A Street Academy*, the film features commentary from both Walters and Lewis on the history of the academy and stylistically embodies the same *safe mode* of production we witnessed at work in films like *Danny and Leo*. While the film unfolds across two shots (with only one edit), the cinematographic approach entails a series of pans and tilts as the camera shifts from speaker to speaker, often zooming in as a way to punctuate a particular sentiment. To be clear, the only words heard on the film come from Walters and Lewis. We receive no aural cues from the filmmakers. Instead, the improvisational camerawork registers both an encounter that unfolds in real time and a deferential posture on the part of the crew as their work implies a willingness to listen while actively observing. The opening two shot also reminds one of *Hector and Ruben*, a film from *The Farmersville Project* that was equally concerned with representing voices who were otherwise ignored. The politics of *A Street Academy* emerge precisely out of the stillness of the film and the filmmakers' willingness to hold back. The *safe mode* of the Fogo process simultaneously reassures the subjects of the film, Walters and Lewis, while also potentially challenging city elites. The film speaks to the city's power structure by presenting an intimate work of cinematic portraiture in which two African American men speak about the intersection of revolutionary politics with the familiar challenges of running a school. At one point, Walters draws a connection between the academy's radical politics and its creative pedagogy:

> The main problem … is that we had ideas in terms of education – like using the Polaroid Land Cameras – to bring out things that a child, student or young man might normally be inhibited about bringing out. He would take the camera and he would go out and he would do some shots and we would

talk about it. This was Jim Scully's class, a prize-winning poet from the university [James Scully, from the University of Connecticut].

Walters' use of the Polaroid cameras to encourage students to see the world differently synchronises with the aims of the Fogo process as a form of filmic community development – recall that the desired aim of the Fogo process is to use cinema as a way to reconfigure a community's sense of itself. The screen is used to stage views of subjects and experiences that are often overlooked or marginalised by a community's power structure. Similarly, Walters deploys Polaroid cameras to engender a resonate posture of passive observation. He offers his students a temporary reprieve from language so that vision can become a source of knowledge as well as play. Walters is also explicit about the academy's revolutionary politics, noting that the school taught American history through the radical political lens of figures like Eldridge Cleaver.

> We found that we could best get history done – by not specifically focusing on black history – but giving it some sort of light through Cleaver's book. We started with Cleaver's book for a history course. [...] We got into 'revolution' in terms of American history, which is founded on revolution. [...]

Figure 23. Oscar Walters (left) and Butch Lewis (right), from "A Street Academy," from *The Hartford Project* (1969).

PROJECTING RACE

We [drew on educational approaches] other than the traditional means of throwing out reading, writing and arithmetic in a very structured manner. We could get to the youngsters a lot better by approaching them in their own manner.

For the organisers of the school, the revolutionary stance is not simply about a particular message. Rather, it also involves a different way of seeing and inhabiting the world.

The other films of *The Hartford Project* remain similarly disciplined in assuming the posture of passive observation, to ensure that repressed voices and experiences are heard and seen. In *Los puertorriqueños y la corte* [*Puerto Ricans and the Court*] and *Y otra mas* [*Another One*] the film crew recorded a pair of conversations with Reverend Charles Pickett, minister of the Episcopal Metropolitan Mission and head of the Spanish Action Coalition; Tito Santiago, who was working with the Community Renewal Team in Hartford (CRT); and María Sánchez, *la madrina* of the Puerto Rican community and who co-founded the Spanish Action Coalition in 1967 (see Cruz 1998: 60). The first conversation centres on the politics of language in the Hartford court system and takes place in Sánchez's store front. The way in which the conversation unfolds in this particular space positions the viewer as a casual observer while also grounding a discussion of social problems with everyday life. Rendering this conversation and this space visible onscreen was a way for the production team to, again, foreground spaces, political views and accents that have been otherwise repressed by the institutions governing the city. It is also crucial to note that the conversation takes place entirely in Spanish. Both the substance of the conversation as well as the language in which it plays out affirm the central point of the film. From the vantage point of all three participants, translation problems saturate the court system, leaving Puerto Rican defendants often at a severe disadvantage. Santiago, who had also worked for Greater Hartford Legal Aid, notes how court-assigned translators are frequently ill-equipped to communicate with Puerto Rican defendants:

Many times the translation [in the courts] is different from the Spanish we speak on the street. For this same reason, we know that to translate is not just to translate the word professionally. Because many of the defendants are not professionals and a qualified translator with a college or a postgraduate degree translates the word finely, like in college. Thus, the defendant doesn't understand what he says in this way. And so it doesn't bother him to say 'yes' or 'no' if they say 'you are guilty of this', he says yes without knowing what they are saying. The translator has to … study for at least a year how this is said by the middle class … especially the middle class people who haven't completed 8th grade … [they are the ones] who have to understand the one who will translate and who will work with them, especially in the court.

Sánchez chimes in with her own anecdote about the risks of poor translation:

I remember that once I was in the court with my husband, and there was a woman [translator] who wasn't Puerto Rican. […] They almost arrested me there because I stood up from the seat to help a Puerto Rican who was there and to whom [the translator] was saying the opposite of what the judge told her, she said the opposite to the Puerto Rican, and she had the boy confused there, so that if I [had not spoken], he would have gotten six or seven months in jail, unnecessarily.

The nature of the conversation and the reliance on Spanish throughout speaks to the crew's adherence to Low's methodological preference. Recall that Low insisted on the team's deployment of a safe mode of production, allowing for various perspectives to be seen and heard without any ideological imposition from the filmmakers. A film like this could hardly be considered a violation of the Fogo process and yet the critical perspective on the court system ruffles feathers, renders the managerial liberal uncomfortable and perhaps explains the negative attitude towards *The Hartford Project* on the part of OEO staffers. As a vertical film, it is not necessarily evidence of the social problems described within it. And yet it is evidence of these leaders' experiences and views. Such a film compels the managerial liberal to actively close the gap between ideological assumptions and the social experiences of those featured in the film. While we as viewers are left feeling as if we are *listening in* as observers, there is a countervailing feeling that the film camera stages this conversation *for us*. The conversation is for the benefit of city leaders and not simply an internal one by Puerto Ricans for Puerto Ricans. And yet the insistence on speaking in Spanish challenges the members of the audience who only speak English to do the necessary work to understand the perspective of the film and the citizens who are featured. In *Y otra mas*, Sántiago notes that the xenophobic reactions to Spanish overdetermines the Puerto Rican experience in the city and differentiates it from African American experiences. 'When the Puerto Rican goes to the factory,' she insists, 'they don't reject him because of the last name or because of the colour, they reject him because he doesn't speak English.' In a sense, this pair of films seeks to turn the tables and normalise what is too often rendered strange and other.

Figure 24. María Sánchez and Reverend Charles Pickett in 'Los puertorriqueños y la corte', from *The Hartford Project* (1969).

While many other films of *The Hartford Project* are portraits of individuals – including *Mrs Blake*; *Mary Gilbertson: A Teacher at Weaver High School*; *Margaret Tedone*; *Jack Dollard: A School Principal*; and *Colin Bennett: A Realtor* – most entail these similar kinds of interactions between community leaders. In the case of the films just discussed – *A Street Academy*, *Los puertorriqueños y la corte*, and *Y otra mas* – the discussions featured the voices and experiences of those who are typically marginalised by mainstream discourses and practices that prevail in the city. By contrast, films like *Problem and Commitment* and *Business and Government* gather together the power brokers of the city and are filmed as Julian Biggs himself moderates the discussion. The subjects of both films include Biggs, George Kinsella (city councilman), Howard Klebanoff (state representative), James English (President, Connecticut Bank and Trust), Norris O'Neal (state representative), George Ritter (state representative) and Nicholas Carbone (city councilman). The opening of the film is indicative of the passive posture promoted by Low and Michaels. After a brief identification of the above individuals, we witness the following exchange in *Problem and Commitment*:

> *Voice*: Are you going to throw out some questions?
> *Biggs*: Only if it stalls.

Voice: Huh.

Ritter: Are you going to start us out with any questions?

Biggs: I don't know. Do you really need any?

English: George Ritter's going to do all the talking [laughs].

Biggs: We found that we can't, we can't do anything really useful if the entire output of three months of work is problem, problem, problem, negative, negative, negative. Nobody would live anywhere if it was all negative; so sometimes we like to hear a few of the positives, too. What keeps a person here? The reasons that you're here might be quite different than the reasons some other people are kept here. From what I've heard already I would strongly suspect that is so. But to begin with, I'll ask a question: What do you think is the most positive or compelling reason for a person to live in this town?

Biggs opens by embodying what Low described earlier as the 'outsider-stranger'. He starts out by repressing any sense of an emotional alignment with a particular perspective. Nevertheless, once prodded, Biggs cracks. His incredulousness at the interviewees' need for questions gives way to his pronouncement of a fatigue with all that is 'negative, negative, negative'. Michaels' earlier sentiments that people are 'basically good' as well as her preference for the 'removal of confrontation' in the Fogo films synchronises with Biggs's exhortation to focus on the positive.

And yet in spite of this set-up for discussion, the participants do not necessarily follow Biggs' lead. English, for instance, reminds Biggs that the circumstances facing Hartford are similar to those facing other American 'urban centers'. He insists people often don't 'have much choice' about where they live: '[One] has to live in an urban center of one sort or another, at least most people do.' This response – coming from the president of a bank – quickly exposes Biggs' initial comment that 'nobody would live anywhere if it was all negative' as a kind of outsider idealism that is blind to the material conditions that govern individual and group behaviour. This exchange, one of the few involving a member of the production team onscreen, sheds light on a fundamental contradiction in the managerial mindset of Low and Michaels. We saw it in Low's methodological blueprint for *The Hartford Project* where he adopts a modest position of the simple outsider while also insisting that there are possibilities, 'human and economic', that the 'establishment' and 'ghetto' do not yet grasp. Even more to the point, recall Low's insistence that his approach will allow ideas to 'emerge' without imposition from the film crew (1969). And, of course, any crew member who prefers 'confrontation … should have the integrity to stand aside' (ibid.).

Perhaps not surprisingly, we have arrived at an almost perfect reiteration of the liberal advocate we saw represented in the more conventional OEO training films of the mid-1960s (see chapter five). We shall recall that the liberal advocacy depicted in many of the OEO training films featured a dialectical tension between *transformation* and *refraction* grounded in the figure of the white advocate. To varying degrees, these films suggest an advocate who intervenes at the behest of the liberal state to transform the downtrodden into newly made citizens prepped and ready to compete in the marketplace. But, of course, a countervailing force intervenes as the advocate – especially in *A Year Towards Tomorrow* (see chapter five) – partly disavows this arrogant charge and sublimates it in favour of refraction. The advocate subsequently claims to be a refractive presence that does not impose change, but merely facilitates the change that lay dormant inside the downtrodden. In the above sequence, Biggs' refusal to commence the proceedings with a key question registers this tendency towards refraction in the Fogo process. 'Do you really need any [questions]?' he asks. This implies a kind of false modesty in that Biggs assumes the passive presence of the liberal observer, cognisant of suppressing his own emotional and intellectual desires as an outsider. Similarly, Low is adamant that emotions should be controlled on the part of the production team in Hartford.

But, of course, this refractive stance conceals as much as it reveals. It exists in tension with Low's follow-up proclamation that he sees something the establishment and the 'ghetto' do not. And when Biggs is compelled by the group to finally articulate a prompt for discussion, the managerial liberal voice rears its head, resonating with Michaels' retrospective comments. The Fogo imagination, at this particular juncture, grows weary of complaints and negativity. For Biggs, conditions in the city cannot be *all* bad. And the embarrassing nature of this sentiment is directly confronted as the president of the Connecticut Bank and Trust reminds Biggs of the crisis of, not just Hartford, but the American city in general.

This mild disagreement speaks to a tension within the films of *The Hartford Project* between the crew's willingness to observe and listen, on the one hand, and the call of the crew's leaders to focus on the positives. The most powerful films are those like *The Street Academy* and *Los puertorriqueños y la corte* where the crew is willing to be still and listen to viewpoints that shed light on deep-seated, structural problems in the city. Lewis's provision of access to voices, experiences and spaces that are otherwise disregarded amounts to a seminal accomplishment of *The Hartford Project*. In this regard, its stillness is the project's most affirming character. The problem from the managerial liberal's point of view was to 'remove' confrontation and anger. And yet many of the films feature expressions of legitimate anger and frustration. *The Hartford Project*, then, inadvertently reflects a form of liberal advocacy that has reached its own outer limits of sustainability, where the contradictions between transformation and refraction implode. The managerial liberal posture of the Fogo process proves somewhat untenable here and mirrors the crisis point of the city itself. *The Hartford Project* fascinates for the same reason it frustrates. The films that resulted produce a fragmented picture of a particular space and time, of 'Harford '69', while also resisting managerial pressures towards rational solutionism.

Aftermath

Upon completion of *The Hartford Project*, the production team offered the films to the local public broadcasting station (see McFarland 2000). They were rebuffed and Lewis later speculated that the films and the experiences they depicted were too 'controversial' for public broadcasting at the time (ibid.). The films were eventually shipped to Washington and Lewis kept 16-millimeter prints of all the films in his basement for the next thirty years. Upon learning about the Hartford Studies Project at Trinity College, he made the decision to donate the films to the school with the hope that this would redeem his efforts decades after the fact (ibid.). *The Hartford Project*, Michaels admitted, 'never really got to where it was supposed to go'. This was largely because, for her, the project was hijacked by people who wanted to 'stick it' to the establishment. Eventually the OEO – under the leadership of Donald Rumsfeld – moved away from sponsoring community programmes, and the opportunity for continued work on *The Hartford Project* or other applications of the Fogo process was cut short (see Pennybacker 2001a).

From Michaels' perspective, not enough time was spent preparing for production activities in Hartford. A minimum of 'six months of preparation' was – in hindsight – needed for the team to properly implement the Fogo process. The end result, without such careful preliminary work, was a sense of disorganisation from the top on down. There was, in her mind, a clear lack of oversight and a failure to properly manage the production so that it was clear – for instance – where all the screenings would take place and that there was a proper means of transportation for locals to attend. Michaels regrets her laissez-faire approach as an administrator ('You don't go in there, as I did, and let a bunch of people loose and try and figure out what they are doing'; ibid.).

The War on Poverty prompted other ventures into the terrain of filmmaking and racial representation. There was, for instance, the launching of the Community Film Workshop Council (CFWC) in 1969 through a collaboration between the OEO and the American Film Institute (AFI). In spite of the deference to feature narratives and commercial cinema evident in the mission of the AFI, it conjoined its educational emphasis with the federal government to develop job skills among underserved, lower income communities through the establishment of the CFWC. Elbert Sampson worked at the New York branch of the CFWC and, in an interview with Pacifica Radio, noted that this effort was the 'result of a very strongly recognised need by people who were working with the AFI to provide a vehicle to get more minorities involved in the film industry here in the United States' (WBAI Radio 1970). Opening up access to the means of film production drove George Stoney's work in Canada as well. As the head of the National Film Board's 'Challenge for Change'/*Société nouvelle* from 1968 to 1970, Stoney led comparable efforts north of the border to encourage marginalised groups to express themselves through filmmaking. The results included films such as *These Are My People* (1969), produced by an all-Aboriginal crew.

The fascinating way in which both Stoney and Low traversed the American/Canadian border in the late 1960s points us toward Low's insistence on a broader 'North American challenge' in the quote opening this final chapter. More than this, Low speaks of 'global situations' that the uprisings in Hartford can only suggest. What we are supposed to make of these global situations is not entirely clear. But, taking the quote at face value, it is evident that the late 1960s as well as the more precise historical marker of May '68 triggers a recognition of a crisis cascading across many interconnected and divergent geographies. As a passage point into late capitalist and postcolonial horizons, we can think of the late 1960s as both an end and a retrenchment of the post-war racial look mapped throughout this book. The documentary films reviewed here chart the racial look of the post-war liberal, from one of psychic fixation (*The Quiet One*) to a more open, but anxious one desiring testimony and participation from marginalised subjects (*The Farmersville Project* and *The Hartford Project*).

Note

1 My interviews with Casey Case and Harry Keramidas confirmed that this is likely the total number of completed films from *The Hartford Project*; see Charbonneau 2015a, 2015b.

CONCLUSION

STILL BURNING:
PEDAGOGY, PARTICIPATION AND
DOCUMENTARY MEDIA

While the dramatic increase in scholarship on the moving image and its historical entanglement with educational institutions yields new data for film historians, this is only part of what is needed. The fact that a film exists is not the same as coming to grips with its significance. Any film scholar invested in uncovering overlooked or ignored orphan films, educational films and training films must also grapple with the stakes of her work, with its ultimate contribution to cinema studies and our shared understanding of the medium and its history. The scepticism and indifference that can greet such research is understandable given the extraordinarily narrow audience reach of these films as well as their failure to fit into more familiar generic categories. Nevertheless, film history is never completely closed and is continuously being redefined. The social and historical impact of cinema exceeds the confines of entertainment and the avant-garde, saturating many undiscovered nooks of everyday life. Research into non-theatrical filmmaking compels a shift in perspective even as it also rightly fields demands to rationalise its efforts. In other words, what is ultimately gained?

I have sought to answer this question at various points throughout this book. Filmmaking and its historical utility appears anew for us when sponsored cinema is accounted for. My discussion of educational film aesthetics calls attention to the work of institutions that we take for granted and reminds us of indiscrete or utilitarian forms of cinema. Bill Nichols has characterised the kind of pleasure one may derive from viewing documentary films as *epistephilia*, or a love of acquiring knowledge (1991: 178). Studying educational films, then, enhances our understanding of how and why knowledge was actively produced or generated. While the degree of procedural specificity and insularity can vary across educational films, the specific ones in focus here mobilise a range of addresses – procedural, affective, narrative, poetic, observational and participatory

– to serve a particular sponsor while also reflecting a broader impulse to capture intimate visions of everyday life. As a result, this study is motivated by not only a desire to share information about understudied or unknown educational film practices, but also by an insistence that these same works help us see film history differently as the medium became a post-war means of knowledge formation on behalf of liberal institutions. I also contend that these films are not merely *about* everyday life, but also *of* everyday life in ways that are distinct from more traditional and theatrical moving pictures. Their presumed disposability and shallow utility is more compelling to me than works of profound 'depth' by more familiar filmmakers, ironically revealing more about past sensibilities precisely because they are designed to have short lives. Such films are produced for the *here and now*, for a pedagogically intense moment that provide us with unique insights into the past.

And yet even as they complicate our perception of the past and enlarge our perspective on film history, these films resonate in light of our contemporary digital media moment. Low's characterisation of verticality is perfectly at home in an era of snack television, or portable media consumption. Moving imagery, video and digital, permeate our educational institutions as well as our everyday lives. Vertical media bombards us now and implies relentlessness rather than the modesty with which it was originally intended by Low. Social media also trends towards abstracting history and experience *from below*, from the vantage point of individual points of view that nevertheless aggregate into increasingly complex networks. The broad trajectory of that post-war *feeling of the new* at work in all of the films discussed here is perpetuated in new media contexts.

Tracing the post-war racial look is, furthermore, as vital as ever in light of present-day uprisings in cities such as Baltimore or Ferguson. Rather than simply account for overtly racist representations in educational films, *Projecting Race* has sought out the thorny racial politics of ostensibly liberal films and their correlative way of looking. What we have seen is a stubborn liberal sensibility that evolves along with the Civil Rights movement, swelling in intensity and focus as neorealist traits eventually yield to new documentary approaches. The paternalism of the white therapist and narrator in *The Quiet One* recedes in similar educational films like *Palmour Street* and, especially, *All My Babies*, where collaboration between the filmmakers and the African American subjects opens up space for conversation and discussion. Such a space is politically crucial in *All My Babies* where an insistence on modernisation must yield to the flexible and resistant legacy of African American midwifery. This fractured racial look is reimagined in the 1960s as new documentary techniques draw it into modes of liberal advocacy that conjoin passive witnessing with surreptitious agency, linking watching with the desire to change from the outside. This dynamic is actively staged in expository OEO films like *A Year Towards Tomorrow* and critically engaged in *With No One to Help Us*. In the latter film, the observational approach foregrounds the entanglement of War on Poverty projects with local struggles; whereas, in *Another Way*, the Drew Associates reassure audiences that tax dollars are being spent wisely on remaking troubled young men into good citizens.

Participatory and observational approaches are, finally, deployed in training and 'community development' filmmaking to cope with crisis in the streets and in the fields. *The Man in the Middle* is a police training film produced by George Stoney that blends a procedural address with an observational and participatory engagement with life in South Jamaica, Queens. Managing the transition between presidential administrations, the OEO finally pursued new communication experiments inspired by the National Film Board of Canada's Fogo process. Colin Low and Julian Biggs sought to help communities overcome internal conflict and strife by forging new lines of communication through filmmaking in Farmersville, California, and Hartford, Connecticut. The racial look of these experiments straddle the managerial liberal belief in rational communication and the anxious passive lens of the outsider crew.

At the end of her book, Alessandra Raengo echoes the ideological field of the documentaries discussed here when she writes that the 'paradigm' of the 'shadow has the ability to bring to the fore the idea that race most prominently inhabits the *state* and not the content of the image' (2013: 166). Read conventionally ('as a mirror'), she continues, 'the racial image is … a tool for knowing' (ibid.). But if we get past the idea of the image as a utility 'for knowing' – or as a kind of liberal pedagogy – we can see the ways in which social and historical fields intervene in and give sustenance to the shadow of race. If Raengo is right to suggest that blackness is not only a 'visual attribute' but an address for a 'place of avisuality' (2013: 17), then the post-war racial look represented by the educational documentaries reviewed here continually circles that place. To reiterate a point made throughout this project: the educational documentary represents an intensified nonfictional experience, balancing a specificity of procedure with the contingent flux of reality. The racial look in these films often sets out to pin down and render racial experiences legible and ultimately pedagogical. To this end, the proceduralism of educational documentaries would seem to flow easily with the dreams of precise fixation associated with the racial look. But we have also seen that the most interesting educational films embrace ambivalence and collaboration, opening up their frame to the contingencies of history.

BIBLIOGRAPHY

Aitken, Ian (1992) *Film and Reform: John Grierson and the Documentary Film Movement*. London: Routledge.

Allen, Robert and Douglas Gomery (1993) *Film History: Theory and Practice*. New York: McGraw-Hill.

Andrew, John A., III (1998) *Lyndon Johnson and the Great Society*. Chicago: Ivan R. Dee.

Anon. (n.d.) 'Discussion Outline for "Palmour Street"', Southern Educational Film Production Service, 1–3. George C. Stoney Papers, 1940–2009, Collection Number 04970, Box 30, Folder 790, The Southern Historical Collection at the Louis Round Wilson Special Collections Library, The University of North Carolina at Chapel Hill.

____ (n.d.) 'Films from Farmersville', The Farmersville Collection. Box 1. Folder 15. Chicano Studies Research Center. University of California, Los Angeles.

____ (1949a) 'Children Thrive on Wise Parental Devotion', Georgia Health 29.4 (April): 1, 4. George C. Stoney Papers, 1940–2009, Collection Number 04970, Box 29, Folder 789, The Southern Historical Collection at the Louis Round Wilson Special Collections Library, The University of North Carolina at Chapel Hill.

____ (1949b) 'Feeling All Right', *Film News: The Newsmagazine of Films and Filmstrips* (September) George C. Stoney Papers, 1940–2009, Collection Number 04970, Box 37, Folder 994, The Southern Historical Collection at the Louis Round Wilson Special Collections Library, The University of North Carolina at Chapel Hill.

____ (1950a) 'Beginning was good...' 2 August. George C. Stoney Papers, 1940–2009, Collection Number 04970, Box 30, Folder 790, The Southern Historical Collection at the Louis Round Wilson Special Collections Library, The University of North Carolina at Chapel Hill.

____ (1950b) '"Palmour Street": A Study in Family Life', The Survey: Family Training for Parent and Child (April), 188–9. George C. Stoney Papers, 1940–2009, Collection Number 04970, Box 30, Folder 790, The Southern Historical Collection at the Louis Round Wilson Special Collections Library, The University of North Carolina at Chapel Hill.

_____ (1968a) 'Agenda', The Farmersville Collection. Box 1, Folder 13. Chicano Studies Research Center, University of California, Los Angeles.

_____ (1968b) Memorandum. 24 Sept. Public Affairs Office, Office of Economic Opportunity. Bertrand M. Harding Papers, Office of Economic Opportunity, 1966–68, and Internal Revenue Service, 1955–66, Box 49, Conference File: Washington, D.C., Canadian National Film Grand [sic] Members, Lyndon Baines Johnson Library.

_____ (1968c) 'OEO-PAC Farmersville Film Project', The Farmersville Collection. Box 1, Folder 11, Chicano Studies Research Center, University of California, Los Angeles.

_____ (1968d) 'Shooting Schedule.' Colin Low fonds, R5667, 'Farmersville', Container 169, File 4. Library and Archives Canada.

_____ (1969a) 'Council Supports Movies in Poverty War', *Hartford Courant*, 18 March.

_____ (1969b) 'Ghetto Film Project Presented to CRT', *Hartford Courant*. 16 March.

_____ (1975) Interview with Herbert Kramer. Oral History. 11 March. Lyndon Baines Johnson Presidential Library.

_____ (1995) Interview with George Stoney. The Center for Media, Culture, and History at New York University. 13 November. George C. Stoney Papers, 1940–2009, Collection Number 04970, Box 7, Folder 185, The Southern Historical Collection at the Louis Round Wilson Special Collections Library, The University of North Carolina at Chapel Hill.

Barnouw, Erik ([1974] 1993) *Documentary: A History of the Non-Fiction Film*, second edition. Oxford: Oxford University Press.

Baron, Jaimie (2014) *The Archive Effect: Found Footage and the Audiovisual Experience of History*. London: Routledge.

Bogle, Donald (1989) *Toms, Coons, Mulattoes, Mammies, and Bucks: An Interpretative History of Blacks in American Films*. New York: Continuum.

Bowser, Pearl (1999) 'Pioneers of Black Documentary Film', in Phyllis R. Klotman and Janet K. Cutler (eds) *Struggles for Representation: African American Documentary Film and Video*. Bloomington, IN: Indiana University Press, 1–33.

Boyle, Deirdre (1997) 'Oh, Lucky Man: George Stoney', *The Independent* magazine, (October), 28–31.

Branch, Taylor (2006) *At Canaan's Edge: America in the King Years, 1965–1968*. New York: Simon & Schuster.

Brauer, Carl M. (1982) 'Kennedy, Johnson, and the War on Poverty', *Journal of American History*, 69, 1, 98–119.

Brill, Lesley (1997) *John Huston's Filmmaking*. Cambridge: Cambridge University Press.

Cartier-Bresson, Henri (2005) *The Mind's Eye: Writings on Photography and Photographers*. New York: Aperture.

Case, Harold (1969) 'Description of the Farmersville Project', Colin Low fonds, R5667, 'Farmersville,' Container 170, File 1. Library and Archives Canada.

Casetti, Francesco (1999) *Theories of Cinema: 1945–1995*. Austin, TX: University of Texas Press.

Charbonneau, Stephen (2012) Interview with Harold 'Casey' Case, 30 March.

____ (2014a) 'Exporting Fogo: Participatory Filmmaking, War on Poverty, and the Politics of Visibility', *Framework* 55.2: 220–247.

____ (2014b) 'John Grierson and the United States', Zoë Druick and Deane Williams (eds) *The Grierson Effect: Tracing Documentary's International Movement*. London: British Film Institute, 13–28.

____ (2015a) Interview with Harold 'Casey' Case, 20 October.

____ (2015b) Interview with Harry Keramidas, 19 October.

Clark, Robert F. (2002) *The War on Poverty: History, Selected Programs and Ongoing Impact*. New York: University Press of America.

Clifford, Bill (1950) Letter to George Stoney. 30 August. George C. Stoney Papers, 1940–2009, Collection Number 04970, Box 30, Folder 790, The Southern Historical Collection at the Louis Round Wilson Special Collections Library, The University of North Carolina at Chapel Hill.

Corrigan, Timothy (2011) *The Essay Film: From Montaigne, After Marker*. Oxford: Oxford University Press.

Crawford, Jay (1968) 'U.S. Pays the Bill: Farmersville a Movie Star', *Tulare Advance-Register*, 2 November.

Cripps, Thomas and David Culbert (1983) 'The Negro Soldier (1944): Film Propaganda in Black and White', in Peter C. Rollins (ed.) *Hollywood as Historian: American Film in a Cultural Context*. Lexington, KY: University Press of Kentucky, 109–33.

Crocker, Stephen (2008) 'Filmmaking and the Politics of Remoteness: The Genesis of the Fogo Process on Fogo Island, Newfoundland', *Shima: The International Journal of Research into Island Cultures*, 2, 1, 59–75.

Crowther, Bosley (1949) '"The Quiet One," Documentary of a Rejected Boy, Arrives at the Little Carnegie', *The New York Times*, 14 February.

Cruz, Jose (1998) *Identity and Power: Puerto Rican Politics and the Challenge of Ethnicity*. Philadelphia, PA: Temple University Press.

De Moraes, Vincent (1950) 'The Making of a Document: "The Quiet One"', *Hollywood Quarterly*, 4, 4, 375–84.

Delisle, Martin (2007) 'Direct Cinema and the National Film Board', *Encyclopedia of French Cultural Heritage in North America*. Société Héritage de Champlain. Available at: http://www.ameriquefrancaise.org/en/article-555/Direct_Cinema_and_the_National_Film_Board.html (accessed 5 October 2014).

Desser, David (1993) 'The Wartime Films of John Huston: Film Noir and the Emergence of the Therapeutic', in Gaylyn Studlar and David Desser (eds) *Reflections in a Male Eye: John Huston and the American Experience*. Washington, D.C.: Smithsonian Institution Press, 19–32.

Diawara, Manthia (1993) 'Black American Cinema: The New Realism', in Manthia Diawara (ed.) *Black American Cinema*. New York: Routledge, 3–25.

Druick, Zoë (2008) '"Reaching the Multimillions": Liberal Internationalism and the Establishment of Documentary Film', in Lee Grieveson and Haidee Wasson (eds) *Inventing Film Studies*. Durham, NC: Duke University Press, 66–92.

Dunne, Philip (1946) 'The Documentary and Hollywood', *Hollywood Quarterly*, 1, 2, 166–72.

Edgerton, Gary (1993) 'Revisiting the Recordings of Wars Past: Remembering the Documentary Trilogy of John Huston', in Gaylyn Studlar and David Desser (eds) *Reflections in a Male Eye: John Huston and the American Experience*. Washington, D.C.: Smithsonian Institution Press, 33–61.

Ellis, Jack C. (2000) *John Grierson: Life, Contributions, Influence*. Carbondale, IL: Southern Illinois Press.

Evans, Gary (1991) *In the National Interest: A Chronicle of the National Film Board from 1949 to 1989*. Toronto: University of Toronto Press.

Everett, Anna (2001) *Returning the Gaze: A Genealogy of Black Film Criticism, 1909–1949*. Durham, NC: Duke University Press.

Fraser, Gertrude J. (1995) 'Modern Bodies, Modern Minds: Midwifery and Reproductive Change in an African American Community', in Faye D. Ginsburg and Rayna Rap (eds) *Conceiving the New World Order: The Global Politics of Reproduction*. Berkeley, CA: University of California Press, 42–58.

____ (1998) *African American Midwifery in the South*. Cambridge, MA: Harvard University Press.

Gillette, Michael L. (2010) *Launching the War on Poverty: An Oral History*. Oxford: Oxford University Press.

Glascock, Baylis (1968) 'Welcome to Farmersville: Democracy, Race Relations, and Class in Rural California', The Farmersville Collection. Box 1, Folder 'To Be Filed', Chicano Studies Research Center, University of California, Los Angeles.

____ (1997) 'Farmersville Proposal – 20 November 1997', The Farmersville Collection. Box 1, Folder 'To Be Filed', Chicano Studies Research Center, University of California, Los Angeles.

Granger, Lester S. Letter to Joan Laird. n.d. George C. Stoney Papers, 1940–2009, Collection Number 04970, Box 37, Folder 994, The Southern Historical Collection at the Louis Round Wilson Special Collections Library, The University of North Carolina at Chapel Hill.

Griffiths, Alison (2002) *Wondrous Difference: Cinema, Anthropology, and Turn-of-the-Century Visual Culture.* New York: Columbia University Press.

Guterl, Matthew Pratt (2013) *Seeing Race in Modern America.* Chapel Hill, NC: University of North Carolina Press.

____ (2014) 'Why Darren Wilson is Driving You Mad', *The Guardian*, 30 November. Available at: http://www.theguardian.com/commentisfree/2014/nov/30/darren-wilson-ferguson-retirement-fear (accessed 5 December 2014).

Harrington, Michael (1962) *The Other America: Poverty in the United States.* New York: Macmillan.

Horak, Jan-Christopher (1997) *Making Images Move: Photographers and Avant-Garde Cinema.* Washington, D.C.: Smithsonian Institute Press.

Horton, Carol A. (2005) *Race and the Making of American Liberalism.* Oxford: Oxford University Press.

Jackson, Lynne (1987) 'The Production of George Stoney's Film All My Babies: A Midwife's Own Story (1952)', *Film History*, 1, 4, 367–92.

____ (1999) 'A Commitment to Social Values and Racial Justice', *Wide Angle*, 21, 2, 31–40.

James, David E. (1989) *Allegories of Cinema: American Film in the Sixties.* Princeton, NJ: Princeton University Press.

James, Rawn, Jr. (2013) *The Double V: How Wars, Protest, and Harry Truman Desegregated America's Military.* New York: Bloomsbury.

Jameson, Fredric (1984) 'Periodizing the 60s', *Social Text*, 9/10, 178–209.

Kahana, Jonathan (2009) 'Introduction: What Now? Presenting Reenactment', *Framework: The Journal of Cinema and Media*, 50, 1/2, 46–60.

Kearns, Doris (1976) *Lyndon Johnson and the American Dream.* New York: Harper and Row.

Kerner, Otto (1968) *The Kerner Report: The 1968 Report of the National Advisory Commission on Civil Disorders.* New York: Bantam Books.

Lanford, Henry (n.d.) 'Application for 'Film in Community Development Workshop', The Farmersville Collection. Box 1, Folder 1, Chicano Studies Research Center, University of California, Los Angeles.

____ (1968) 'Farmersville Diary', Colin Low fonds, R5667, 'Farmersville,' Container 169, File 43, Library and Archives Canada.

Lee, Rohama (1950) 'Editorially Speaking: Looking South', *Film News: The Newsmagazine of Films and Filmstrips*, 10, 8 (May/June), George C. Stoney Papers,

1940–2009, Collection Number 04970, Box 37, Folder 993, The Southern Historical Collection at the Louis Round Wilson Special Collections Library, The University of North Carolina at Chapel Hill.

Low, Colin (n.d.) 'Objectives', Colin Low fonds, R5667. 'Farmersville,' Container 170, File 3, Library and Archives Canada.

_____ (1969) 'Notes on Hartford', The Farmersville Collection. Box 1, Folder 19, Chicano Studies Research Center, University of California, Los Angeles.

MacDonald, Dwight (1963) 'Our Invisible Poor', *The New Yorker*, 19 January. Available at: http://www.newyorker.com/magazine/1963/01/19/our-invisible-poor (accessed 7 March 2016)

MacKenzie, Arch (1968) 'U.S. Adopts Plan from Newfoundland', *The Evening Telegram*, 8 October.

Marchant, Elizabeth (1963a) Letter to George Stoney, 9 May. George C. Stoney Papers, 1940–2009, Collection Number 04970, Box 6, Folder 162, The Southern Historical Collection at the Louis Round Wilson Special Collections Library, The University of North Carolina at Chapel Hill.

_____ (1963b) Letter to George Stoney. 13 May. George C. Stoney Papers, 1940–2009, Collection Number 04970, Box 6, Folder 162, The Southern Historical Collection at the Louis Round Wilson Special Collections Library, The University of North Carolina at Chapel Hill.

Marchessault, Janine (1995) 'Reflections on the Dispossessed: Video and the "Challenge for Change" Experiment', *Screen*, 36, 2, 131–46.

Marin, Niebla E. (1951) Letter to George Stoney. 13 August. George C. Stoney Papers, 1940–2009, Collection Number 04970, Box 29, Folder 789, The Southern Historical Collection at the Louis Round Wilson Special Collections Library, The University of North Carolina at Chapel Hill.

Massood, Paula J. (2003) *Black City Cinema: African American Urban Experiences in Film*. Philadelphia, PA: Temple University Press.

Mayers, Arthur (1949) 'Documentary Dilemma', *Southern Film News* 3.1 (January): 1–2, 5. George C. Stoney Papers, 1940–2009, Collection Number 04970, Box 17, Folder 438, The Southern Historical Collection at the Louis Round Wilson Special Collections Library, The University of North Carolina at Chapel Hill.

McFarland, Steve (2000) Interview with Butch Lewis. 29 July. Hartford Film Project 1969, Hartford Studies Project, Watkinson Library and College Archives, Trinity College.

Metz, Christian ([1977] 1986) *The Imaginary Signifier: Psychoanalysis and the Cinema*. Bloomington, IN: Indiana University Press.

Meyer, Sylvan (1950) '"Palmour Street" Acclaimed Here; Second Health Film Set Here', *The Times of Gainesville*. 22 May. George C. Stoney Papers, 1940–2009,

Collection Number 04970, Box 30, Folder 790, The Southern Historical Collection at the Louis Round Wilson Special Collections Library, The University of North Carolina at Chapel Hill.

Michaels, Anne (1968) Memorandum, 20 Sept. Bertrand M. Harding Papers. Office of Economic Opportunity, 1966–68, and Internal Revenue Service, 1955–66. Box 49. Conference File: Washington D.C., Canadian National Film Grand [sic] Members. The Lyndon Baines Johnson Library.

Montgomery, Meadie (1950) Letter to Ledford C. Carter. 2 August. George C. Stoney Papers, 1940–2009, Collection Number 04970, Box 30, Folder 790, The Southern Historical Collection at the Louis Round Wilson Special Collections Library, The University of North Carolina at Chapel Hill.

Morin, Edgar (2003) 'Chronicle of a Film', *Ciné-ethnography: Jean Rouch*. Steven Feld (ed.) Minneapolis, MN: University of Minnesota Press, 229–65.

National Film Board of Canada (n.d.) 'Film and Community Development', Fogo Island Project. Record Group: R5667, Box 253, File 2 of 13. Library and Archives Canada.

Newhook, Susan (2009) 'The Godfathers of Fogo: Donald Snowden, Fred Earle and the Roots of the Fogo Island Films, 1964–1967', *Newfoundland and Labrador Studies*, 24, 2, 171–97.

Nichols, Bill (1985) 'The Voice of Documentary', in Bill Nichols (ed.) *Movies and Methods, Vol. II*. Berkeley: University of California Press.

____ (1991) *Representing Reality: Issues and Concepts in Documentary*. Bloomington, IN: Indiana University Press.

____ (2008) *Introduction to Documentary*. Bloomington, IN: Indiana University Press.

Noriega, Chon A. (2000) *Shot in America: Television, the State, and the Rise of Chicano Cinema*. Minneapolis, MN: University of Minnesota Press.

Office of Economic Opportunity (n.d.) Public Affairs Office, Contract No. B89–4577. Bertrand M. Harding Papers, Office of Economic Opportunity, 1966–68, and Internal Revenue Service, 1955–66. Box 49. Conference File: Washington, D.C., Canadian National Film Grand [sic] Members. The Lyndon Baines Johnson Library.

Pennybacker, Susan (2001a) Interview with Ann [sic] Michaels. 24 May. Hartford Film Project 1969, Hartford Studies Project, Watkinson Library and College Archives, Trinity College.

____ (2001b) Interview with Colin Low. 24 May. Hartford Film Project 1969, Hartford Studies Project, Watkinson Library and College Archives, Trinity College.

Poinsett, Alex (1965) 'Poverty amidst Plenty', *Ebony*, August, 104–12.

Popham, John N. (1950) 'The South Sees Itself Via Its Own Educational Films', *New*

York Times, January 22. George C. Stoney Papers, 1940–2009, Collection Number 04970, Box 37, Folder 993, The Southern Historical Collection at the Louis Round Wilson Special Collections Library, The University of North Carolina at Chapel Hill.

Quadagno, Jill (1994) *The Color of Welfare: How Racism Undermined the War on Poverty*. Oxford: Oxford University Press.

Rabig, Julia (2010) 'The Laboratory of Democracy: Construction Industry Racism in Newark and the Limits of Liberalism', in David Goldberg and Trevor Griffey (eds) *Black Power at Work: Community Control, Affirmative Action, and the Construction Industry*. Ithaca, NY: Cornell University Press, 48–67.

Raengo, Alessandra (2013) *On the Sleeve of the Visual: Race as Face Value*. Hanover, NH: Dartmouth College Press.

Reiley, Linda Cobb (1969) 'Attempting to Achieve Public Consent for the War on Poverty: An Historical Study of the Public Relations Program of the Office of Economic Opportunity Compared to Newspaper Response to the Program from August 20, 1964 to July 1, 1968.' Master's Thesis. American University. Ann Arbor: ProQuest/UMI, Publication No. AAT 1302157.

Roemer, Michael A. (1960) Letter to George Stoney. 9 March. George C. Stoney Papers, 1940–2009, Collection Number 04970, Box 4, Folder 102, The Southern Historical Collection at the Louis Round Wilson Special Collections Library, The University of North Carolina at Chapel Hill.

Rosenthal, Alan (1971) *The New Documentary in Action: A Casebook in Film Making*. Berkeley, CA: University of California Press.

Scythes, Ted (1950) 'Yoke Fellows of Athens', *Film News: The Newsmagazine of Films and Filmstrips*, 10, 8 (May/June) George C. Stoney Papers, 1940–2009, Collection Number 04970, Box 37, Folder 993. The Southern Historical Collection at the Louis Round Wilson Special Collections Library. The University of North Carolina at Chapel Hill.

Sieving, Christopher (2011) *Soul Searching: Black Themed Cinema from the March on Washington to the Rise of Blaxploitation*. Middletown, CT: Wesleyan University Press.

Simmon, Scott (2007) 'Let There Be Light (1946) and Its Restoration', Program Note. National Film Preservation Foundation. Available at: http://www.filmpreservation.org/userfiles/image/PDFs/LetThereBeLight_ProgramNote.pdf (accessed 28 May 2014)

Sklar, Robert (2012) 'James Agee and the U.S. Response to Neorealism', in Robert Sklar and Saverio Giovacchini (eds) *Global Neorealism: The Transnational History of a Film Style*. Jackson, MS: University Press of Mississippi, 71–86.

Snowden, Donald (n.d.) 'Film and Cummunity [sic] Development.', in Baylis

Glascock, The Farmersville Collection. Box 1, Folder 5. Chicano Studies Research Center. University of California, Los Angeles.

Sobchack, Vivian (1992) *The Address of the Eye: A Phenomenology of Film Experience.* Princeton, NJ: Princeton University Press.

Solbrig, Heide (2007) 'Henry Strauss and the Human Relations Film: Social Science Media and Interactivity in the Workplace', *The Moving Image*, 7, 1, 27–50.

Southern Educational Film Production Service. 'Palmour Street.' George C. Stoney Papers, 1940–2009, Collection Number 04970, Box 37, Folder 992, The Southern Historical Collection at the Louis Round Wilson Special Collections Library, The University of North Carolina at Chapel Hill.

____ 'Palmour Street (A Study of Family Life)' George C. Stoney Papers, 1940–2009, Collection Number 04970, Box 37, Folder 992, The Southern Historical Collection at the Louis Round Wilson Special Collections Library, The University of North Carolina at Chapel Hill.

____ (1948) 'Productions Completed – Where to Get Them' (30 November) George C. Stoney Papers, 1940–2009, Collection Number 04970, Box 37, Folder 992, The Southern Historical Collection at the Louis Round Wilson Special Collections Library, The University of North Carolina at Chapel Hill.

____ (1951) Georgia Department of Health. Agreement. 21 June. George C. Stoney Papers, 1940–2009, Collection Number 04970, Box 4, Folder 105, The Southern Historical Collection at the Louis Round Wilson Special Collections Library, The University of North Carolina at Chapel Hill.

____ (1952) Georgia Department of Public Health. All My Babies: Sneak Prevue. 8 December. George C. Stoney Papers, 1940–2009, Collection Number 04970, Box 4, Folder 105, The Southern Historical Collection at the Louis Round Wilson Special Collections Library, The University of North Carolina at Chapel Hill.

Stoney, George (n.d.) 'Report from Canada.' George C. Stoney Papers, 1940–2009, Collection Number 04970, Box 37, Folder 994, The Southern Historical Collection at the Louis Round Wilson Special Collections Library, The University of North Carolina at Chapel Hill.

____ (n.d.) Curriculum Vitae. George C. Stoney Papers, 1940–2009, Collection Number 04970, Box 17, Folder 460, The Southern Historical Collection at the Louis Round Wilson Special Collections Library, The University of North Carolina at Chapel Hill.

____ (1952a) Letter to Dr David S. Ruhe, 15 February. George C. Stoney Papers, 1940–2009, Collection Number 04970, Box 25, Folder 671, The Southern Historical Collection at the Louis Round Wilson Special Collections Library, The University of North Carolina at Chapel Hill.

____ (1952b) Letter to Robert Galbraith. 3 March. George C. Stoney Papers,

1940–2009, Collection Number 04970, Box 25, Folder 671, The Southern Historical Collection at the Louis Round Wilson Special Collections Library, The University of North Carolina at Chapel Hill.

_____ (1959) 'All My Babies: Research', in Robert Hughes (ed.) *Film: Book 1: The Audience and the Filmmaker*. New York: Grove Press, 79–96.

_____ (1963) Letter to Elizabeth Marchant, 10 May. George C. Stoney Papers, 1940–2009, Collection Number 04970, Box 6, Folder 162, The Southern Historical Collection at the Louis Round Wilson Special Collections Library, The University of North Carolina at Chapel Hill.

_____ (1989) 'Appendix: Documentary in the United States in the Immediate Post-World War II Years', in Jack C. Ellis, *The Documentary Idea: A Critical History of English Language Documentary Film and Video*. Englewood Cliffs, NJ: Prentice Hall, 302.

_____ (2000) Letter to Lynne Jackson. January. George C. Stoney Papers, 1940–2009, Collection Number 04970, Box 7, Folder 181, The Southern Historical Collection at the Louis Round Wilson Special Collections Library, The University of North Carolina at Chapel Hill.

Sussex, Elizabeth (1976) *The Rise and Fall of British Documentary: The Story of the Film Movement Founded by John Grierson*. Berkeley, CA: University of California Press.

Truffaut, François (1974) 'A Certain Tendency of the French Cinema', in Bill Nichols (ed.) *Movies and Methods, Vol. I*. Berkeley, CA: University of California Press, 224–37.

Vitello, Paul (2012) 'George C. Stoney, Documentary Filmmaker, Dies at 96', *New York Times*, A22, 15 July.

Wallace, Michele (1993) 'Race, Gender, and Psychoanalysis in 1940s Film: Lost Boundaries, Home of the Brave, and The Quiet One', in Manthia Diawara (ed.) *Black American Cinema*. London: Routledge, 257–71.

WBAI Radio (1970) 'Minorities and the Media'. Broadcast Date: 31 December. Pacifica Radio Archive.

Weisenfeld, Judith (2007) *Hollywood Be Thy Name: African American Religion in American Film, 1929–1949*. Berkeley, CA: University of California Press.

White, Jerry (2009) *The Radio Eye: Cinema in the North Atlantic, 1958–1988*. Waterloo: Wilfrid Laurier University Press.

Wiesner, Peter K. (2010) 'Media for the People: The Canadian Experiments with Film and Video in Community Development,' in Thomas Waugh, Michael Brendan Baker and Ezra Winton (eds) *Challenge for Change: Activist Documentary at the National Film Board of Canada*. Montreal: McGill-Queen's University Press. 73–102.

Wilkins, Roy (1949) Letter to Joan Laird. 17 October. George C. Stoney Papers, 1940–2009, Collection Number 04970, Box 37, Folder 994, The Southern Historical Collection at the Louis Round Wilson Special Collections Library, The University of North Carolina at Chapel Hill.

Winston, Brian (1995) *Claiming the Real: The Griersonian Documentary and Its Legitimations*. London: British Film Institute.

INDEX